Marshall M. Kirkman

Railway Rates and Government Control

Economic Questions surrounding these subjects

Marshall M. Kirkman

Railway Rates and Government Control
Economic Questions surrounding these subjects

ISBN/EAN: 9783337191726

Printed in Europe, USA, Canada, Australia, Japan

Cover: Foto ©Andreas Hilbeck / pixelio.de

More available books at **www.hansebooks.com**

RAILWAY RATES

AND

GOVERNMENT CONTROL.

ECONOMIC QUESTIONS SURROUNDING
THESE SUBJECTS.

.

———

BY

MARSHALL M. KIRKMAN.

CHICAGO AND NEW YORK:

RAND, McNALLY & CO., PUBLISHERS.

1892.

PREFACE.

The object of every intelligent, honest, and patriotic man is the attainment of that which is best. What I have to say in regard to railway rates and government control is actuated by this desire. It is based on what is practicable and true; on what is attainable. If it runs counter to the opinions of the public, or of those to whom the public looks for information, I am sorry. I do not write from the standpoint of the railways, but from that of an observer and student; from the standpoint of one interested in the prosperity of his country, and believing in the intelligence and uprightness of his countrymen.

CONTENTS.

(5)

RAILWAY RATES

AND

GOVERNMENT CONTROL.

CHAPTER I.

THE ETHICS OF TRADE, INCLUDING THAT OF CARRIERS.

The principles that govern producers and manufacturers generally, govern railroads. But the latter feel more quickly than other property any fiscal disturbance, because they are nearer the people than any other industry; because their relations are more intimate; the association of interest stronger and more sensitive. Reciprocally, anything that injures the business or credit of carriers, injures other industries.

The commercial interests of a people are indissoluble.

Anything that injures one class, eventually injures all. The source from which the injury arises is immaterial, whether from unwise legislation, denial of justice, over production, improvident management, or failure of crops. The effect is the same.

The interests of the railroad companies and the community are indistinguishable. Their objects and aims are the same. Each is necessary to the other. Each must perform its part. They are mutually concerned that each should progress; that each should be prosperous. They participate in each other's prosperity, as they do in each other's misfortunes.

The greater the interest that is stricken down, the greater and more lasting the effect on surrounding industries. Witness a monetary panic, a failure of crops, a prolonged strike, a disturbance in the value of land. It is quite as marked in the case of railroads, though the community rarely, if ever, in such instance, trace the cause of their misfortunes to its true source. The prosperity of the laborer, merchant, land owner, manufacturer, and farmer, can only be temporary if railroads are unremunerative. One class can not successfully prey upon another.

Capital is exacting; its requirements cannot be evaded. Without its confidence, improvements can not be made, and those in existence languish and die. In commercial affairs, enterprises widely separated and seemingly having no connection, wait on each other's prosperity. An attack upon one recoils upon the other. The bond of sympathy is complete.

Interference with trade destroys its equilibrium, its natural adjustment, and this is as necessary to its proper fruition as the equal distribution of the forces of nature is necessary to their harmonious action.

The commerce of the world adjusts itself according to natural laws. Any interference with these laws superinduces artificial action, and injures and retards trade. There are no exceptions to this rule. Particular interests cannot be separated from others. Thus railways cannot be singled out. They must be allowed to prosecute their affairs in accordance with the economic laws that govern such properties. The disasters that follow refusal to recognize these laws will not be offset, as we might hope, by temporary successes. They will occasion injury, through the mistrust they will engender, long after the incidents themselves have been forgotten.

Commercial and social prosperity go hand in hand. The former is necessary to the latter. Recognition of natural laws, of equity, of the rights of labor, of moral obligation, and of the duty we owe society, is necessary to success in commercial affairs. It is bound up in the success of railroads.

Trade must be allowed to work out its destiny, to accomplish its ends in its own way, in accordance with its environment and in harmony therewith. We can not put it in a strait-jacket. This is true of railways, of farming, of the manufacture and sale of iron. A change in prices, say in the rates of railways, can not be brought about arbitrarily without subsequent injury, any more than we can bring about a change in the price of farm products at will.

Railways are based on the needs of the world. They are a necessary of life. They require to be untrammeled to attain their maximum usefulness, just as farming requires to be untrammeled. Nothing but harm can come from interference with their affairs. Their environment, the action of commercial and social usages and needs, will secure their equitable management.

Governmental regulations in harmony with these conditions may be enforced without harm. No . others can.

The railway interest, by its greatness and beneficence, merits our esteem. It answers a universal want. It is an integral part of our being, of our social and commercial system. It must conform to our peculiarities in its government and affairs. This it will freely do, if left untrammeled, but not otherwise.

Railroads are not different from other trades that respond to general needs. They are self-adjustive. They are governed by what we may term God's natural laws—the laws of trade, universal, adaptable, and just. All other laws are limited or accidental in their application.

In every business definite knowledge of the influences likely to operate for or against an enterprise is necessary to its greatest prosperity. Until these can be ascertained, the enterprise languishes. This being the case, we can estimate the injury that may be done a community (though quite likely without its being cognizant of the fact) by ill-considered legislation affecting great business enterprises like railways; by denying them protection; by separating them from other industries; by throwing around them an air of mystery and uncertainty. A community may do the same thing by fostering a belief that the owners and managers of railways are more selfish than other men, less efficient, less patriotic, less honest; by interfering arbitrarily in their affairs; by seeking to make them subservient to other influences; by confiscating their revenues, wholly or partially, through enforced reduction of rates, or other measures. And yet this is exactly what is being done to-day, more or less actively, in every quarter of the world, but more particularly and especially in the United States. In every direction the ignorant, fussy, idle, and vicious are stirring up strife, creating distrust.

Assimilation and distribution are coincident in commercial affairs. Thus, the collection of the revenue of a railroad and its disbursement are simultaneous acts. In many cases the revenue is expended in advance of its being gathered. The receipts from merchants and others for transportation services do not remain in the vaults of the carrier, but pass back without sensible interlude into the possession of the persons from whom received. The proceeds of the check given by the grocer or hardware merchant for the carriage of his goods, he receives back directly, with its accretions, through the medium of purchases made by the carrier, or those directly or indirectly dependent upon him.

The remunerative revenue of railroads is largely disbursed in improving the property or adding to it. No portion is hoarded or lost. It passes without a moment's delay into the circulation of the world, giving employment to men and adding to their field

of usefulness.   It is estimated that the direct outlay
of railways for labor is thirty-eight per cent. of
their gross earnings.   This amount, therefore, is at
once returned to the community.   Twenty-six per
cent. is returned for taxes and supplies.   A part
is paid out in interest, a part for dividends and for
the improvement of the property.   Both interest and
dividends find their way without delay into useful
circulation; a part goes to pay for labor, and the
necessaries and comforts of life; the balance is used
to start new enterprises or develop old ones.   No
portion is lost.   The community derives benefit to
the utmost farthing.

   This much by way of preface to a more minute
consideration of the question of railway rates and
government control.

CHAPTER II.

RAILWAY RATES — THEIR BASES, AND THE INFLU-
ENCES AFFECTING THEM.

Public injustice is the result of misapprehension—
rarely, if ever, of criminal intent; it originates in
ignorance. The injustice railways have suffered in
the United States, at the hands of the people, has
been due to a lack of knowledge of the principles
that govern carriers. The owners of railways are
largely to blame for this. Many of them know
little about political economy, and, while they have
conformed to its laws, have not recognized its presence in their work. It is a common belief of the
public, that all that is necessary to make a rate is
the disposition — that it may be put up or down at
will. This is not true. Rates are governed by influences beyond the control of the carrier. Some
of these influences I propose to notice.

Those who have charge of the traffic of railroads
must conform in all they do to the laws governing
commercial affairs; otherwise their work would be
fruitless. They are practical economists. While
they may not have studied political economy, they
are yet thoroughly versed in its subtleties, so far as
relates to their business. They may not understand
the theory; but they understand its bearings, and
conform thereto in everything they do.

The rates charged by carriers affect the cost of everything we use. They appeal especially to the producer and consumer. Each sees that the amount is added to the cost. The subject is, therefore, one of universal interest. Each day adds to its gravity. It is a favorite theme with those who wish to catch the public ear—to pose as reformers. The effort to make the masses believe that, through legislative action, they may arbitrarily regulate the affairs of railroads, without detriment to themselves, has been persistent and adroit. The idea sought to be conveyed is, that railroads are something apart; that their traffic is not governed by laws known to regulate other commercial transactions—to fix the price of other commodities. The credence these misrepresentations have met with encourages those who utter them to pursue the subject. The outcome can not be foretold. Railways, like other institutions, are capable of withstanding a certain amount of pressure—a pressure equal to their reserve. Then they collapse. The subject is one of the greatest importance, and worthy of careful examination—of honest and intelligent action.

The rates of railways are governed by the same laws that fix the price of other necessaries of life. There are no exceptions to the rule. We can no more change them arbitrarily, than we can the price of fish or flour. The same principles govern in each case.

In considering the question of railway rates, one of the first questions asked is: What is a reasonable rate? What may be a reasonable rate in one section or country may not be in another. The question is purely a local one. It can not be generalized or made to fit any formula. It is a practical, not a theoretical, question. There is nothing ideal about it.

In the enunciation of theories regarding rates, the fact that particular railroads are intended to serve particular districts is oftentimes overlooked, and an attempt made to make them conform to the interests of the country as a whole. This, practically, is the confiscation of private property to the general public—the robbery of individuals and communities to benefit other individuals and communities. It is wrong, unnecessary, and indefensible. Generally speaking, reasonable rates are such as enable carriers to furnish the accommodation the communities they serve require; to keep their property in repair; to pay necessary expenses; to make a reasonable return on the capital invested. The last named governs only qualifiedly, however. The question is a practical one.*

---

* "To determine whether a rate is reasonable it is necessary, in every instance, to go beyond the single article and consider the whole subject of classification and the whole business of the carrier under it. To challenge the charge for the carriage of a single article is to challenge to some extent the whole rate sheet, and calls for careful consideration of the question whether the rate to be charged to the one article is out of just proportion, when all the circumstances and conditions which the railway officers must be supposed to have had in mind in making the classification and the rating are considered. . . . If policy or necessity requires the giving of unprofitable rates as to one article, compensation is expected to be made by a proper adjustment of charges in respect to others. . . . A rate imposed upon any article of commerce may affect rates in distant parts of the country, so that an intelligent consideration of the sub-

So far as the use of mechanical appliances is concerned, common carriers are not different from other people. Their revenues are wisely disbursed. When these revenues fall below reasonable requirements, properties deteriorate and companies become bankrupt. The community suffers in both cases. "The people want good railroad service, and they ought to have it at fair rates; but to give them this, it is needful that the road be kept in good condition and well equipped; that the trains be sufficiently manned and well handled; that competent servants be employed and fairly paid, and that the company avail itself of all new appliances which are calculated to make the service more speedy, more convenient, or more safe. Good service and unreasonably low rates are antagonistic ideas; if the latter are insisted upon, the former is not to be

---

ject will require study of the railroad situation in every part of the land. . . . Relative charges between any one article of commerce, and the others which the carrier transports, are made from considerations of policy and in the discretion of the carrier, so that a rate may be, if considered by itself, unreasonably low or unreasonably high. . . . Railroads, in the matter of rates, can not be considered singly. When a road, favorably situated, charges but reasonable rates for its own service, it may be impossible for a rival road, which was built perhaps without any sufficient demand for it, or which is unfavorably situated for successful competition, to maintain such rates as will give to it a corresponding return upon the investment. It will be compelled to measure its rates by its more fortunate rival, whether its stockholders receive returns upon their investment or not, for reasonable rates to the one may determine what the other shall receive, notwithstanding anything the management can do or that can be done for it by the public authorities." —"Fourth Annual Report, Interstate Commerce Commission," pages 16, 17, 20, 28.

expected. Many times in railroad history it has been found, on inquiring into the cause of some great railway calamity, that it was due to the fact that some bridge had become weak, some tunnel was insufficiently guarded, some machinery defective, or some employe incompetent or wanting in vigilance because of overwork. If the road was prosperous, the management would thus be shown to be inexcusable, perhaps criminal; but, if the road was not prosperous, and for some reason the management had been forced to make such rates as would not give the necessary revenue for a safer service, the blame for such a calamity may be fairly subject to apportionment. The public can never be in the wrong in demanding good service when fair rates are conceded; and an enlightened public sentiment will never object to fair rates, when it is understood that good service is conditional upon them." *

The rate influences the cost of railroads and the outlay for operating.† It also affects the accommodation.

It is never designed to invest more in a railroad than its traffic will yield a return upon. Accommodations conform to the price paid therefor.

If properties are not remunerative, capital will no longer seek such investment. That already placed will shrink in value. This shrinkage entails hardship both on the owner and the community. It is, however, unavoidable when not precipitated by governmental interference.

---

* "Second Report, Interstate Commerce Commission," page 23.

† When I speak of operating expenses, I mean, generally, working expenses, taxes, and cost of maintenance.

In practice, carriers oftentimes find it expedient
to do business that barely covers cost of operating.
This is so when maintenance of organization needed
in other directions is sustained thereby. Such instances are rare, however. Except in cases of rate
wars, business is not done that does not pay a margin of profit over cost of operating.

While rates must be generally remunerative, they
can not be uniformly so. They are the result of
innumerable conditions, compromises, and adjust-
ments. The first tariff was constructed as a child
builds a highway of blocks. It did not remain
unaltered an hour. It was found that the traffic
determined the rate, and not the traffic manager.
His action was mechanical. He was merely carrying out a law.

The rate must be such as to stimulate the effort of
every party in interest. The moment it does not,
business ceases. There must be present or prospective gain in every case. To determine whether a rate
is reasonable or not, we must take the business of a
carrier as a whole. If his gross profits are not unreasonable, particular rates are not unreasonable.

The rates of a railroad are the outcome of natural
causes. There is nothing artificial about them ; the
flow of water, the movement of the clouds, the
reverberation of thunder, the falling of rain, the
warmth of the sun, are not more natural. They
grow out of the action of men, are based on their
needs, on the worth of the thing handled. The
process is extremely simple, but because of its varying conditions is not generally understood. An able

and fluent writer has written a book to make it
appear that the transportation system is artificial,
and is carried on mainly by ignorant, grasping, and
rascally railway owners and managers.* He assumes
rates are based on cost, and craves legislative interference because like service is not charged a like
price. He says the public "demand that the same
method of determining the cost of transportation
shall apply to all classes alike, and that railway
managers must not have one standard for such
freights as they wish to favor, and a higher one for
those which they desire to burden. That all the
services of the railways shall be performed with impartiality, and at charges based on the same standard of cost."† Underlying all he says is the studied
effort to make it appear that carriers are interested
in favoring particular industries; in breaking down
others. Nothing can be further from the truth.
They are absolutely impartial. He particularly
deprecates special rates and the opportunities they
afforded shippers. He devotes many condemnatory
pages to special instances of wrong-doing, among
others to the case of the Standard Oil Company.‡
The benefits this great aggregation of capital has

---

* J. F. Hudson, "The Railways and the Republic."

† His arguments are fanatical and misleading. His basis of rates
would exclude from the markets of the world the cheap beef and
grain of remote districts, because they cannot pay the same rate per
ton per mile for one thousand miles, that local producers can pay for
fifty miles.

‡ A corporation controlling the bulk of the output of oil in Ohio
and Pennsylvania.

conferred on the community, he adroitly ignores. The fact that sixty millions of people are able to buy their oil to-day for one-half what they would, except for its enterprise, sagacity, and economical methods, he passes by in silence. The merging in it of innumerable petty producers, and the avoidance thereby of expenses for services, rents, agents, commissions, and kindred outlays, he ignores, or esteems a commercial crime. He would have had the government keep each little trader alive; have compelled the people to support them, notwithstanding competitive influences amply protect them from arbitrary exactions in other ways. It is apparent from results that the industry referred to has been managed throughout by sagacious and prudential men, and that the people have been greatly benefited thereby. Government interference at any time would have been unwise. It would have kept alive myriads of middlemen, a dead load fastened on the back of the people. The benefits attained are not lessened by the fact that men claim great wrong has been done. In the good accomplished we see the difference between theory and practice; between sense and foolishness. There was no wrong. It was purely imaginary. There was no oppression. A few sharp traders were overreached by other sharp traders. That is one of the incidents of trade, and out of it good arises. It eliminates the drones. The community is benefited. And so it has been generally with all the practices of railroads.*

* I bring up the case of the Standard Oil Company here, and thus prominently, because it is cited in the United States as the most

If every sin attributed to railroads were true, all their shortcomings would be but as a grain of sand in the sea, a star in the sky, compared to the good their unrestricted management has conferred upon our people. I use the word unrestricted advisedly. Railway owners are not different from other traders. They conform to their surroundings. Their methods are the same as those who haul by water. The rates they charge adapt themselves to the law of supply and demand as naturally as does the price of corn.

The rates of railroads can not be the same from month to month, or year to year, any more than they can be by water. They are the center of conflicting interests, of incessant fluctuations. Those who advocate legislative interference would change all this. They would substitute for this natural world an artificial one, a world filled with block houses, wooden horses, impossible men, impracticable theories. They would sweep away that which is good because evil has attended it; would make the government the instigator of commercial enterprise, rather than business men; substitute auto-

---

glaring instance known of railway discrimination and injustice. The country has rung for years with condemnatory speeches, editorials, and enactments based thereon. If, however, all that has been said were true, it would only be an exception, an isolated instance, something special, and not by any means sufficient ground upon which to predicate wholesale warfare upon carriers. As a matter of fact, however, the action of the railways in connection with the Standard Oil Company was involuntary, unavoidable, and natural; was such as the necessities of business required, and the needs of the community demanded. Their action was not predicated upon a desire to please the Standard Oil Company or benefit it, but upon the necessities of the case.

matic action for genius. When they have achieved this, they "look to see the great principle of competition work so freely that wild fluctuations of freight rates, the injustice of special rates, the restrictive influence of pools, or the creation of monopolies, and the crushing out of independent industries by discriminations, become as impossible on the railways as it is upon our lakes, rivers, and canals."* The picture is beautiful, but misleading. The so-called evils are really blessings, and attend transportation by water quite as much as by land. They are the natural tools of commerce, are such as facilitate trade, and should be fostered and encouraged, not condemned.†

Every kind of competition in trade is beneficial. That of carriers is no exception. Particular properties or neighborhoods may momentarily suffer, but the result will, on the whole, be good.

The money that active competition loosens is not wasted, albeit superficial lookers-on esteem it so. It sets in motion forces impossible to animate in any other way. The perfection of the railroad system of the United States is due to it. Managed arbitrarily by a single man, or by the government, it would not be what it is. It would be tyrannical, inadequate, and inefficient.

The wastage of competition is only apparent. It

---

* J. F. Hudson, " The Railways and the Republic," page 23.

† I use the terms "commerce" and "trade" in a general way. They imply buying and selling, bargaining, the effort to make money, the interchange of products and commodities, and include all the agencies incident thereto, such as transportation and warehousing.

is returned tenfold in the intense activity of men, in multiplied interest, broadened intelligence, new inventions, new industries, increased trade, increased consumption, cheapened processes. This is what active rivalry between our railroads has brought us. The future holds out equal promises, but conditioned upon our allowing the capital invested in railroads to manage its own affairs in its own way, conformably, as heretofore, to the greatest good to the greatest number.

The relatively small profits that carriers realize on competitive traffic (discriminating business, so-called), is thus measurably offset by its stimulating effect. The smallness of these profits is explained by the fact that they must be shared with the shipper. Mutuality of interest is present here, as it is everywhere else. Its operation is as unchangeable as cause and effect. While the fruits of competition are wholesome, its processes are curious, oftentimes apparently absurd.*

Wise saws and instances, actual and hypothetical,

---

* Thus, Mr. Hudson thinks it extremely ridiculous that iron should be shipped from Pittsburgh to New York, to be there re-shipped through Pittsburgh to points in Texas, the object in shipping to New York being to get the benefit of the competitive rate by water from there to the Texas coast. Just as if the shipper in Pittsburgh could expect to get the benefit of the New York rate unless he is on the ground! Can sophistry or legislation put Pittsburgh on the same footing with New York, so far as the advantages that the latter enjoys from transportation by water along the coast are concerned? Manifestly not. The advantage is a natural, indisputable, inalienable one, and one that can not be corrected by extraneous action without endangering the whole commercial edifice.

have not been wanting to demonstrate how oppressive and unjust railroads are. They are, however,
generally fallacious. The methods of railroads, if
not interfered with, are wise, far-seeing, and such as
to build up the internal commerce of a country.
Instances of venal, arbitrary, and foolish acts upon
the part of particular men prove nothing. We
might, with equal wisdom, condemn civil liberty
because public servants are sometimes venal.*

An effective means of crippling railroads is to
deny them power to protect their interests and
the interests of those who look to them for transportation. The author quoted above would not
permit them to do business, unless the rate they
received therefor was uniform in every instance.
Thus, industries (among them farming remote from
market), that could not afford to pay the highest
rate would die out. The carrier now keeps them
alive by assuming a portion of their burdens. Millions of industries are thus carried on. It is, however, discrimination. That baleful word! That
scarecrow of theorists and knaves!

Where a producer can not pay the maximum
rate, the carrier aids him if he can. The effect
is to stimulate competitive markets; to cheapen
the cost of the necessaries of life. Countries are
thus built up and enriched. Each industry pays
what it can, without reference to what other industries pay.

---

* Moreover, is it probable that the servants of the government would
be more honest, more impartial, more efficient than railway managers
are? Nothing in the history of the world warrants such belief.

Nor is it a valid objection to a special rate that it is not generally known; that it is secured by a particular merchant. The fault is not the carrier's, and if, by aiding his customer, he creates a new industry, both he and the community are benefited. Railways can not make men equal. The shrewd, experienced, and energetic business man must not be handicapped because his dull and plodding brother possesses neither ingenuity nor foresight. Nor can his methods justly be made common property, to be heralded broadcast for the benefit of others less capable. I do not consider worthy of notice the statements and innuendoes that carriers have been in collusion with shippers in connection with the use of special rates. There undoubtedly have been instances of that character, but they are unworthy of notice, except to brand as dishonest those who have been guilty. To change our system of commercial practice, because of such instances, is as foolish as to deprecate rain, because the crops of individuals here and there have been ruined thereby. Trade of every kind abounds in special instances. It is creative. It is built up of wise discriminations. Railways are not an exception. Uniformity, here as elsewhere, is the shield of mediocrity, the refuge of the ignorant, stupid, and lazy.

It would be impossible to enumerate the instances that call for the special intervention of carriers. They come into play wherever a mutual benefit may be derived therefrom. The business of railroads is dependent upon the patron being benefited.

Thus it is self-corrective. The occasions of special rates are infinite. Thus a special rate may be given by a railroad in consideration of the shipper forwarding nothing by water; of giving it his whole business. Such an arrangement is natural and legitimate ; of general utility. It has been instanced as oppressive. It is directly the reverse. It adds to the business and the profits of the carrier, and incidentally redounds to the benefit of other patrons. It is also sometimes expedient to reduce rates, in order to move a crop, or the traffic of a place or district, at a particular time, just as a prudent merchant reduces the price of his goods for a few days to clear his shelves. It is impossible to enumerate the instances that call for special intervention. They will occur to the reader. They are as countless as the incidents of trade. The enemies of railroads refer to them to strengthen their case. They, however, prove nothing. If attentively examined, they will be found to be based on good business usage, and to be, on the whole, beneficial. It does not strengthen the arguments of unfriendly critics, that instances are not wanting where railway managers have been ignorant, dishonest, and foolish ; where they have made a dishonest use of special rates. The acts of railroad managers, as a whole, have been wise and salutary, in harmony with those about them, answering the wants of the country, fostering and extending its trade.

The making of a low rate never has the effect to raise another rate. Each is independent and co-existent ; a unit of the service. The act of raising or lowering is the result of cause; of commercial necessity, not of chance or caprice. A rate can not be raised without cause any more than we can break a link in a chain without ruining its strength.

Public opinion has never made a rate either higher or lower, any more than it has changed the price of potatoes. The reason is because it is based on natural laws. Many traffic managers may, it is possible, believe that they are potent in such matters. But this only shows how ignorant a man may be, and still perform a duty creditably. Public opinion is useful in enlightening the minds of such men; but to assume that it attracts or diverts trade, or lightens its physical burdens, is absurd.

Wherever commerce is remunerative and men are free, it will be carried on. When greatly extended, it requires the coöperation of many, among others, carriers. This means a division of the profits. Each gets his share. The division is the result of compromise — mutual adjustment. It is the duty of the government to protect all the parties in interest. To except the carrier is to cripple his usefulness. If left free, he will perform his part; otherwise not.

It is a great mistake to suppose the country has been benefited, or will be benefited, by laws restricting the freedom of railways. The people may think so, just as they used to think the burning of our grandmothers at Salem benefited them. The task of disabusing their minds from such delusions is a laborious and thankless one. As soon may we

hope to purify water by damming it, as to build
up the internal commerce of a country by placing
restrictions upon it. Every restriction placed on
railroads cripples, to the extent it is enforced, the
industries of a country.*

To restrict the right of carriers to change their
rates at will, is like entrusting one's breathing
apparatus to the will of another. The commerce
of a country thus hampered can not be healthy and
vigorous. The carrier must be in constant and
familiar touch with markets and the local and
general needs of business, and must be able to
respond to them instantly, otherwise opportunity
will be lost and business die from lack of attention
and encouragement.

The belief that carriers may use the power to
make rates to oppress others, is absurd. They are
the creatures of circumstances. They originate
nothing, and their prosperity depends upon their
conforming quickly and accurately to the needs and
equities of business.

The evils that attend railway management are
ever in process of extinguishment, because they
antagonize the interests of others and minimize the
usefulness and profitableness of such properties.
The management of railroads is neither blind,
dumb, nor brutish. It is instinct with life, at once

---

* General supervisory and judicial powers, such as those belonging to the Interstate Commerce Commission of the United States
or the Board of Trade of England, may be both wise and salutary,
if the law under which they are exercised is not oppressive. The
law in the United States is oppressive in many respects, but the
Commission referred to is not responsible for this.

kindly and complaisant, because its welfare is insep-
arably bound up with those it serves.

The sins and shortcomings of carriers are those
common to merchants, bankers, manufacturers, and
farmers. They are not criminal. They are not
such as to merit special mention or reprobation.
Wherever harmful, they will be corrected much
more effectively without legislative interference
than with it. However, I do not by any means
wish to say that they should be overlooked. Criticism is beneficial here as elsewhere. It is like a
lash across the back of a lazy horse. It enlivens,
but let it be intelligent and temperate—such as the
case requires. Let us not damn them as a class,
because of isolated instances of wrong, any more
than we damn farmers as a whole, because one
farmer seeks to repudiate his debts, or has been
caught stealing his neighbor's oats. Above all, let
us not mix up ignorance, jealousy, and hatred with
our justice.

The era of railways precipitates new conditions.
These are not yet fully understood. They affect
governments as well as individuals. The constitu-
tions of the last century are thought by many not
to be able to cope with our gigantic interests, our
concentrated efforts, and intense activity. If that is
so, let us remodel them so that they will conform
to our needs, rather than the needs of our grand-
fathers. If the central government is not strong
enough, let us add to its strength; let us make its
constituency represent a higher ideal; let us make
its civil service more industrious, intelligent, and

honest: its judgeships a life tenure, to be filled by conscientious men.   Every railway owner, employe, and manager will applaud, in common with others, such a resolve, and will aid in every possible way to bring it about.   They are all interested in a stable, wise, and beneficent government.   There is no antagonism here.   They are as one with the community.

A prime factor in determining the rates carriers charge, is the value of the service to the shipper. This is the basis of remuneration for labor in every field of industry.   Any other would be oppressive, if not prohibitory.   Its operation involves the exercise of discrimination.   But discrimination is the instinct of trade, its intelligent, directing, and governing force.   The ignorant, the vicious, and the superficial speak of it, when exercised by railroads, as something oppressive, something to be discountenanced.   This is because they do not consider the analogies of trade, or its methods.   The charge of carriers can not be disproportionate to the thing handled.   If more is charged than I can reasonably pay, it prohibits me from doing business; but if I am charged what I can afford, I am not treated unjustly, so long as the general profits of the seller are not unreasonable.   It is not an act of injustice to me that a carrier charges a higher rate for my blooded horse than for my neighbor's mule, although they both occupy the same space.   I can not afford to pay the same rate for the brick used in the construction of my house that I can for the carpets that cover its floors.   Rates are based on discriminations of this kind, at once practicable, necessary, and wise.

Value is also the basis of discriminations between places. Thus, the numerous land and water routes between Chicago and the seaboard render the service of the carrier less valuable than it otherwise would be. It is a fact in political economy that competition lessens value. If such rates, therefore, are low, they have merely adjusted themselves to this well-known law. The carrier must, under such circumstances, take less. To prohibit him from doing so, will only be to enhance the profits of the water carrier, without lessening the burden elsewhere.

Any business a carrier can get that affords him a profit, however small, helps him to that extent to accommodate other interests. It does not matter how this profit arises, whether from concessions to a weak and struggling manufactory, or a city where competition between carriers is active. In either case, the rate is a special one.

. Rates must at least equal the cost of operating and maintenance. They ought also to render a reasonable return on the original investment. How the amount shall be divided, how apportioned, is governed by economic laws that we must acquiesce in but can not govern. The adjustment is a natural one, based on the values of the things handled, and is governed by reciprocal interests. It is as unnecessary to say that railway rates shall be reasonable, as it is to say that men shall not drink when they are not thirsty. Rates conform, like every other par-

ticular of business, to their environment. They are
an incident merely; a link in a long chain. Anything abnormal that attends their operation, is
corrected as quickly and as surely as abnormal
action is corrected in other fields of industry.

A city on a highway is better off than one that
is not. So, a city located at the junction of two or
more highways, is better off than one by the way-
side. It is, to a certain extent, a competitive point,
and in commercial affairs every competitive point is
more or less a point of distribution. Because of
this, it is especially advantageous to the country
round about. The value of what it has to sell is
increased, while the value of what it has to buy is
lessened. The advantage is a natural one. It affects
the traffic of the carrier and modifies his practices.
It prevents uniformity of rate. But this does not
matter. No one is harmed.

A uniform rate is a delusion, the utopia of theorists, the hiding-place of those who seek through it
to destroy or confiscate the capital of others. It is
the delusion of dreamers and the weapon of their
less honest brothers. Rates are governed by the
markets of the world. Commerce reaches its destination by the most advantageous route. "Trade
seeks the easiest path from the producer to the
consumer. The history of a hundred generations
shows great cities which have grown rich and
powerful along the line, or at the termini, of some
great transportation interest, sinking into decay
and ruin when a nearer or easier route is discovered. Commerce, like water, seeks the lowest level.

It rebels at unnatural restrictions. Temporary obstructions may be put in its way, just as one may dam a stream, but sooner or later, over the dam or through its ruins, the stream will find its natural channel." *

Extraneous causes influence rates where the competition is wholly between railroads. They also influence competition between water and land carriage. In the latter case, competition is further enhanced in value to the community by the exceptionally cheap facilities of water transportation. Between Chicago and New York, the water routes determine the rate of the railroads for six or seven months of the year, as much as the price of sugar in one store is determined by the price in another store. Nor is the effect of competition confined to the prescribed limits of the particular routes over which it operates. It affects, directly and indirectly, every collateral route and interest. Thus, "whenever rates are reduced on account of the opening of navigation from Chicago and the lake ports, the same reduction is made from all interior cities, not only from New York, where the canal runs, but to Boston, Philadelphia, and Baltimore. Although the latter cities have no direct water communication with the West, yet they receive the benefit, as far as low railroad rates are concerned, to the same extent as if a canal were actually running from the lakes direct to those cities, because whenever rates from Chicago to New York are reduced, it becomes absolutely necessary to reduce correspond-

---

* George H. Lewis.

3

ingly the rates from Chicago to Boston, Philadelphia, and Baltimore; otherwise these cities could do no business, as it would all go to New York. The reduction of the rates from Chicago and St. Louis to New York, Baltimore, etc., reduces the rates from Western points via New York, Baltimore, and ocean to the Southern Atlantic points. . . The railroads running directly from Chicago and St. Louis, via Louisville, Nashville, and Chattanooga, to the same points, are obliged to follow the reductions made via the rail and ocean routes. . . The same is true in relation to the west-bound traffic." *

In considering the influence of water routes on railway rates, it may be said that shippers will never in any case forward by rail wholly, unless it is to their advantage; unless the benefit is greater than to ship by water. There can be no coercion about it. Herein lies one of the advantages derived from water routes to shippers. It also enables them to secure concessions outside the limit of water area not otherwise attainable. The compulsion is not put on the shipper, but on the carrier. In order to secure a part, he must make concessions on the whole. This is, to the community, the most effective and valuable competition of all.

Without competition, every man would be at the mercy of his neighbor. Competition is the life of trade; its balance wheel—protecting and shielding all alike. It is to be encouraged. It should be

---

* Letter, Albert Fink, Commissioner Associated Trunk Lines, to Senator Windom, Chairman Committee of the United States Senate on Transportation Routes to the Seaboard.

unrestricted. The clash of contending influences, the strife of rival interests, should be given full play. Their effect is to better and to cheapen. Unrestricted competition is the greatest blessing a people can possess. Mr. George L. Lansing, who has given the subject of traffic considerable study, says that the effect of competition is to bear most strongly on those things in which there is the greatest trade. Thus, the smallest margin of profit, over the cost of production, is on the necessaries of life; the next smallest on the common comforts, and the largest on the luxuries. This effect is not caused by design. It results from the operation of natural laws of trade. The operations of the same laws produce the same effect on the rates of transportation. We find, as a rule, the lowest rates on the products of the farm, coal, wood, petroleum, iron, and lumber, etc. The forces of competition, which tend to reduce the rates of transportation, coöperate in producing discrimination in favor of those things which are moved in the largest quantities, and which are, of course, consumed in the largest amounts. The aim of the carrier is to secure the traffic. To do this, he must make low rates on cheap commodities. This results in distributing the charge for transportation where it is most easily borne. Not only do necessaries have low rates, relatively, but necessaries consumed in the largest quantities have lower rates than those consumed in smaller quantities.

These practices are not discretionary with the carrier. They have the binding force of principles.

They are necessary conditions of business, of progress. It is not necessary to make them the subject of legislative enactments or other governmental interference. They are inherent. They are, however, subject to these limitations: in carrying out the principles that govern carriers, as well as other traders, equal intelligence will not be exercised in every instance. There will be sagacious traffic managers and dull traffic managers, just as there are shrewd merchants and stupid merchants. But they are all animated by the same idea, by like conscientiousness. What they lack in comprehension is not to be made good by extraneous action. Time will cure the evil in every case. Intelligence will finally govern here, as it does elsewhere.

CHAPTER III.

The value of the service to the consumer, its
cost, and the competition of carriers and markets,
will ever be potent factors in determining the rates
carriers of every description charge. The demand
for transportation increases each year; so long as
it is remunerative, the supply will keep pace therewith. Its character is at once varied and picturesque. We are more concerned, however, in that of
railroads. But the water-courses of the world are of
supreme importance. "The Almighty has furnished
by far the most important avenue of transportation;
our navigable rivers furnish it; our artificial canals
furnish it. Our water-ways are abundant and varied.
We have thousands of miles of rivers that go un-
vexed, unharassed, untaxed, to the sea. We have
lakes which are inland seas, and upon which there
are no charges; they roll and shine perpetually—
ceaseless, constant, everlasting competitors of every
artificial form of transportation. In their quiet
way—as quiet and as resistless as the tides—they
confront every railroad corporation in the country
and say to it: 'In the regulation of your charges,
thus far shalt thou go and no farther.' "* These

---

* Emory A. Storrs before the Committee on Commerce, February,
1882.

conditions, while potent factors in the United States,
are also noticeable in every other country.

The rate-making power of railways is an adaptive
one.   It must take into account the producer, middleman, and consumer, as well as the carrier.   It
must conform to the market and the competitive
influences of other carriers.   It is only in isolated
and petty cases that the rate-maker exercises any
discretion whatever.   It is never greater than that
of the merchant who puts a price on his wares.
"The commercial and industrial forces of the country are much more potential in determining rates
than are all the railroad managers of the country,
either when acting separately or in concert.   .   .   .
The commercial and industrial forces of the whole
country have been brought into instant and intense
competition with each other.   This struggle imposes
restraint upon freight charges which the railroad
manager is powerless to withstand."* Not only is
this so of our own country, but the commercial and
industrial interests of the whole world are so interwoven—compete so actively with each other—that
they affect the rates of local carriers quite as power-
fully as do local interests and rivalries.

Primarily, the cost of a property, and the expense
incident to its operation, would, conjointly, it was
thought, determine arbitrarily the price that should
be charged.   Experience has proven that this expectation was not well founded.   It has been found that
the cost of the property influences the rate only in
those cases where monopoly exists, or where govern-

---

* Joseph Nimmo, Jr.

ments assume to fix the rate. In the latter case, any other basis would be an acknowledgement of the right of the government to confiscate private property. The result is that the rates made by monopolies and governments are frequently prohibitory.

The profits of the carrier are unequally distributed. He is the creature of circumstances. "A rule that should measure charges by cost would work an entire revolution in the business of transportation, since it would no longer be practicable to make articles whose value was great in proportion to bulk or weight aid in transportation of articles of a different nature, and the carrier would be compelled to demand, upon the traffic in heavy and bulky articles, such compensation as in many cases the traffic could not possibly bear. . . . Nothing more disastrous to the commerce of a country could possibly happen than to require the rating for railroad transportation to be fixed exclusively by this one rule."*

In measuring the elements that enter into cost of constructing and operating railways, the reader can not but be impressed with the scope and magnitude of the subject.† He can not but be struck with the multitude of things to be considered, many of them of petty consequence, but in the aggregate of prodigious importance and perplexing uncertainty. He

---

* "Fourth Annual Report, Interstate Commerce Commission," pages 15 and 16.

† This phase of the subject will be explained in volumes devoted to "Construction, Capitalization and Maintenance," "The purchase, care, and use of Material," "Railway Disbursements and Accounts," etc.

will see that they absolutely and forever negative legislation or other governmental action based on uniformity of conditions and cost, and constitute a fatal drawback to any attempt to impose the same obligations upon different properties.*

It needs no argument or illustration to prove that, equitably, a railway company is entitled to base the price of its services on a reasonable return on the cost of its property and the expense of operating. The right is inherent. Rates thus based may be termed the maximum. In practical application, however, the basis is that which will secure a profit to the railroad company over and above the cost of operating, and, at the same time, stimulate, to the greatest extent possible, the production of the article carried. This purpose underlies all rates. It applies to passengers as well as freight. Rates are in every instance fixed with a view to their favorable effect on the thing transported.

Innumerable conditions surround and govern the making of rates. The value of the product measurably influences it, but not proportionately. A tariff based on the relative value of the articles

---

* "A rate that would be just to the trunk lines of the Central States, would be destructive to expensive railways reaching the mines of Colorado or California. Rates which the mines in the Rocky Mountains or Sierra Nevada can pay, and must pay, if railroads are to be built for them, would amount to confiscation if applied to the coal mines of Pennsylvania, or the grain of Iowa and Nebraska. The schedule which would be just for a railway at one time would be unjust at another. The branch line through a new country must collect higher rates at first, than when it has developed the productive power of the region."—J. F. Hudson, "The Railways and the Republic," page 339.

carried would be prohibitory in many instances. The space occupied and the attendant risk are factors. The indirect advantage to be derived from a business also affects the price charged. Railways do a wholesale and retail-business, and the rate in particular cases is governed, more or less, as it is with all manufacturers, by the amount of the product. In other words, quantity influences the price. The exceptional relation that certain articles of a standard character bears to the community has been thought to affect favorably the price asked for carrying. The influence, however, arises from the quantity offered, its competitive character, and its relatively small value, and, not from the fact that it represents a necessary of life.*

Traffic classifications of railroads are a means of indicating the rate. Local conditions do not affect them, except in purely local matters. Relative values, weight, bulk, and risk, are prime factors. While still imperfect, the thought and labor that have been given them render them marvels of commercial wisdom and skill. The results arrived at embody, as nearly as human intelligence can, the experience of trade and the wants of commerce, the

* "The discretionary power which the managers of railroads are able to exercise in the adjustment of freight tariffs, and which they are able to bring to bear toward influencing the course of trade, is subject to several very important qualifying and limiting conditions, proceeding from competition exerted through the markets and from the direct influence which merchants and other citizens are able to bring to bear toward regulating freight charges in the general course of trade. . . . This is especially the case with respect to the rates for transportation of grain, flour, provisions, and the other necessaries of life."—Joseph Nimmo, Jr.

machinery necessary to set it in motion and develop
it. The burdens enforced are equitably distributed,
and intended to be so apportioned as to create the
least embarrassment to trade, to engender the least
complaint, the least hardship to the community.
They conform in all things to the law of supply and
demand; to the laws of trade.

The rate foreshadows the concern the people have
in the product. Thus, if the cost of carriage "constitutes a large part of the ultimate price of the
article, it is classed low, and the rate is made very
little above the bare expense of carriage. On the
other hand, if the cost of carriage constitutes but a
small part of the ultimate price, the article is classed
high."* This is in accordance with the practices of
business, based on economic grounds everywhere
recognized, that the price of a thing shall be such as
it will bear. If railroads were to attempt to assess
"low-class traffic with its ratable proportion of all
expenses based on cost of service, . . . the consumer, unable to pay the cost of production and
high transportation charges, both of which enter
into the cost of the article to him, would seek a substitute either in a different article or from a different
field of production."† If a substitute could not be
found, the expense of living would advance to meet
the enhanced cost.

We grow each day in our comprehension of
the laws governing transportation. "The earliest

---

* W. D. Dabney, "The Public Regulation of Railways," page
163.

† *Ibid*, pages 164, 165.

freight tariffs involved little or no classification. Each step toward our present system has been accompanied by increased efficiency. It has made cheap traffic possible, has helped high-class traffic."* In other words, as the owners of railroads have become better acquainted with the natural laws governing their properties, they have been able to make them more generally useful.

Rates are based upon what the traffic will bear. For instance, a ton of lumber has such small intrinsic value, that if the same rate were charged upon it as is imposed upon dry goods, there would be no lumber carried, for the lumber traffic would not bear the high rate placed upon dry goods. "We hear a great deal said about charging 'what a traffic will bear;' and the man who avows this as his principle is compared by anti-monopolists with the robber barons of the Middle Ages. In the proper meaning of the principle, the case is just the opposite. Charging what the traffic will bear is a very different thing from charging what the traffic will not bear. . . High rates are not to be regarded as a tax which could be removed if the low rates were abandoned. When we come to examine the practice of European countries, where the attempt has been made to base rates on the cost of service, we shall find these views confirmed; and we shall further find that the effort to prevent discrimination as a system results in leveling up rather than in leveling down."†

---

* Arthur T. Hadley, "Railroad Transportation," page 113.

† *Ibid*, pages 76, 124.

Intelligent discrimination is the governing principle of railway classifications, as it is of everything else connected with trade. Uniformity is
impossible. The rate takes cognizance of the traffic
from every point of view. To attempt to base it on
any other ground " would give us dear food and
dear fuel, and would injure both the railroads and
the districts which they serve."*

Railways may and do agree among themselves to
maintain a uniform rate; that they will act together
in increasing or diminishing it. This is both practicable and just, and in harmony with well-established practices. It is not inconsistent with the
adjustment of rates based on their value and the
fluctuations of markets. Managers may think they
raise or lower rates of their own volition. They do
not. Conditions are superior to men, and while
carriers are sometimes loth to recognize it, they are
made aware of the fact by their inability to maintain a rate inconsistent therewith. Herein lies the
protection of the community from acts of injustice
upon the part of railroads; from anything more
than momentary hardship. If carriers, and not the
markets of the world, fixed the rate, then it might
be wise perhaps, (I don't say it would), to ask the
intervention of the government. But the carrier is
a passive agent merely. Wherever a product must
seek a general market, or its price is thus determined, the law of supply and demand fixes the rate
the carrier shall charge for transporting it. In
other cases special influences intervene. In prac-

* Arthur T. Hadley, " Railroad Transportation," page 114.

tice, an arbitrary rate may be enforced within a
limited range on merely local traffic. But it must
be reasonable, must be clearly within the means of
consumers, and generally fair to all parties, otherwise production will cease or seek other means of
conveyance. Its loss would react disastrously on
the carrier in many ways, because his interests are
as much bound up in the prosperity of the communities he serves as are those of the people themselves.
He is, therefore, interested in fostering them. This
fact many who are in the habit of discussing railway matters persistently ignore or deny. It is all
important, because more potent in securing fair rates
than any interference from without can possibly be.
Community of interest and the governing force of
markets everywhere render extraneous interference
unnecessary.

Carriers could not, if they would, combine among
themselves to do an unjust thing. To combine to
maintain an unfair rate, would be to combine to
destroy their traffic. Equity must be observed,
otherwise business will cease. This proposition is
self-evident.

The demands made upon railroads are oftentimes
picturesque in their grotesqueness. The moral
claim the people assert over them is also oftentimes
absurd. Thus the claim that the government may
arbitrarily interfere in the affairs of railroads,
because of the right of eminent domain exercised by
them, is a case in point. As if the right had any
inherent value to those who furnish the money to
build railways! Its exercise primarily is valuable

to the community, but to no one else. Those who
build railways pay fourfold for every rood of land
they get. But while the right of condemnation possesses no inherent value to capitalists, its exercise
is of enormous value to the people, because without
it a railroad could not and would not be built. In
such case, who would be the sufferer? The people
who were denied facilities of transportation, or the
capitalist? Certainly not the latter, because he has
other ways of investing his money. If property
acquired by railroads by act of condemnation could
be used for other purposes, the right might, under
remote contingencies, possess a possible value. But
property thus acquired reverts to its original owner,
when no longer used as intended. This franchise,
therefore, upon which so many demands are predicated, like many other imaginary benefits conferred upon railroads, will be found to be valueless
when critically examined. But oceans of ink and
tons of paper will continue to be wasted upon it
annually, so long as ignorant or designing men write
and silly people can be found to read. The excessive prices that railway companies are compelled to
pay in the exercise of the right of eminent domain,
rob the privilege of anything like favor, and give it
the appearance of robbery, carried on under the
guise of law by complaisant courts and aggressive
juries.* The experience of railroads is uniform in

---

* Here again, in the matter of eminent domain, it is sought to
make it appear that the railroad interest is *sui generis*, that it differs
from all others. The fact that it has been accorded the power to
take from individual owners and use in its business the land it requires, albeit it must pay the owner more than the value thereof, is

the fact that justice and common honesty are systematically denied them in the exercise of the right of condemnation. It is not a favor, but a legal means of plundering them.

---

cited as a reason why the government may interfere in the conduct of its affairs. The fact that railroads have been donated land by the government, or have been accorded the power to acquire such land as they need in their business upon payment therefor, does not place them in a category by themselves. Other interests have been accorded gifts, dispensations, and privileges by the government. But one instance seems closely to parallel that of the railways, namely, the agricultural interest. This has received at the hands of the government something far more valuable, far more tangible, than the right of eminent domain. It has been granted millions of acres of fertile land, and may to-day acquire many millions more, at merely nominal cost, and this is so in all countries save those of Europe. The agriculturist has but to adapt the land by his labor and skill to his purpose, just as the railways have. The products he reaps from the face of his government-granted acres are not less matters of public concern than the transportation which the carrier vends; his corn, his wheat, his cattle, are no less a necessity to the community than the means of carriage the railway provides. Yet we do not hear it suggested that the government shall interfere in the affairs of the farmer, shall prescribe the rules that shall fix the price he shall receive for his products, shall create or annihilate his markets, shall dictate the kind and quantity of crops and stock he shall raise, shall exercise a minute supervision over his methods and appliances, shall see that his revenues are wisely applied. Yet, if the farming interest is wasteful, shiftless, or incompetent, it works a public injury by keeping down production and enhancing the price of its products; if it withholds its crops in its storehouses, it heightens the cost to the consumer. But these things have not as yet invited legislative interference in agriculture. The farmer, with the staple of his business furnished him by the government, conducts his business as he pleases, sells his products how and when he pleases, or stores them away till he can get his price, and the community does not suffer, because experience has proven that natural laws are fully adequate for the regulation of the matter. And this is right. But it is as true of railway transportation as it is of the products of the farm.

The discussion of railway rates takes on a wider range each day. One writer likens the charges of carriers to tolls. Another to the duties of governments. Very well! Call them tolls or duties. But the fact that they represent actual disbursements for material, labor, and other necessary expenses incurred in operating, including a return on the money used in building, remains. There is a *bona fide* consideration in every case. Moreover, through association of interest, the people receive, in exchange for a nominal return on the capital invested in railroads, the experience, energy, and wisdom of an army of resolute and sagacious business men, gifted with a knowledge of the needs of the community, and possessing the capital and disposition to meet such needs. Their services could not otherwise be obtained. If the business were carried by the government, we should have to be content with hired agents of a perfunctory and very commonplace kind. The difference is the difference between genius and mediocrity, between energy and sloth, between experience and the want of it, between knowledge and ignorance, between wisdom and folly. This is one of the resultant benefits that grow out of the private ownership and management of railroads.

In the regulation of rates it has been claimed that they should be based on the average received by the carrier for the whole service rendered, after taking into account special rates, rebates, free transportation, and other necessary discriminations. The claim is based on the theory that these concessions are unnecessary; that the business that is done on reduced rates would be carried on without such concessions; that they are, in fact, the result of collusion. I cite the case merely to illustrate the length to which folly and ignorance may extend, not as requiring an answer.

The carriers of the world reach every important source of supply and demand. This is why an unjust rate is impossible. To attempt its enforcement would be to cripple the industry it is to the interest of the carrier to foster. Markets are no longer local. Railroads have ceased to be so in their ability to control rates. A consolidation of all the railroads of a great country, like that of the United States, would, however, destroy competition in many minor directions, and would, consequently, entail more or less hardship. But it would still be preferable to government management, because it would be intelligent and business-like. A combination of all the carriers of the world is necessary to the creation of a complete monopoly. The railroads of every country, "the tides of the seas, the currents of rivers, the swells of lakes, the waters of canals, and the rivalry of adjacent nations, enforce transportation conditions."* Combinations of a local nature do not destroy or cripple competition. Nor do limited pools sensibly affect it. On the contrary, they strengthen it, because they render it more intelligent. Monopoly is no longer possible, except in the case of local products, such as gas, water, street railways, and the like. So long as car-

---

* G. R. Blanchard, "Politico-railway Problems and Theories," page 43.

4

riers serve a common purpose, and their interests lie
apart, there can be no such thing as a monopoly of
rates. When competition ends, legislative interference may begin. Such interference under other
conditions is not, however, necessarily injurious.
If honestly, temperately, and discreetly exercised,
it may prove highly beneficial. Its effect is to
silence unjust clamor. It is only injurious when
ignorantly or demagogically exercised. But in
regard to the regulation of rates, so long as the
markets of the world are supplied by carriers acting
independently of each other, competitive forces are
more effective in preventing injustice than the perfunctory act of any man or body of men. The
beneficent effect of competition can not be overestimated. Its forces are " the efforts of rival sellers
to secure a market for their goods, each striving to
offer better terms than his competitors. Competition is what prevents any individual from fixing
prices to suit himself, because his rivals will give
lower prices, and he will get no business at all."*
Railways have not destroyed the principle of competition nor lessened its value. It has simply taken
on a wider field than formerly. They have made it
universal. But the great and varied interests that
cluster about it, as exercised by them, render it
difficult for the student to discover and analyze its
operations. It affects everything we eat or wear.
"The wheat of Dakota, the wheat of Russia, and
the wheat of India come into direct competition.
The supply at Odessa is an element in determining

* Arthur T. Hadley, " Railroad Transportation," page 63.

the price at Chicago. . . . Cabbages from Germany contend with cabbages from Missouri in the markets of New York."*

In the operation of carriers, discriminations not based on natural causes are impossible. When thus superinduced, they are irresistible and irremediable. To attempt to enforce uniformity, under such circumstances, would be to entail evils infinitely greater than the nominal ones sought to be remedied.

The complaint so often put forth, that railroads have favored one individual at the expense of another, except on sound economic grounds, beneficial to the community, is generally untrue. Isolated exceptions to the rule prove nothing.

Much of the criticism bestowed upon railroads is sentimental, demagogical, or communistic. Much of it is merely the mouthings of ignorant men talking to ignorant men. It has, however, been an avenue to public notice and favor; a political "fad." Production is not retarded, but in every case expedited by the rates of carriers. They are nominal only — a pittance merely.† "The cost of delivering bread from the baker to his customer is a larger element in the price of bread than the cost of getting wheat from the farmer to the miller, and flour from the

---

* Arthur T. Hadley, "Railroad Transportation," pages 65 and 66.

† "The value of the product of five hundred operatives in a coarse cotton factory in Massachusetts is over $1,000,000. All the western flour and meat which these operatives need in a year, can be moved from Chicago to Lowell at a cost of $600, and sometimes for less." — Edward Atkinson, "The Distribution of Products," page 38.

miller to the baker, though the one is but a few
hundreds of yards, and the other as many hundred miles."*

The influences to which we owe the low rates of
American railways—rates much less than those of
other countries—are, in the main, due to better facilities and more economical methods, superinduced
by intense and widespread rivalry. The immense
distances traversed, and a desire to secure a load both
ways, have had something to do with it. The amal-
gamation of rival and continuous lines has been
beneficial. Combinations of sympathetic interests
that are the result of natural causes are always
good. Among these may be mentioned the consolidation of continuous railways and the formation of
pools. On the other hand, combinations occasioned
by extraneous influences, such as those caused by
the interference or oppression of the State, are not
likely to be so beneficial, because they are more or
less artificial.

Englishmen and Americans make the same complaints in regard to the rates of railways, namely,
that they are excessive; that special advantages are
afforded competitive interests; that goods are in
some cases carried at unduly low rates, losses being
recouped elsewhere. Heretofore, England has permitted carriers to charge what the traffic will bear,
to make special rates to meet particular circumstances. The necessity and value of these provisions
have been generally recognized in every country where railroads are operated, save the United

* Arthur T. Hadley, " Railroad Transportation," pages 103, 104.

States. In the United Kingdom the supervisory
power of the government has been merely nominal.
The people have had greater confidence in the ability
and wisdom of their business men than in their government.* On the other hand, the belief in the
efficacy of State interference in the management of
railways is cardinal in many parts of the United
States. Thus, the commissioners of one great State
openly boast of their active influence in determining
what railroads shall charge, claiming that within the
restricted area of their activity they have, through
arbitrary action, placed competitive and non-compet-
itive business on the same plane; that they have, in
fact, subverted the law of competition upon which
the world is dependent for its development, and the
comforts and the necessities it enjoys. They openly
boast that, under the powers they exercise, "competition which could only operate at certain points
touched by independent lines, if left to natural laws,
is, by the statutory penalties denounced against discrimination, made to operate equally at all points,
intermediate as well as directly competing." I leave
the reader to judge as to what the effect would be if
similar powers were exercised by every government.
Nine-tenths of the world would have to be abandoned. No more monstrous proposition ever found
birth in the brain of civilized man. The commissioners in question do not regard the exercise of
their prerogatives as unjust or oppressive. "To
say a railroad company may discriminate in any

---

* Their disposition to depart from this practice, as evinced in a
recent act of Parliament, is to be deplored.

degree between different places or between different
persons, or that the case should be left to the vague
and inadequate remedies afforded by the common
law upon the subject of discrimination, would be to
advocate the practical subjection of all other interests to that of the railroads." In other words, they
would have us believe that railroads are governed
by mechanical agencies, which only the intervention
of the government can prevent becoming oppressive.
Self-interest and competitive forces are alike ignored.
The picture is an exaggerated one; an extreme view
of the virtues and benefits of government interference. It is, however, shared in by many. It does
not matter that it is contrary to generally accepted
practices recognized in every country save the United
States that special rates are necessary; that discrimination is not only unavoidable, but beneficial; that
rates must adjust themselves to localities and markets; that competition is a recognized principle, to
be encouraged, rather than condemned; that self-
interest is a potent factor in ensuring equitable rates.

On the other hand, another State commission* is
disposed to trust rates largely to natural causes.
"It seems apparent, from results of operations in
this State, that a conservative policy, rather than
one too exacting, as illustrated in the enactments of
some of our sister States, is the one best serving the
real interests of the public, and most certain to
secure fair rates of transportation. While the law-
making power should see that our railroad corporations are not in a position to impose unfair, excessive

* That for Michigan, U. S. A.

or discriminating charges upon the business of the State, still, if lines of railroad shall be multiplied, opening up competing ways to important trade centers, and affording to large manufacturing communities choice of routes in the shipment of their products to market, in the securing of their trade, the intelligent management of our railroad properties, which sharp competition also makes liberal, will leave but little to be desired in the way of legislation for the regulation of tariff rates.''* Such a policy will not only ensure equitable rates, but will invite the confidence and respect of men who have money with which to build railroads and otherwise enrich the State, while the policy of the commission previously mentioned will be directly the reverse.

A favorite assumption of those who discuss railway subjects is, that wherever aid is extended in the building of roads, it affords just grounds for State interference afterwards, among other things, for the enforcement of abnormally low rates. · The point is not well taken. Wherever aid is extended by donations of money, bonds, right of way, or other gratuities, the donors receive an equal or greater consideration in return. It may be assumed, in every such instance, that the railroad would not be built except for the aid extended; that the field is not such as to invite capital. If it were, capital would neither receive nor solicit such assistance. It is too embarrassing. No ground, therefore, exists for enforcing subsequent obligations in cases of this kind. Besides, railroads thus built are as a rule

*Report of Commissioner of Railroads for Michigan, 1888, page ii.

unproductive, at least for a long time. But the districts they traverse derive instant and abnormal advantages from their presence. If obligation rests on either party, therefore, it is clearly on the people and not on the railroad.

The right of the legislature to control the rates of carriers is not questioned. However, such interference is neither necessary nor wise. It is as impolitic as it would be in the case of other manufacturers and middlemen. But the semi-public character of railroads, the mutuality of interest, as between private owner and public use, seem to make the right a natural one. Therefore it is not disputed. "It has been conceded that the States generally have control of railway rates, the ground for the exercise of such power being the doctrine of the inalienable nature of the sovereign powers of a State, such as the police power and eminent domain; that when a franchise to take a toll is granted, it must be considered as being in the hands of the subject, but still belonging to the States and fully under State control; that the right of eminent domain can only be delegated, not alienated, and that corporations exercising it, therefore, possess a public character, must perform a public function, and in their nature and origin are subject to the sovereign authority. There is also a broader basis of support for such control. That is the natural and circumstantial monopoly that railway companies possess over the traffic tributary to them. The State's right to regulate tolls rests upon the consideration that the State has assisted to erect a monopoly, against which the people have no adequate protection but its sovereign power. Again, the railroads may be said to lie at the very foundation of society, as organized in America. In the west, at least, the whole social fabric rests on railroad transportation, which brings into play the common-law axiom that 'When private property is so used that a public interest attaches to it, it is no longer strictly private property, and the right of the legislature to exercise control of it by statute can not be questioned.' " * When we remember that the traffic of railways is governed by competitive influences as much as that of water transportation, the concessions of the government are found to be nominal, rather than real. They do not create a monopoly, or special privilege, any more than they do when the government licenses a steamboat, and so far as the justice of the case is concerned, the government has no more right to interfere in the case of railways than in the case of steamboats. All arguments predicated upon the assumption that railways are monopolies are fallacious and misleading. But if the right of the State to interfere is allowed, the manner in which that right shall be exercised is still of the greatest importance. Its enforcement requires the exercise of candor and tact; a due observance of the natural laws that govern trade. "The right of public control must be exercised within those constitutional and legal limitations which environ all legislative or administrative acts. Regulation does not mean con-

* From a paper read before the Engineers' Society of St. Paul, by Edwin E. Woodman, in April, 1889.

fiscation, nor the right to authorize rates ruinous to
the public, nor can a railroad be compelled to carry
without reward." *

Public control, when exercised, should not be perfunctory or superficial, but minute, and as far reaching in intelligence and interest as when exercised by
the railways themselves. But this is impossible.
The structural forces of government do not permit
it. A supervisory power may, however, be maintained by a government in a less minute and practical way, and without the danger that attends active
interference. The exercise of the rate-making
power involves preparatory education, familiarity
with business methods, intimate knowledge of properties, rival routes, markets, sources of supply,
every attendant detail that governs the business
handled and the district provided for. No one
but practical men, present on the ground, can
possess this experience and knowledge. The competitive influences of markets are too acute, the
influences that govern trade too subtle, to be settled
out of hand. The farthest we may go blindly in
fixing rates, is to say that between any two points
they shall be the same for all shippers, time, quantity, quality, and service being alike.† Except
within these narrow limits, no one can say off-hand
what is or what is not a just rate.

Much diversity of opinion exists as to the unit of
service for railway traffic. Extremists profess to

* " Report of Committee of State Railroad Commissions and Interstate Commerce Commission."

† The car lot, for instance, being the unit of quantity for freight.

believe that the same rate should be charged, relatively, for car lots as for one hundred pounds; that one hundred pounds should be the basis. The effect of this, of course, would be to reduce enormously rates on small shipments. Car lots afford a more rational basis. The train load is a still more conservative estimate. That a distinction should be made between wholesale and retail shipments, there can be no doubt. "Railroad transportation is a commodity which is bought and sold as much as coal is; and to say that it should never be dealt in except at retail prices, or, as has been said, that one thousand cars should never be shipped at a less rate per car than one train or one single car, is the same as saying that coal should be sold as cheaply for one car load as by the cargo making a hundred car loads. It is wholly a question of expediency, to be answered only by those directly interested. To do away with wholesale trading would limit distribution and consumption, and would, in the end, hurt the small consumer. The world needs wholesale traders as much as it needs retail traders. Wholesale prices, whether of transportation or other commodities, so far from being an unjust discrimination, are of the greatest benefit, because they encourage distribution, and make possible the carrying of large local stocks, thus enabling the retail traders to do a large business on small capital, which means a small profit on each transaction."*

Generally speaking, the interference of governments in the commercial differences of a people is

---

* Letter of C. E. Perkins.

harmful. Every evil carries its cure. Its correction, moreover, serves to make those concerned self-reliant; it teaches a people self-control, manliness, acuteness, independence, ability to look out for themselves, self-government. Such interference, in the case of England or America, is unnecessary; the people do not generally need it. It only delays justice, does not accelerate it. This has been abundantly attested in the case of America. Her great and rapid development evinces the self-reliance of her people. " In the adjustment of commercial and trading relations, the American people exhibit a very high degree of shrewdness and sagacity. It can scarcely fail to strike an observer that, in the so-called struggle between the railroads and the people, each party has in the past substantially obtained pretty much what it wanted and was entitled to have. . . . The people were determined to have low rates; and it soon became apparent that they could get them, if they permitted the railroads themselves, within rational limits, to work out the problem in their own way. They enjoyed, prior to the passage of the interstate commerce act, the benefit of low rates and a good service. A reasonable *modus vivendi* had been arrived at, and the great bulk of the community was fairly well satisfied. In the writer's opinion, the experience of the past affords the best key to the future; and what has happened before, in connection with the railroad situation, is likely to happen again. If this be so, the new legislation would appear calculated to challenge the vigilance, but not necessarily to excite the alarm, of the foreign investor."*

Rates, to be equitable, must be self-adjustive; must conform to their environment; must be based on the property of the carrier, and the traffic handled. "The more the attempt is made to control the rates of traffic by statute, the higher the rates charged must be, because it is very plain that the rates on railways, which have a small traffic, can not be reduced by statute to the level of those which have a heavy traffic, unless the State takes them and operates them at a loss; and therefore it follows of necessity that statute interference can only end in an advance of the low rates now charged on the lines having a heavy traffic to the higher rates of the lines having a small traffic, if the statutes do not prove to be inoperative."†

The principles of transportation, and the competition of carriers, occupy the attention of writers and publicists more and more, as the relation of the subject to the internal commerce of the country becomes more and more apparent. The capable, the superficial, the ignorant, and the vicious, alike have a word to say. A recent writer‡ devotes a volume to the competitive practices of railroads. He sees no cure for the petty acts of injustice he chronicles, except legislative interference. It is very much like devoting a book to the disputes of

---

* John Swann, M. A., "An Investor's Notes on American Railways," page 183.

† Edward Atkinson, "The Distribution of Products," page 309.

‡ A. B. Stickney.

boys; boys are not always truthful; boys will sometimes fight; boys are not actuated by an exalted
sense of justice in every case. Therefore, lock up
the boys, or appoint tribunals to supervise their
affairs. What kind of men would such boys make?
Similar interference in the affairs of men destroys
their manhood. It is called "coddling." In passing judgment on the affairs of railways, men
oftentimes make the mistake of confounding acts
with conditions; mistake incidents for principles.
On these mistakes they found systems, or tear them
to pieces. To change a method of business because
its working is not perfect, is very much like oblit-
erating the sun because it has spots on its face;
like imprisoning a population, or disfranchising it,
because particular men are hot-headed, foolish, or
dishonest.

It is a favorite assertion of writers, as I have
already noticed, that carriers should derive an
equal profit from all their business. "It seems
impossible that any set of men could become so
befogged by a form of words as to suppose that it
was profitable for a railway to haul a ton of freight
five hundred miles at substantially the same price
as for hauling it two hundred miles, yet a reference
to the tariffs of these railways would tend to show
that such is the fact."* Doubtless the profit is
less for the long distance, but if it is all the traffic
can pay, and if there is a margin in it over operating
expenses, the transaction is right and proper. The
margin of profit, whatever it is, inures indirectly to

* Stickney's "Railway Problem," page 52.

the benefit of the short-haul shipper. It would not make the rate of the latter smaller to have the carrier refuse the less productive business. Whatever profit he derives from it, helps to pay interest on the capital invested, helps to make the railroad profitable, and, consequently, to multiply railroads. The business would not be done if attended with loss.

So long as values, rather than bulk, determine the measure of commercial profit, so long will it be impossible for carriers to frame a tariff that will distribute its burdens alike. Such time will never come. This is why the cost of a railroad, or the amount of its capital, has little or no influence in fixing the rate. Rates adjust themselves to the thing carried, and not to the tools of the carrier. Hence, watering the stock of a railroad does not affect its rates.*

A theory more or less regarded is, that the rate-making power of railroads should be separated from the rate-maintaining power.† This would be true if rates did not adjust themselves naturally. A rate that may be moderate this week, may be high or low next week. The purpose sought by the separation, is the prevention of rate-cutting, undue competition, prevention of strife. A better remedy is to be found in permitting railroads to enter into

---

* "Watered stock and bonds can not affect the charge for transportation in any manner."—Edward Atkinson, "The Distribution of Products," page 259.

† *Vide* circular of Aldace F. Walker, Chairman Interstate Commerce Railway Association of railroad companies.

contracts to pool their competitive business. That is the method of procedure in other countries. It should be here.*

Not only do the roads of England and the continent make pools, but the use of preferential rates is universally recognized as necessary and beneficial.†

To separate the rate-making power from the rate-maintaining power, is to separate the body from the mind, to prevent concerted action, flexibility, facility, knowledge of the situation. No one save the carrier can fulfill the duties that attach to the power to make rates. He is in daily and hourly contact with shippers. A remedy for the evils of rate-cutting is not in taking the busi-

---

* Those who are able to judge believe that the law of the United States prohibiting pooling, if not repealed, will have the effect to bring about a consolidation of all the railroads in the country ; unless, indeed, railway owners find some practical means of avoiding it, i. e., of operating their roads according to the real interests and wants of the country.

† Thus, the rate per ton on meat from Liverpool to London is 25s., while it is 45s. from London to intermediate points. To the local mind this is aggravated by the fact that the smaller rate is on imported meats. Another instance is the tariff on sugar from Greenock, at a rate of 1.09d. per ton per mile, while from London it is 2.13d. This last was made a matter of complaint to the government of Great Britain. The conclusions of the latter were as follows : " It does not appear to your committee that such a result" (as the closing, namely, of southern markets to Greenock sugar for the benefit of London refiners), "would be either just or reasonable. . . This competition can not but be advantageous to the public. That Greenock sugar refiners should be in the same market as the sugar refiners of London, while it may be a grievance to London refiners, must be an advantage to Greenock refiners, and can not be a disadvantage to buyers of sugar." — W. M. Acworth, M. A., " The Railways and the Traders," pages 14, 15.

ness out of his hands, but in permitting reasonable combinations between carriers, sanctioning such
combinations by law, and enforcing them by penalties, such as those imposed by the interstate commerce law of the United States for disregarding
its requirements. It is probable that a central tribunal, composed of the local traffic managers of
the railways interested, having the power to make
or amend rates, would work well. But it must be
so located and constituted as to be in hourly contact with those who use the rates it makes, otherwise they will not represent the requirements of
either the carrier or his patron.

The rates of railroads represent the adjustment of
a part to the whole. The details of this adjustment
can not be explained any more than any other
natural phenomenon. The rate is an incident
merely, a link in a chain of transactions, and adjusts itself within its environment as unreservedly
as the atmosphere conforms to its sphere, fitting
like a glove, yet not bearing perceptibly upon any
particular part. So long as a railroad, or group of
railroads, does not possess the monopoly of a
product and its substitutes, interference is posi-
tively harmful.

Interference in commercial affairs precipitates
evils worse than those sought to be remedied.

There is no patent way for ascertaining what a
rate should be; the power to determine it is not
easily acquired. It must be such as to foster the
growth of the product, and at the same time afford
the carrier a profit. Both objects must be attained.

5

If left free to adjust themselves, rates will conform
to these conditions with the precision of a mathematical demonstration. The process is one of evolution, of natural adjustment. However, man's work,
here as elsewhere, is not perfect, but it approxi-
mates perfection. His success is dependent upon
his industry, experience, and breadth of knowledge.
When he errs, he will quickly learn the fact from
those about him; from the shipper or the carrier.
His errors injure the carrier as much as they do the
patron. The efficiency of traffic managers is not
uniform. Some come much nearer than others to
the measure of their duty. However, the mistakes
that are made are not permanent. The necessities
of trade compel their daily reconsideration and re-
adjustment. Out of this evolution there comes
equity; a tariff in which every interest is considered.

Those who make rates come in hourly contact
with the producer, merchant, and consumer. Out
of this interchange of views the truth is evolved,
errors are corrected, omissions remedied, every
interest reconciled. The work is coöperative,
economic.

Those who formulate rates may not always be
aware of the facts underlying them, but they are
facts nevertheless. Men oftentimes obey a law while
thinking they lead. This is true of carriers. The
aggregate number of men engaged in the duty of
classifying, revising, and fixing the rates of railroads
constitutes an army. Its bulk is made up of assist-
ants, clerks, and agents. They are, however, quite

as experienced, patient, and discerning, in their way, as the chiefs they follow; quite as necessary in carrying on the business. They are not clerks, in the common acceptation of the term, because each one is endowed with special knowledge, talent, and discretion. This is the rate force of a country. No body of men less experienced, less wise, less discreet, less industrious, less in number, less adaptable in their ways can take their places. They possess the knowledge and instinct of trade. They know what traffic is natural and possible to a section, what is not; the business that may be encouraged to become profitable, that which can never become profitable. Their methods are simple and practical, and so long as a country conforms to commercial usages and principles, rather than political emergencies, they will continue to be followed.

Rates are based on barter. A traffic that affords the carrier gain is sought, but not at the expense of more profitable business. They follow in their natural order.

The issuance of a special or discriminatory rate does not involve any obligation or understanding. The favor is not a particular one. The profit that enures from it accrues to the community. Its purpose is to create trade that would not otherwise exist, to increase production, to lessen cost, to stimulate consumption, to benefit mankind. No business is ever done that involves a permanent loss. A profit must accrue in every case, directly or indirectly. Rates conform to circumstances. They fluctuate. If the necessity of the situation calls for

low rates, we have low rates. It is not necessary
that the legislature should interfere to secure them.
The process is natural and inevitable. So long as
the rate affords the carrier a measure of profit, he
will adapt himself to it, if the circumstances of
trade require it, piecing out the poor with something
better. If his income as a whole is sufficient, his
property will be prosperous. If it is not, it will be
depressed; and as it is prosperous or otherwise, so
will other interests be. The bond of sympathy is
complete. We cannot cut an artery, or deny any
part of our body its just proportion of food, without weakening the whole. So a great interest can
not be crippled by the State without other interests
being crippled.

Wherever competition is free, the rates of carriers will be such as to facilitate transportation,
to increase production and consumption. Why?
Because competitive influences overlook nothing.
No interest is too small or too unimportant for it to
notice and provide for. Traffic, that will only pay
the carrier a molecule of profit, will be attended to
as conscientiously as if involving millions; a traffic
that will afford a margin of profit, be it ever so
slight, he accepts with eagerness, if it is all it can
pay. No one is harmed thereby, but both the community and the carrier are benefited. Out of these
small ventures a profitable trade oftentimes grows.
The commerce of the world has grown up in this
way. Particular items of traffic can not be considered by themselves, but must be viewed in their relation to the whole. The fact that shippers are not

charged relatively the same rate per mile, grows out of forces beyond the control of the carrier. He would gladly charge everyone the same. The discrimination he is compelled to exercise stimulates production, cheapens cost, increases consumption.

The rivalry of carriers also benefits. It begets better service, better roads, better cars, quicker transportation, greater safety.

Uniformity of rates must not be looked for, except in conformity with the markets they supply. Each company must be considered by itself. A traffic that may be carried profitably upon one road, it may be impossible to carry at all on a neighboring line. Cost of operating is never the same. It may be greater in December than in June; more in March than October; more on one section of a road than another. On one day the load may be light, the next day it may be heavy; facilities, terminals, labor, expenses, climate, and innumerable other things affect cost.*

---

* "The underlying principle governing the fixing of rates is that the railroad company is not merely a common carrier, but is also the *owner of a roadway*, and it charges, not only for the work of moving freight as a common carrier, but also *toll for the use of its roadway*. Now, in the United States it requires nearly forty per cent. of the receipts to pay the toll on this roadway, that is the interest on the investment, and within that forty per cent. the railroads have great latitude in making their charges. The other sixty per cent. goes to pay the cost of operating the road; that is to say, of moving and handling the freight. In making competitive rates, therefore, the question is presented to the railroad manager whether he can reach a certain business at certain rates, and if he finds he can not get his forty per cent. on that business, he takes twenty or even ten. . . .

 . The higher charges made upon some classes of freight com-

It is a favorite theory, and one we meet with every day, that managers of railroads may build up a town or destroy it at will. The theory is not true, but is carefully perpetuated by those who seek to breed distrust of railway methods. Managers do not fix rates any more than brakemen. They record them merely. Conditions determine the status of cities, as they do of men. Trade centers are determined by sources of supply and distribution. A town at the junction of two or more roads ought, naturally, to possess an advantage therefrom. It is in harmony with just laws that it should. If its growth is stimulated by competitive practices, so much the better, not only for the town, but for the community.

Men will never be able to legislate rightly for railroads until they learn that the interests of the people require that these carriers should be allowed the same latitude, in collecting and distributing the products of a country, that private individuals are. The carrier does not determine the product or point of distribution. Natural causes do this. The distinction thus created, however, affords a fine opportunity for the maliciously inclined to excite suspicion, create jealousy, foster animosities, stir up the ignorant. Whenever a product or a town no longer responds to a natural requirement, its decline is certain and inevitable, and while carriers may temporarily stay its downward progress, they

---

pensate the railroad companies for the lower charges upon others. They must be regulated according to what the articles will bear."— Albert Fink, before Committee on Commerce, February, 1882.

will not attempt to do so when they discover the nature of the load they are carrying. Neither cities nor carriers find occupation or place longer than they respond to a natural want of the community. Trade centers, maintained by rival markets and the influence of competitive carriers, are valuable to a community. Those maintained by government bounty are not. The community in one case receives the benefit of a local tax. In the other, a neighborhood is made the beneficiary of a general tax. Similarly, this is a distinction between private and public ownership of railroads.

In America, competitive influences have from the start had free play in the building of railroads, and the adjustment of rates. To this fact we are indebted for our unexampled commercial wealth. England more nearly resembles us in this respect than any other country. Practices elsewhere are generally alike; Germany is, in the main, typical of the whole. Its system, like its army and civil service, is a cast-iron one: "So far as they can, they have eliminated competitive rates altogether. America has given free play to competition. England has taken a position midway between the two. . . Every time we (the English), yield to German ideas, and move away from the American principle of giving competition full swing, we may do injustice between two competitors, whether they be individual traders or rival towns, but we unquestionably raise the general average of English rates."*

---

* W. M. Acworth, M. A., "The Railways and the Traders," page 227.

In America, action has heretofore been impersonal; has been responsive to the natural conditions of trade fixed by the world. Germany has tried to make the world respond to merely local desires—to an autocracy. Naturally, she has not been successful. Her action has not been materially different from other governments owning and operating railroads.

The interests of a community and the carriers who supply it are one, and while they will have many differences, many heart-burnings, they must mutually support and protect each other. One can not be crippled without injury to the other. Left to their own devices, carriers will, so far as they can, adjust rates, so that every interest shall derive some advantage. That is the limit of their power. Interests that can not conform to this just requirement, without trenching upon the just profits of others, are abnormal, artificial, hurtful to a community. Business that can not be handled under such circumstances, should be allowed to die out. To seek to perpetuate it, is to seek to fasten a burden on the community. But this is just what governments do whenever they meddle in commercial affairs. The votes of the improvident town are quite as potent as those of the prosperous town. Governments carry out in trade the principles they endeavor to enforce in their courts, namely, absolute equality, without reference to capacity or fitness. White and brown sugar are to them the same; capable and incapable men are alike their children. They place the burdens of the weak on the strong, and thus render all weak.

The rates of railroads react naturally when too high. But reduction will be dependent upon ability to heighten. Obligation and privilege must go hand in hand. It is not necessary that the carrier should have an order to reduce rates. His interests are more potent to move him than any statute; his instincts more facile than the reason or logic of men.

America bases her rates on the value of the service; the ability of the traffic to pay.* The Germans have sought to base them on cost entirely. They have made the experiment under the most favorable circumstances. The unity of the country, and the exceptionally high character of its civil service, made this an exceedingly favorable field for demonstrating theories of this nature. But, notwithstanding her exceptional service and autocratic power, it was found impossible to operate railroads except in harmony with the laws of trade, the supplying of markets from the cheapest sources and by the cheapest routes. The desire of Germany to build up distinctively German railroads, fostering distinctively German interests, failed. The system was accordingly changed, but begrudgingly, and in that retroactive, combative way so peculiar to governments—and crabs! However, natural condit' ns have gradually re-asserted themselves, until to day fifty per cent. of the tonnage of Germany is carried under special arrangements, preferential rates, contracts, agreements, and understandings. The Ger-

---

*Cost is considered to this extent, that the rate must at least equal the cost.

mans found that a tariff based distinctively on cost
was an impossibility. The competition of carriers and
markets forbade it.   A well-known writer on the
subject* says that a tariff based on cost would result
in three things: " Either of which would upset the
business of the country: 1st. There would be little or
no classification of freights. Grain, lumber, coal,
iron, shoes, dry goods, groceries, drugs, and chemi-
cals, would all have to pay near about the same rate
per hundred pounds per mile, and that rate would
have to be something like the average of the present
rates charged upon the different classes of freights.
The higher classes of freight would be a good deal
lowered, and the lower classes would be materially
raised.   The result would be that cheap and heavy
products could be no longer transported over the
distance that they are now carried. 2d. The rates
on through freight would have to be proportioned
very nearly to the distance hauled; the rate from
Chicago to Boston, for instance, would be materially
higher, and the rate from Chicago to Baltimore
materially lower, than the rates from Chicago to
New York, because there is difference enough in
distance to make a difference in cost. 3d. Roads
having lowest grades and most favorable alignments
would have lower rates than their competitors, and
would monopolize the business, to the entire exclusion of those lines which traverse more difficult and
expensive territory, and upon which the cost of
transportation was greater. And the tide once
turned, the evil would multiply itself; for the rates

*E. P. Alexander.

would decrease rapidly on the favored roads, with the increase of business, and would increase on the unfortunately located roads, with the decrease in volume of their freights, until the latter would be left with nothing but their local business to support them, which would then have to be advanced to the highest figures possible.''

Dissimilarity of cost of operation and construction would prevent cost being made the basis of rates, if other and more potential causes did not intervene. "The average cost of transportation over one line of railway may as much exceed that over another, which reaches the same competitive point or region, as the average cost of transportation over the latter exceeds the average cost of water carriage." * Those that would base rates on cost go hand in hand with those who believe that all rates should be relatively the same. The latter believe (or profess to believe) that rates based on mileage are alone equitable; that they prevent discrimination; that they treat all alike; that everyone pays according to the distance he travels, or the length of line over which his goods are hauled. Such a rate is, however, an impossibility. A tariff thus predicated might be possible within the boundaries of a small and isolated country. But not elsewhere. Mathematically arranged, rates for near-by freight would not be enough to cover cost of carriage and terminals, or, if made to cover these expenses, would soon reach a point where they could not be further increased, in which case business would have to be abandoned, or a less

---

* W. D. Dabney, "The Public Regulation of Railways," page 115.

rate relatively exacted. The latter will be conceded
in every case where carriers are left untrammeled.
An equitable tariff may be illustrated in this way:
Between Georgetown and Norfolk, four hundred
and twenty miles apart, the rate on wheat and flour
at ten miles will be fifty-five and seven-tenths per
cent. of the whole rate; at fifty miles it will be ninety
and one-tenth per cent. of the whole rate; at eighty
miles it will be the same as for the whole distance.
The reasons are obvious. The roads must either refuse to do business near Georgetown, or charge a
sufficient rate to pay carriage and terminal charges.
This they do. The people near Georgetown do not
suffer in any way by the arrangement; they would not
get a lower rate if the business outside their restricted
circle were refused unless it paid a corresponding rate.

The impracticability of a progressive tariff is
well understood by those versed in such matters.
It not only restricts the movement of traffic, but
retards railway development.* The long and short

---

* Arthur T. Hadley, referring to this phase of the subject, says:
" Suppose it is a question whether a road can be built through a country
district, lying between two large cities, which have the benefit of
water communication, while the intervening district has not. The
rate between these points must be made low to meet water competition; so low that if it were applied to the whole business of the
road it would make it quite unprofitable. On the other hand, the
local business at intermediate points is so small that this alone can
not support the road, no matter how low or how high the rates are
made. So that, in order to live at all, the road must secure two different things — the high rates for its local traffic, and the large traffic
of the through points which can only be attracted by low rates. If
the community is to have the road, it must permit the discrimination."
—" Railroad Transportation," page 115.

haul clause (progressive feature) of the Interstate Commerce Act of America, by which a railroad is prohibited from carrying passengers or freight for a particular distance at a lower rate than it charges for a shorter distance, is happily qualified by the statement that the prohibition applies only where the circumstances and conditions are the same. The law is defective in this, that it does not give sufficient discretion to those in charge of the traffic of railroads. It permits "a greater charge on the shorter haul, when the conditions and circumstances seem to justify it, even permitting what may be called a suspension of the law in special cases, if, in the opinion of the commission appointed to regulate interstate traffic, it should seem after investigation to be reasonable to do so."* Getting an opinion from the commission, crowded as it is with cases, is, however, like sending a thousand miles for a busy doctor in a case of life and death. The delay it necessitates in a great measure destroys the value of the concession. Carriers should have the right to make such charge as in their judgment is necessary. If afterwards the commission, on reviewing, esteem it improper, its further use may be prohibited. If application must be made in every case calling for such concession, they would be so numerous that their adjudication singly by the commission would be impossible. Requiring the consent of the commission in advance in such cases, is tantamount to prohibiting all traffic falling under such regulation.

---

* "Fourth Annual Report, Interstate Commerce Commission," page 44.

Competition and circumstances of a like nature are recognized abroad as justifying discriminatory rates by railroads. They are professedly so regarded by the government in America, but we are disposed to surround our carriers with such restrictions and delays as to greatly impair their usefulness, and greatly restrict and injure the business of the country.

In reference to the local business of railroads, the petty traffic that passes back and forth on a line between stations, is a thing apart. The rates that govern it, however, are distinctly influenced by those made to cover the surplus of the district, including the through traffic that seeks a wider outlet. It is, therefore, assured of favorable conditions; of a rate that will develop and maintain the country.

As a general thing, local rates are influenced unfavorably by lack of return load, by a short haul, by restricted use of rolling stock, by delay at stations in loading and unloading, by the limited quantity of the traffic offered, and by relatively increased expenses for handling and accounting. On the other hand, they are affected favorably, from the standpoint of the shipper, by the constant and intelligent effort of carriers to build up business along their lines; to make their properties independent and self-sustaining. This leads them to make especially favorable rates, wherever necessary to encourage new enterprises, or perpetuate those already in existence. They are partners in interest, and the regard paid is that which such conditions engender. The fact that it is largely selfish does not detract from its value; on the contrary, it adds thereto by insuring its perpetuation; by making it more sustained, intelligent and discriminating. Intelligent selfishness is the basis of commercial wisdom and energy — the basis of commercial growth and perpetuation.

Local rates, quite as much as others, are based on equitable grounds. Production could not thrive otherwise. Water does not more surely seek a lower level, than trade abandons a location unfavorable to it. Railroads can not, if they would, maintain an inequitable local tariff. To do so would be to depopulate the country tributary to them. Local rates must be such as the nature of the traffic requires and in harmony with good business usage and the customs that govern such matters. Every carrier puts his patrons on an equality with others, so far as he can. He aids them in every way. But it is not a matter he can wholly regulate. Location and adaptation have much to do with it. If the producer is unfavorably located, it is not in the power of the carrier to remedy his lack of judgment. If the latter locates his road wisely, builds cheaply, and operates economically and efficiently, he has done everything he can to aid the community he serves. All these conditions have been observed in America. Our railroads are not only built more cheaply than in other countries, but they are worked more economically. Their operations, however, are not generally understood. Many of our laws are predicated upon a belief that they act automatically. The competition that exists in the carrying trade of the world is too subtle to be generally analyzed, too far-reaching to be generally described. It is, however, universally felt. Monopoly among carriers is impossible, because combination is impossible. Conflicting interests can neither be reached nor governed. They are too widespread, too diversified, too indefinite. "A monopoly must either be one secured by public authority, or one that results from the practical impossibility of competition; and in making out the latter, it is going altogether farther than the common law has ever gone, to say that competition is impossible, because one mode of transportation has an advantage in the public estimation over another. That advantage is continually varying. It varies with the season of the year, with the state of trade, and the particular objects which individuals wish to accomplish. It is now on the side of the railroads, and now on the side of other means of transportation. One man may wish to make a long journey with the utmost rapidity, and he can afford to pay the highest railroad fare. Another man is not so pressed for time, and he can take the slower, and perhaps cheaper, conveyance by water. One person employs the more expensive communication by telegraph, because he is in a hurry; another can use the cheaper communication by a letter dropped in the post office, because he is not in a hurry. In short, every mode of conveyance of persons, or things, or information, is incessantly engaged in competition with other modes; and there is no one of them that enjoys a monoply, in the only sense that the common law attaches to that term, namely, an exclusive privilege secured by public authority, or resulting from the practical exclusion of all competition."*

Competition governs prices where we least expect it, and controls industries that are apparently without rivalry. It governs the local rates of railroads, as well as those recognized as competitive. A particular district or carrier does not exercise a monopoly in any article, so long as that article is produced in appreciable quantities elsewhere. Nor can the carrier exercise a monopoly unfavorable to local patrons, so long as others are not governed by similar conditions.

* George Ticknor Curtis, "The Doctrine of Presumed Dedication of Private Property to Public Use," pages 8, 9.

CHAPTER IV.

RAILWAY RATES—THEIR BASES AND THE INFLUENCES AFFECTING THEM.

An important factor in determining the rate is the attendant risk of handling the traffic. Common carriers are insurers, within certain prescribed limits. The insurance covers loss, breakage, and fire, in the case of goods, and accident and life, in the case of passengers. In many instances the risk is scarcely appreciable—does not sensibly affect the rate; in others it is as marked as the cost of handling. Whatever it may be, it influences the rate to that extent, and being of universal application, is general in its effect.

The principles that govern the making of rates, while in the main identical in different countries, are affected somewhat by local conditions. In England and the United States, two things, above all others, operate: the value of the transportation, (determined by the thing transported), and the cost of carriage. The value of the service rendered is generally the difference between the value of a thing at the point of shipment and at its destination. More than this can not be charged. If it were, traffic would not be offered. In determining the cost of transportation, averages only can be safely used. We can not assume that new business will

cost less than the average of that which already
exists. A French writer,* however, disputes this.
He thinks the lowest price at which a carrier
can transport a unit of traffic, or ton of freight,
one hundred miles, with advantage to himself, is
not the average cost of carrying a ton one hundred miles, but is the cost of carrying an "additional ton" one hundred miles. He says: "If
trains are run empty, the cost of handling them
is a trifle less than if they were run full; but the
difference is not large; and so long as there is not
traffic enough to compel an increase in the number
of trains, the transportation of a ton, in addition
to that which already exists, involves, so to say,
no additional expenses. Even when the number '
of trains is increased, the increase in the expense
is far from being proportional to the increase
in traffic." Mr. Colson's argument is more specious
than trustworthy. No rate can safely be made
that does not assume that the cost is equal to the
general average for such freight. Any other basis
would quickly bankrupt a company, because it would
leave no margin for the constant enlargement of
expenses that is going on. Not only this, but provision must be made for a return on the additions
to the property that new business engenders. For,
while the original cost of a property is but little
considered in making a rate, additions to a property
are not lost sight of in that connection. Thus, if
rates are unprofitable, no additions or extensions to

---

* C. Colson, of the Government Council of the French Railway
Service.

a property will be made. If they are made, it is
because the rate on the business they are intended to
provide for is sufficient to cover a return thereon.
To this extent, therefore, the cost of a property
affects the rate.*

The large financial interest which the French
government has in its railways suggests to it that
the rate shall not only cover the cost of carriage,
but also a proportionate charge on account of the
original investment. The French are handicapped
to this extent. The conditions in France are not
the same as in the United States, where free railway
construction is permitted. In explaining the French
system, Mr. Colson says the cost of transportation
involves, not only the expense of moving the traffic,
but also a charge for using the road, which charge
may properly be called a toll. On this charge the
"additional ton" has but little effect, for the cost
of the road remains the same until a very large
additional traffic necessitates extensions and improvements, and much of the cost of maintenance
is affected but slightly by the volume of traffic.
Mr. Colson claims that the law of supply and
demand is not free to act in the fixing of railway
rates; that it is restricted and trammeled. The
supply, for instance, is represented by facilities
created by capital. But when once capital has been
invested therein, it can never be withdrawn from

---

* While this applies generally, it does not apply in every case.
Many additions and improvements are made to a property with a
view to cheapening the cost of operating. Thus a company whose
traffic is unproductive may, by certain additions or improvements,
so cheapen cost as to make its business profitable.

that enterprise, if it be a failure, and put into more profitable ventures. This is only negatively true. If the original cost of a property determined the price asked for service, the law of supply and demand would not operate in fixing the rate. But it does not. The rate traffic will bear and the cost of service determine finally, as in every commercial transaction, whether business can be done or not. Wherever railways are unprofitable, other lines will not be built, and those in existence will dwindle. Unprofitable roads quickly adjust themselves to their environment, and if, with the increase of business that follows the introduction of every railway, properties that are at first unprofitable are able to earn abnormal returns, other lines will be constructed. From whatever point of view the subject is considered, the law of supply and demand operates untrammeled as effectively and inevitably in the case of railways as in the case of other industries. But this is only true where railway construction is free—wherever railroads are owned by private individuals, wherever unrestricted railway construction is permitted. wherever carriers are allowed to make their own rates.

In making rates, each company endeavors to make the traffic it handles cover a reasonable return on the first cost of the property; but its ability to do this is governed by influences beyond its control or that of the shipper, and when traffic can not pay its proportion of fixed charges, it is yet taken, if it can contribute something, no matter how small the amount may be. This is not true of government railroads, or of monopolies.

Rate-making is a purely practical question. And
here is where so many writers and theorists fail to
understand the problem. It is not, to them, coldly
a matter of business, a thing governed by the same
principles as the production and sale of turnips; a
question of barter and sale, of giving every man his
due. They look at it from a sentimental point of
view. Properly, however, the subject can only be
considered from the standpoint of the trader. Only
on this basis can railways be made self-sustaining;
only on this basis can those who use them be made
to pay therefor. On any other basis the load would
have to be borne, partially at least, by others. It
would be class legislation of the most unjust kind.
Professor Cohn likens the rates of railways to taxes:
" All experience shows that railway rates are based,
not on the cost of furnishing the service, but on
what the purchaser can afford to pay, and ought to
pay. . . . The problem at bottom is one of
ethics, involving those considerations of public
policy and of right and wrong which recur in the
discussions of proportional or progressive taxation."
Because of this, curiously enough, he argues that
private persons can not be entrusted with the delicate duty of determining what the charge shall be;
that the government only can do this. It is very
much like saying that because air is necessary to
man, its distribution can not be left to natural laws,
but must be looked after by the government. Rate-
making is purely a commercial question, like the
supply of corn. " The main peculiarities in railway
rates are not to be explained on a supposed basis of

justice and right, by which the well-to-do are
charged high, and the needy are let off easily.   One
might as well say that the prices of rump steak and
of tenderloin were fixed as a matter of mercy on the
poor consumers of rump and of tax on the rich
consumers of tenderloin, and argue thence that,
since the delicate business of adjusting this apportionment could not be entrusted with safety to
private persons, the State should take into its hands
the business of cattle raising."*

Rates are relative in this, that they are governed
by their value, exactly as rump steak and tenderloin are.   Transportation commands a proportionately big rate if its service is unavoidable, a less rate
if not: i. e., it may dictate terms in cases of monopoly, but not in other cases.   "It will contribute
more and sell proportionately high, if the demand
does not need to be tempted by low prices, and
will contribute less and sell proportionately low, if a
high price tends to choke off the demand.   Traffic,
which will continue to come, even at comparatively
high rates, will continue to be taxed high, and
will contribute largely to fixed charges."†   Thus a
railway lying in a densely populated country, or
connecting two great cities, having a large passenger traffic, has a great demand for such kind of
service.   This bears a proportion of the joint expenses and the fixed charges, according to its volume
and the profit it can be made to contribute.   This

---

* F. W. Taussig, "A Contribution to the Theory of Railway
Rates."

† *Ibid.*

profit helps to eke out less productive traffic; to make the railway as a whole productive. On the other hand, "traffic for which the demand is sensitive to price, and which can be got only at low rates, will contribute little."*

The business of railways governs itself. It adjusts itself on equitable grounds of the greatest good to the greatest number. If carriers charge too much, their business diminishes or ceases, their revenues are cut off, their bonds and stock depreciate, that upon which they depend to live ceases. Self-interest constantly intervenes. Herein lies the protection of the community. Governments are not influenced by this subtle and all powerful law; they may make arbitrary rates, and if industries are ruined thereby they claim the crown of martyrdom as public benefactors, in this, that they have prevented discrimination! They pose as public benefactors, when they ought to be branded as asses.

The distinctions that exist between natural and artificial laws, between a temperature regulated by the atmosphere and one fixed by individuals, is not more marked than the difference between a business carried on independently by private parties and a business in which the government presumes to meddle. Governments should have nothing to do with railways, except of a supervisory character, in countries having the commercial enterprise to construct and operate such properties. The intelligence and facilities of government are but one step above

* F. W. Taussig, " A Contribution to the Theory of Railway Rates."

the barbarian. We appeal to it only when men can not be found to carry on a needed enterprise.

Those who use railroads should pay for them, the same as those who use street cars, omnibuses, drays, gurneys, hacks, wheelbarrows, and donkeys. Professor Cohn, who is peculiarly parental in his ideas, would distribute a part of the price paid over the public generally. He would make the industrious carry those who are lazy; make those who save do so for the benefit of those who spend. He can not accustom himself to the thought that anybody or anything can be self-sustaining. He looks upon the whole human race as a race of imbeciles, *quasi* paupers, needing constantly the strong arm of the government.

The rate carriers charge is purely a question of business, of expediency, of private contract. Any other basis would quickly make the citizen an object of public aid; the carrier an object of charity. We have the same concern in building up a prosperous railroad system that we have in building up prosperous manufactories. An unremunerative railroad is a burden to the community, as much as a tax on real estate or personal property. If existing railways are not profitable, no more will be built. Thus competition is lessened. In this sense the cost of a property affects rates. Railways already constructed are fixtures bound to the soil. On these traffic will be carried, if it yields a return over and above cost of operating. "As to any particular item of traffic, the only question is whether it pays more than the cost of

moving it. If it does, the traffic is advantageous to
the railway, even though the excess over operating
expenses is so small that, if the same proportion held
on all traffic, very little would be earned towards
interest and dividends. It is a commonplace in the
discussion of railway rates that different sorts of
traffic contribute in very different degrees toward
paying fixed charges and dividends. Some classes
of traffic, of the sort that can be got only if the rates
are low, contribute little; others, of the sort that
come even though rates be high, contribute much."*
In considering the relation of rates to cost, we must
remember that there are two kinds of expenses:
those relating to traffic, and those not directly
affected by traffic. Their influence is not the same.
Economists illustrate the principle of cost as it
affects the price by the case of wool and mutton.
The producer can not base his price on the cost of
producing the wool and mutton separately; but he
will not sell his wool for less than it costs to shear,
nor his mutton for less than it costs to dress.
Beyond this, the price he obtains for his products is
determined by the law of supply and demand. So
in the case of railways and manufacturers making
a diversity of articles. Their products are the
result of joint cost. The manufacturer will not sell
for less than the separate cost of the distinct classes
of goods he manufactures; beyond this, the prices
he obtains are fixed by the law of supply and demand. Nor will the carrier, as a rule, transport

* F. W. Taussig, "A Contribution to the Theory of Railway
Rates."

any particular shipment for less than it costs to carry it; the price he gets over and above this, is determined by the nature of the demand for the transportation furnished.

Direct cost is always considered in fixing the rate, but it is not imperative that traffic should pay its proportion of fixed expenses, i. e., the expenses that would go on, whether or no. These last are considered incidentally in fixing the rate; if the traffic will bear its proportion, such proportion, or even more, is added; if it will not, and yet will return something over bare expenses incurred, it is still taken. The ethics of trade govern. In the case of passengers, the amount charged those of the first class in excess of others, is not the additional expense the company is put to, but is based on ability to pay—on what the traffic will bear.* But in the case of freight, the principle is modified or applied in a different way. The rate is based on the value of the thing carried. It is higher on silk than on fuel. The fuel that is to be consumed by the rich pays no more than coal to be consumed by the poor. If the use could be traced, the latter would doubtless influence the price. But it can not. In one sense, the principle applied to passengers and freight is the same, considering the

---

* "The items which are separable — such as the more expensive fitting of the first-class carriages — are insignificant. Wages of trainmen and engineer, the only considerable remnant which can, under any circumstances, be separated from the 'general' costs, are here incurred for all three classes of passengers together. It would be difficult to find a more complete illustration of the application of the principle of joint cost." — F. W. Taussig.

passengers as commodities merely, possessing relatively different values analagous to the different
values of other commodities.

[NOTE. — Even so imperfect an explanation of the interests that
affect transportation, and that are in turn affected by it, as I am
able to give here, necessitates, in their collateral bearings, frequent
repetition of certain cardinal principles. This the reader will understand, and, I trust, excuse. I have endeavored to restrict this reitera-
tion as much as possible. — M. M. K.]

CHAPTER V.

The question of discriminatory rates is not a new one, nor confined to any particular country. It has been the subject of frequent investigation in Europe, but always with the same result, namely, that they are necessary and proper. "The unlimited power of varying their charges to the public, which the companies now use, ought not to be limited."[*] The abolishing of special rates, or the basing of rates on distance, the English government has found would prevent the railways competing with traffic by sea, canal and other routes, and, because of this, result to the detriment of the community, besides robbing the carrier of a profit legitimately belonging to him. The conclusions of the French authorities are the same. "The operation of railroads, like all other industries, is subject to the great law of economics; prices should be regulated according to the value of the transportation, as determined by the action of supply and demand. When different bases are adopted, such as the length of haul or the amount of cost, we are led into contradictions and impossibilities. . . . . A railroad, in its own interest, and in that of the country, ought not to

---

[*] Royal commission, 1872.

(95)

neglect any traffic of a kind that will increase its
receipts more than its expenses."*

Competition enforces equitable rates, and is the
only guarantee we have of their maintenance. It
secures the lowest possible rates (*a*) on the necessities of life, (*b*) on the comforts of life, (*c*) on luxuries and similar articles. It affects most favorably
the poorer classes whose purchases are confined to
the common necessities of life. To disturb competition, is to increase the burdens of such class, to
make its struggle harder, to put the comforts of life
farther and farther from its reach, to entirely
deprive it of the hope of possessing a luxury.

The word "discrimination," in modern railway
literature and discussion, has become perverted.
An improper meaning attaches to it. Rightly inter-
preted, it presupposes the exercise of a discretion
at once wise and salutary; the act of dissecting and
placing in proper relation the component parts of
a subject. For instance, it indicates, when applied
to rates, that the necessities of trade, and the
equities and rights of all concerned, have been considered. Unfortunately, this, the true meaning of
the word, no longer attaches to it. It has been so
frequently prefixed with the adjective "unjust,"
that, insensibly, the people have come to attach
that qualification to it. To them a discriminative
rate is synonomous with an unfair one. The word
has thus become misleading. Let us rejuvenate it.
When a rate is spoken of as discriminatory, let us
remember that it is not necessarily wrong, but that

* M. de la Gournerie, Inspector General.

in its exercise experience, intelligence, and due regard for the necessities of commerce and the rights of all concerned, have been duly considered. If a rate is unjust, let us call it so. Properly, a discriminatory rate is just, because intelligently made. There doubtless have been cases where it was unjust. But such cases do not constitute a rule; are not to be set off against the general good, any more than defects in particular individuals outweigh the strength of all. The marked disposition of railway critics to attach a general and exaggerated importance to particular acts, renders all they say unworthy of confidence. They manifestly lack either honesty or intelligence. If a railway manager is dishonest, let us put him in jail. But let us not handicap all railway managers because of his sin. Making discriminatory rates is not discretionary with railroads. It is a duty they owe the community—an obligation. This they have recognized and carried out.* For these reasons, the attempt to make it appear that the exercise of discriminatory power by railroads in making rates is injurious to the interests of the people, corrupt, unbusiness-like, or abhorrent, can not be too severely condemned. Likewise, public intelligence should condemn those who claim that carriers should enforce equal charges for

---

* "Every step leading to the establishment of the rates that shall be charged for transportation begins and ends in the exercise of discretionary authority. Rates are never measured exclusively by the weight of the articles carried, or by the bulk, or by the cost to the carrier of transporting them, or by the value to the owner in having them transported."—Fourth Annual Report Interstate Commerce Commission, page 14.

7

equal services; that charges should be based on the same standard of cost, etc., etc. How far those who give utterance to such statements are ignorant, how far they are intentionally misleading, we can not tell. A tariff based on cost of service would be prohibitory. Railroads would stop when the maximum rate was reached. Necessity and interest alike compel the carrier to reduce maximum rates, when traffic requires it, provided there is left a margin of profit over the cost of operating. This is discrimination. It lies at the base of every special rate. It is one of the concomitants of business.

Further, it is also the duty of carriers to make lower rates on cheap freights, like corn and fuel, than on cotton, furniture, and trotting horses. This also is discrimination. It is adaptation. Its exercise is necessary to build up a country.

If a railroad refuses to one shipper what it concedes to another, everything being alike, article, place, time, quantity, risk, and service, that is not discrimination, but robbery. Petty instances of this kind have occurred in the history of railway management. But they are only instances. They are, however, the stock in trade of railway critics. They are unworthy of notice. They form no appreciable element, and are not to be compared for a moment to the benefits that grow out of the ability of carriers to adapt their properties to the varying needs of those they serve.

"No law . . is more definitely established than that . . accommodations must be extended to all persons on the impartial principle of exactly equal

rates for equal service."* This is misleading. Such
a law would forever prevent the internal development of a country; would confine improvements to
the sea-coast, to the borders of navigable rivers.

Much of that which is said against railroads is
dictated by ignorance. But much more is actuated
by hatred, by a desire to injure, to mislead; it mis-
interprets every act, miscalculates every aim, wrong-
fully interprets every motive. It ignores the fact
that while railways are built to make money, they
must be operated afterwards to meet the wants of
the community they supply, sharing with it the fortunes of the day, be they good or bad.

A railroad is not a money-making machine, in the
sense that a banker is, who may leave the country if
the rate of interest is not such as to satisfy him. It
must share the profits of those it serves. Its lot is
cast irrevocably with them. Could there be any
greater bond of good behavior? But those who seek
to mislead the people, and the dishonest among the
latter, are not satisfied to share and share alike with
the carrier. They want the lion's portion. Sometimes they have succeeded in getting it. However,
wherever they have, the misfortunes of the carrier,
it is gratifying to know, have reacted fourfold on his
persecutors. Dishonesty, here as elsewhere, carries
its own punishment.

No just ground of complaint against the practices
of railroads exists or ever has existed. Particular
things may have been reprehensible. But we do
not imprison a community because a man does a

* J. F. Hudson, " The Railways and the Republic," page 149.

dishonest thing; we do not eschew eggs because dogs suck them when opportunity offers. No great and beneficent thing was ever more unjustly abused, more grossly misrepresented, more maligned, than our railroad corporations. The vastness of the theme, the little knowledge that the majority possess of it, the universal interest attached to the subject, conspire to make it the focus of public misrepresentation and fraud. "By open discrimination, or by secret rates, drawbacks, and rebates, a few railway managers may subject to their will every business in which transportation is a large element of cost, as absolutely as any Oriental despot ever controlled the property of his subjects. No civilized community has ever known a body of rulers with such power to distribute at pleasure, among its mercantile classes, prosperity or adversity, wealth or ruin. That this is no abstract or remote danger to society, is plain to any man who will look at the condition of trade and of mercantile morals in the United States to-day."* How vivid! But how absurd! how untrue! Our commercial morals are equal to the highest in the world—to those of any people who ever existed. The picture is overdrawn, feverish, fantastical, untrue. Managers have no such discretion. They could not exercise it if they had. The idea that a great internal industry upon which the convenience, profit, and enrichment of the world rests, is dependent upon such discretion, is unworthy the intelli-

---

*J. F. Hudson, "The Railways and the Republic," pages 178 and 179.

gence of a child. That a book containing such statements should receive the compliment of a third edition, indicates a lack of public intelligence or honesty that is anything but creditable to America.

No business can be carried on successfully that deals with the products of the world that is not accorded abundant discretion, that is not trusted, that is not worthy of being trusted. Every fluctuation of markets, of competitive practices, must be considered and acted upon by it, not at some indefinite time, but instantly. Failure to do so is to lose the golden opportunity, to cripple, to destroy.

Commercial prosperity and growth are dependent upon promptness and unity of action. It is sought to deny carriers this necessary discretion, lest some rascal should receive an unmerited favor, should be temporarily benefited. It is sought to cripple our greatest interest because of exceptional acts. It is to be made the football of idealists and charlatans because, forsooth, particular men are dishonest, foolish, or ignorant. The malignancy of those who seek to mislead the public mind in regard to railroads is on a par with that of those who deliberately corrupt the sources of life.

Every enactment that curtails the discretion of railway owners will result disastrously in the end, will heighten rates, increase prices, lessen production, reduce the area of business activity—is in the interests of the few.

Many of the regulations it is sought to enforce in the practices of railroads, while ostensibly in the interests of the people, are really in the interests of the few; of a particular individual, district, class, or interest. ·Every' such advantage is esteemed fair. In trade, misrepresentation is a common weapon. No argument is too absurd, no utterance too puerile, if it accomplishes its purpose. Men go to every extreme to make money or to gain the end they seek.

In one breath the critics of railroads deplore competition between railroads as injurious to the interests of such carriers. In the next they refuse them the right to pool. They advocate competition, but deplore its effect as distributing the burdens of life unequally. They clamor for governmental intervention, but see only ruin to the country if it is necessary for capital to secure the approval of some official body before embarking in railway construction; they would not "place the freedom of trade under the control of bureaucracy and set the claims of spurious railway issues above the freedom of honest capital."*

So far as a uniform rate can be applied to traffic without transgressing any law of trade, it is enforced by carriers. They should be accorded

---

* J. F. Hudson, "The Railways and the Republic," page 291. I trust Mr. Hudson will excuse me for quoting him so often. The reader will understand, however, that I recognize in him an honest exponent of that enormous army of writers and talkers, who, with an exhaustless rhetoric and abundance of time, use up both in citing special cases of wrong on the part of railways, and from these special cases seek to deduct general conclusions. Mr. Hudson is brilliant, vehement, excitable, tempestuous, flooding his subject with a torrent of words and ideas; the ablest of his class; a writer worthy of a better cause.

every facility in this. The right to pool their interests at competitive points is one means. The purpose of a pool is to eliminate the merely fictitious in competition. The principle remains undisturbed. Unnecessary waste and undue expenditure are prevented, both at the junctions of carriers and at points where railroads compete with water routes and other carriers. The benefits growing out of it are quite as important and valuable to the community as to the carrier. They can not be consummated in any less practical way, unless, indeed, we can find some means of preventing rate wars, some means of allaying the natural rivalry of carriers.

In practice, carriers must be allowed discretion to make such rates as are necessary to secure business. But it is sought to use the exercise of this discretion as a club to compel them to make discriminatory rates the normal basis of their tariffs; to make a benefit accorded mankind an occasion for robbing the benefactor; to make an abnormal rate normal.*

---

* " There are few important lines in the country that have not, at some time in their history, been carrying freight at prices that, if long continued, would cause bankruptcy. But to a large proportion of the public the fact that the rates were accepted was proof that they were reasonable; and when advanced rates are complained of, the complainants, to demonstrate their unreasonableness, go back to the war prices, and cite them as conclusive proof of what the companies then charging them can afford to accept. Many popular complaints have their origin in the ideas regarding rates which these wars have engendered or fed, and the evils of the controversies do not end when the controversies are over, but may continue to disturb the relations of railroad companies with their patrons for many years afterward."—First Annual Report, Interstate Commerce Commission, page 37.

No country can prosper that denies to its carriers the right to make a lower rate when the maximum can not be attained. No country can be built up, or its greatness maintained, in any less practical way. But a low rate will never be granted, if afterward it is sought to make it the basis of other and more productive business. Fairness and frankness, here as elsewhere, are the price of commercial activity, of investment, and business association.

In conceding to rival carriers the right to pool, it must not be forgotten that the laws that govern rates, namely, competitive markets and the self-interest of carriers, operate just as effectually where there is a pool as in other cases. Rates must always be such as to secure the business, such as to afford every one a margin of profit. The mechanical effect of a pool is to mollify the natural jealousy and distrust that exist between carriers; to prevent their making ruinous concessions under the apprehension that their rivals are thus acting; to prevent injurious rate wars that react unfavorably on both communities and carriers.

Pooling does not have the effect to make carriers neutral. Their desire to maintain their strength and add to it, will always lead them to exert themselves to the utmost to popularize their routes and attract business to them. Its effect is to steady rates. It does not prevent legitimate competition. A pool is, at best, only temporary. For that reason carriers dare not let their properties run down, dare not let their traffic be diverted for lack of facilities or effective service. The public, therefore, is assured of as good, if not better, service where a pool exists as in other cases. It does not prevent the strife of carriers, but adds to their ability to meet the just expectations and desires of their customers. It prevents extravagance, waste, unnecessary expenses.

In order to secure the highest advantages from pooling, it should have back of it the authority of the law, should be binding on the carriers interested. Its infringement should be a misdemeanor. This protection is due to the country; it is due to the owners of railroads and investors, to whom we are indebted for the unexampled development of the country. Its effect is to measurably remove from designing persons the ability to increase or diminish the price of stocks by manipulation of rates at competitive points. Not that practices of this kind have been usual or general. They have not. They cut no figure. They are like all other exceptions.

There can be no possible objection to a pool, save in the possible instance where it covers a monopoly of a product, including all its substitutes. Such an instance is improbable.

Pooling is in accordance with good business usage and the conservative instincts of trade. It prevents foolish extravagance, and materially lessens cost of operation. To prevent it, is unfair to the carrier and generally harmful to the community. Oppression could hardly be carried further; it can only be excused on the ground of public misapprehension, of public delusion. Its prevention is contrary to the customs of every enlightened country save ours. While governmental authorization of pools is desirable, it is not absolutely necessary. Indeed, it would not be at all desirable, if it were the entering wedge to governmental interference generally. The ingenuity of carriers will provide a way to make it effective, if they are left unimpeded. Its purpose is not to carry out private measures. Such a purpose would be reprehensible. It is a matter of public concern, because its object is the protection and perpetuation of the properties it affects. Instances may have occurred where the purposes of pooling have been perverted; but they cut no figure. No one thinks of putting the world under police surveillance because particular men have gone astray.

We do not refuse to recognize an economic law because it is sometimes abused. The instances that are cited where private greed has taken advantage of pooling to accomplish personal ends, are something apart and exceptional; do not in any way vitiate the principle of good that lies back of it; do not lessen, generally, the desirability of permitting men to enter into business contracts and agreements with each other, and of protecting them therein.

The principles of pooling and the benefits it confers have been lost in a maze of untruthful and sophistical statements. One of its objects is the prevention of unnecessary discrimination between persons and places. A directly contrary purpose is ascribed to it.* So long as rates are determined by

---

* " Admitting that the pool will abolish the discriminations complained of, it will also abolish the freedom of trade movements and the operation of natural laws of commerce, in whose defense alone the

influences over which particular carriers have no control, it will be safe to entrust the latter with discretionary power. Moreover, their interests and the interests of their patrons are inextricably interwoven; the injury of one is the injury of both. Herein is a country's safeguard—a safeguard simple, effective, and intelligent beyond extraneous influence or authority; a safeguard always present, alert, and apprehensive; a safeguard upon which the commerce of the world has depended from the start, and upon which it must depend to the end.

One object sought in pooling is the reduction of expenses. This is in the interest of the shipper, because it places the carrier so much nearer the goal of a maximum return on his capital. It also prevents rate wars. These latter are an incident of railway practice. While in many respects deplorable, they have not been wholly bad. They have had the effect to stimulate carriers, to sweep away obstructions, to eliminate the wrecking enterprises, that have from time to time sprung into being for blackmailing purposes, or as a means of making money out of the sale of securities or construction contracts. Generally, however, they are harmful. Railway strife here, as elsewhere, requires to be tempered and its action minimized by conservative influences. Hence the device of pooling.

---

practice of discrimination is resisted. The railway pool, as a remedy for discrimination, is a leap, from the frying-pan of inequitable and partial exactions by the railway power, to the triple-heated furnace of absolute and arbitrary rule."—J. F. Hudson, "The Railways and the Republic," page 232.

Mr. Hudson is always picturesque, albeit somewhat trying. He writes by far too much for the galleries.

The owners and managers of railroads are not different from their neighbors. They are no better, no worse. They must be judged from the same standpoint; not the standpoint of the purist, but the standpoint that has animated business men, from the time of the Phœnicians down to the present moment. Their methods and aims are honorable, laudable, beneficial to mankind. If not meeting our approval in every respect, we must not condemn them wholesale, but leniently, leaving the correction of their mistakes (never heinous or unmixed with good) to the mollifying influence of time. Why should they be singled out for reprobation and spoliation more than the merchant, farmer, or blacksmith?

The device of pooling is as old as the practice of barter and sale. Certain destructive effects that attend competition have, in every age, been modified by private agreement among local traders. Such agreements do not prevent competition or sensibly allay competitive effort. They are beneficial, because conservative in their tendencies. They can not be made sufficiently far-reaching to constitute monopolies.

A monopoly can only be made effective by being made universal. And if it were possible, those interested in it would still find their advantage in the direction of low prices and increased consumption, rather than in high prices and moderate consumption. The distinct divisions of the human race and the multiplicity of its interests prevent combination. Trade can not be bound. Man's methods, needs, instincts, and selfishness prevent it. He is too solicitous of personal gain, too wary, too unstable, to be controlled, except in a limited way.

The purpose of a pool is not to make rates high, but to maintain reasonable rates; to preserve the revenues of the carrier that he needs in improving and operating his property.

The apprehension that pooling prevents competition would be true, if competition were merely local. But it is not. It is animated by the action of railroads in every part of the world, by water routes, by other means of carriage; by the energy, versatility and covetousness of men; by the abundance of capital; by the law of supply and demand.

Pools place the competition of railroads on a rational basis—on the basis of common interest, as between the carrier and his patrons. They eliminate the element of chance, of hasty and inconsiderate action, of indeterminate causes. Beneficial competition will still remain, because founded on conditions that are constant and unchanging, on natural laws that are not determined by particular persons or groups of men, but by the concurrent action of the whole world.

In every country save the United States, pooling is recognized as an essential element, a necessary concomitant of railways. It, or some effective substitute, will again be so recognized here, or, failing in this, we shall sooner or later see a practical consolidation of all our railroads. Pooling does not necessarily invite governmental supervision. But carried on under the eye of the government, the apprehensions of the suspicious and timid would be allayed. In the United States, it would be carried on under the supervision of the Interstate Commerce Commission. This commission has already done much, and promises to do much more, to correct popular prejudice, and allay public passion against railways. As it studies the laws governing railway transportation, it will discover that they are superior to men; that they are natural and equitable; that, while the practices of carriers are sometimes reprehensible, they are, in the main, of unexampled benefit. Thus, the scope and color of the duties of the commission will take on a complaisant hue; it will occupy the position of an alert, unprejudiced tribunal; it will discover that the law under which it operates is not so much harmful as misleading; that active, aggressive, constant discrimination is a necessary element of transportation; that the traffic of the country can not be handled effectively under any other less comprehensive system; that favoritism is not now, and never has been, the practice of railroads, except in isolated and unimportant instances; that shippers can only claim equality when time, place, and circumstances are alike; that rates must be such as circumstances require and the wants of commerce demand; that pooling is not iniquitous, but wholesome, an essential element of railway traffic; that it is not monopolistic; that reductions in rates, brought about by governmental or other extraneous influence, are to be deplored because harmful alike to carrier and customer; that to be permanent and valuable they must be self-imposed. In reference to railway owners and managers, it will find that they are not here as moral examples or object lessons for purists, but as engines of material good to mankind; that they possess the virtues and weaknesses common to business men; that they are generally worthy of trust; that they alone understand the transportation question and its needs; that they alone are able to fully meet these needs; and finally, that they must be accorded a liberal discretion to enable them to withstand the endeavors of the public and rival enterprises. These self-evident truths are everywhere recognized by those who have given the subject of railways unprejudiced thought. They are recognized by foreign governments. Our Interstate Commerce Commission will secure their general recognition in the United States.

Enactments prohibiting pooling are not only unwise, but they are grossly unjust; the railway companies are injured, while the community generally is not benefited. Any law or restriction that deprives a carrier of an opportunity to add to his profits, "under circumstances where the enforcement of the prohibition will result in no benefit to the community, but will deprive the company of any adequate return on the just value of its property,"* is to be condemned from every point of view. Such restrictions are, in the main, the result of ignorance. They are, however, in some instances planned maliciously to meet interests antagonistic

---

* W. D. Dabney, " The Public Regulation of Railways," page 59.

to the general good. In any event they are deplorable, but doubly so if they deprive the owner of revenue, necessary to the maintenance of his property or a reasonable return on his investment. The equity of this is recognized by the courts, but in practice it is much impeded. " Where the proposed rates will give compensation, however small, to the owners of railroad property, the courts have no power to interfere."* But if the rates fixed by carriers will not "pay some compensation to the owners, then it is the duty of the courts to interfere to protect the companies from such rates." † In no case, however, have they ever done so. For this abstinence we should be thankful.

The circumstances of business that render it impossible for traffic to pay the same rate per mile, have been referred to. The carrier is an impassive agent. He does not create conditions, but obeys them. What he does " is not done wantonly for the purpose of putting the one place up, or the other down; but only to maintain its business against rival and competing lines of transportation." ‡ His action is precipitated by the nature of competition, by the advantages of one location over

---

*Judge Brewer in the Federal Court.

" State statutes, expressly forbidding a greater charge for the shorter than the longer transportation, have sometimes been violated by railroad companies, with the tacit consent of the authorities, where their enforcement would manifestly have been unjust to the companies and productive of no public good."—W. D. Dabney, " The Public Regulation of Railways," page 183.

†Judge Brewer in the Federal Court.

‡ W. D. Dabney, " The Public Regulation of Railways." page 65.

another, of one market over another. What he
does is in the interest of the community, because its
comforts and necessities are augmented thereby.
"The general public welfare demands the maintenance of this salutary principle of railroad transportation" (i. e., charging less relatively for a longer
than a shorter haul). "Upon it is based the immense internal commerce of the country, whereby
exchanges of products are effected between the most
distant portions of the Union, and all sections bound
together by the strongest ties of mutual interest.
By it the fields of production are enormously ex-
panded; the values of lands remote from markets
are enhanced; the price of every necessity of life is
reduced; the surplus products of the interior,
amounting to hundreds of millions in value, are
thus brought to the seaboard. In the United States,
the application of this principle has produced
great hardships, especially to the agricultural interests of the Atlantic States."* But these hardships
were unavoidable. It would not have helped the
eastern farmer, located on a line of railway compelled to abandon its competitive traffic, because of
an enactment preventing its charging less for a
longer than a shorter haul. Such prohibition would
diminish the revenues of the road, but "would not
enhance the price of his products in the markets of
the world, for they are governed by the cost of
transportation over the cheapest routes by which
the demand can be supplied. It is cheap trans-

* W. D. Dabney, "The Public Regulation of Railways," pages
104, 105.

8

portation over other routes which puts him at a
disadvantage, much more than the discrimination in
favor of the longer haul by the line over which he
ships."* An unanswerable argument against prohibitory enactments of this kind, is the double
injury they inflict—injury both to the community
and the carrier; increasing the cost of living to the
former, and depriving the latter of a just return on
his property. "Discrimination which produces no
injury can not be considered unjust; if it can be
shown that discrimination may in certain cases be
actually beneficial to the community apparently
discriminated against, it should, instead of being
denounced, be encouraged."† The influence that
governs carriers is not local; the power that propels
them is as wide as the industrial world. As I have
had frequent occasion to state: "It is not the commerce of one nation or continent alone, that determines the conditions of transportation within its
limits, but that of the civilized world." ‡

The advantages of competitive traffic, as between
the carrier and local shipper, are reciprocal. The
latter is directly concerned in adding to the income
of the former in every proper way. This interest is
based on enlightened selfishness—on that of part-
nership. The profit the carrier derives from
competitive traffic he shares with his clientage.
"By taking competitive traffic, even at excessively

* W. D. Dabney, "The Public Regulation of Railways," page
118.
† *Ibid*, page 111.
‡ *Ibid*, page 113.

low rates, the railroads, to the extent that any net revenue is derived from it, are enabled to reduce the rates on local traffic;" * i. e., they will be able to reduce rates when the return on a property equals the maximum interest allowed on such investments.

Under the beneficent law of exchanges, communities far removed from each other receive the reciprocal benefits that flow from active competition, when, under other circumstances, they would be subject to local monopoly. Thus, the farmers in the north and south of England are enabled to buy their plows and wagons at a much lower price than they would if manufacturers located at these extremes were not able to offer their products in competition with each other; if they were not allowed, by low rates, to ship their goods from one end of the country to the other. The value of the principle is not restricted to particular articles of commerce. A community derives benefit and profit from its application in proportion to the need that exists for an article. Its exercise is dependent upon the discriminatory rates of carriers.

It has been suggested that long and short haul rates should be exercised only under the supervision of the government; that it should be the duty of the latter, among other things, to see that no traffic is handled by railroads improperly, or that does not pay a profit to the carrier. The precaution is an unnecessary one. Self-interest will prevent carriers making an unremunerative rate. They may do so

---

* W. D. Dabney, "The Public Regulation of Railways," pages 114, 125.

in isolated and exceptional instances. But such instances cut no figure in the operations of railroads as a whole. However, the supervision can do no harm if wisely exercised. It may tend to placate public opinion, which, in the United States at least, regards every railway corporation "as the natural enemy and oppressor of the masses of the people, to be despoiled and warred upon whenever occasion offers." * This antagonism lies at the bottom of every unjust verdict against railroads; lies back of the oppressive legislation that disfigures our law-books, and that makes our railroad companies little better than common outlaws.

---

* W. D. Dabney, " The Public Regulation of Railways," page 280.

CHAPTER VI.

I have referred to the question of special rates in the preceding chapter, but not extensively. The subject merits more extended notice. A rightful solution of it is of the greatest importance.

Every rate made by a railway is a special rate, because conditions are in no two cases exactly alike. Special rates, however, are generally understood to mean those that are given to particular individuals to meet especial emergencies—a rate lower than the established tariff. It is in this sense that I use the term in the following chapter. The interstate commerce act, already referred to, restricts the use of special rates. The carrier must, in every case where he gives a special rate, print and post a tariff therefor. Thus the railway companies are annually subjected to the expense and annoyance of printing millions of tariffs, each tariff particularly governing a particular rate for a particular individual. This supposed publicity is thought to be necessary to protect the community from collusion between carriers and shippers; a most absurd precaution, and one that involves enormous expense and annoyance, alike injurious to the carrier and to the community.

No doubt instances have occurred where the use of special rates has been attended with favoritism, where there was an understanding between the agent of the carrier and the shipper, where the agent derived some personal advantage therefrom. But such cases have neither been frequent nor general, and are unworthy of notice in comparison with the good that has grown out of the unrestricted use of special rates. To condemn them because of such practices, is very much like condemning the banking system of a country because a cashier, or half a dozen cashiers, are rascals.

The economic principle that underlies the making of a rate finds more apt expression in the special rate than in any other. It more nearly accords with business practices than any other; more nearly represents the measure of value between what a thing is worth at the point of shipment and the price it will bring at the place of consumption. In the practical conduct of traffic such rates are made, in particular cases, when business can not afford to pay regular rates. They are made after the most searching inquiry as to what the traffic will bear. Their purpose is to stimulate production; to facilitate exchanges. "The principle which governs a railway company in fixing the rate is that of creating a traffic by charging such sum for conveyance as will induce the product of one district to compete with that of another in a common market."* If left unobstructed in the operations of their property, special rates will be made by carriers whenever necessary to encourage trade or foster new enterprises. In some instances, they will be made at a

---

* Royal Commission on Railways' Report, page xlvii.

loss, in the hope that a remunerative traffic will grow out of them. They may be likened unto the principle of protection, so necessary in the youth of a nation, and so unnecessary when its industries are once established. "The power of granting special rates permits a development of trade that would not otherwise exist, and it is abundantly evident that a large portion of the trade of the country at the present time has been created by, and is continued on the faith of, special rates."*

Special rates benefit both producer and consumer, render possible an exchange of commodities not otherwise practicable. They facilitate trade and cheapen cost to consumers. The isolated instances of wrong that grow up under them are unimportant, are not to be compared to the general good they engender. To restrict their use because of these wrongs, is to deprive the world of a good because individuals are sufferers; is to make the convenience or profit of particular persons the measure of commercial activity; is very much like abolishing passenger trains because individuals are injured by them. Those who inveigh against the use of special rates do not recognize the effect upon the commerce of the world that their prohibition would engender.

Special rates are the buttress and foundation of business, without which it could not be carried on. Under them communities are lifted out of the slavery of local environment, are generalized, are made the beneficiaries of an extended market. It is claimed

*Royal Commission on Railways' Report, page xlvii.

that they are unnecessary and unjust. They are both necessary and just; both equitable and fair. They represent a need and its gratification. While special in their issuance, their purpose is the general good. They represent an integral part of business.

Rates that can not be adjusted to meet the exigencies of the hour are apt to be a drag on the commerce of a country, are mischievous, are likely to cripple the interests they should serve. Special rates are discriminatory; are a recognition of the immutable law of trade, of its fluctuations and inequalities; a relinquishment of a part to avoid losing the whole. They represent in transportation the practice of commercial life that accords something to every one who handles a product.

The purpose sought in giving a special rate is selfish. But its value to the community is none the less material on that account. The industrial interests that crowd the lines of our railroads owe their inception and growth to the special rates that have been granted them. Without the use of such rates, the undeveloped portions of the country would, in the main, remain as destitute of manufactories as the bridle paths of Afghanistan. It is possible—probable—that special rates are sometimes granted unwisely, are used improperly; but this is only saying that man is fallible. They are none the less necessary, none the less valuable because of it. They are the delicate fluid that anoints and lubricates the joints of the transportation body. Without them the wheels of commerce would cease to turn; we should revert to the period when the stage coach and the overland teamster fixed the limits of commerce and the status of cities. They represent an effort to adjust business to the requirements of trade; are the highest evidence we have of commercial wisdom and acumen; are a concurrence in the customs and needs of particular industries; an intelligent recognition of God's natural law of trade—the adjustment of prices according to the requirements of supply and demand. Almost every great industry that has grown up owes its inception to a special rate. Without this aid, it could not have started, would not have been persisted in. It has been to manufacturers the mother's milk of our time. Other countries recognize and utilize this truth, and will continue to do so, so long as commercial needs, rather than theories and abstractions, govern.

The right governments claim to fix the rates of carriers, is probably the last authoritative expression we shall have, in our time, of the practices so common with mediaeval and barbaric governments, of fixing the price of the necessaries of life—meat, potatoes, bread, etc.—a practice at once autocratic, restrictive, and narrow. It represented paternalism; timid, stiff-necked, distrustful, and baneful. The practice created distrust. If the price fixed was too low to afford a profit, scarcity ensued; want, distress, and famine followed. It repressed production. Attempts to fix the rates of carriers will not be persisted in when its baneful effects are generally known. Its apparent success, within the limited area of a small State, is not to be accepted as an evidence of its practicability. Local losses thus engendered may be overcome elsewhere. If made general, such recuperation would be impossible.

Business takes on the peculiarities of those who handle it. In our progressive country, the special, or discriminatory, rate of to-day becomes the standard of to-morrow. The tendency of rates is downward.* Against this all the resistance of corporate forces is directed to counteract contrary efforts on the part of the public. To the extent that reduction is practicable or necessary, it is unavoidable. But to precipitate it heedlessly is to disturb the commercial interests of a country and retard its growth.

It is assumed by those who inveigh against carriers fixing rates, that the power is used improperly. Ignorance, here as elsewhere, is critical, suspicious, credulous, intolerant, unjust. Undoubtedly acts of injustice have been perpetrated; foolish things have been done; unwise measures enforced. But this was to be expected. Are we to condemn a just and necessary thing, because it is sometimes attended with wrong? We often have rain when we do not want it, and our crops are scorched by the sun. But do we inveigh against rain and sun because of this? No. They are the accompaniments of generally beneficent laws And so it is in regard to the discretion of railroad managers to make rates, special and otherwise. Misuse in isolated instances does not prove that its exercise is not generally beneficial. It is. It everywhere quickens the seed of com-

---

* It is based on increase of business, increased skill, and heightened facilities, etc., etc.

merce, causing it to flourish where it would otherwise remain unfruitful.

Mutuality of interest, the practice of enlightened selfishness, is the sustaining and perpetuating influence that governs commercial affairs, and has been in every age. It compels the carrier, while fixing his charge, to regard his partners, the producer and consumer. It modifies the rule of life that leads us to take all. Except for the exercise of this principle, business could not be done, properties and trade would languish. It is strengthened and perpetuated by competitive practices, by the absence of monopoly. These last are in themselves determining causes, and in transportation matters fix the price as absolutely as competition fixes the price of calico. Like other traders, the efforts of carriers are directed to increasing their profits by adding to their business. Their aim in making rates is to obtain the medium " between an excessively high and an excessively low charge, where the product of the rate and the volume of the traffic will be the maximum."*

Contention in regard to special and so-called discriminatory rates is not confined to the United States, but is common to every country. In England the law provides a maximum rate. Heretofore this rate has been greatly in excess of the rate used. The carrier has thus been left free to charge all the traffic would bear. This is the only just or practicable basis of rates; the only one that is free from criticism or abuse. Its equities, however, are not gene-

---

* W. D. Dabney, "The Public Regulation of Railways," page 91.

rally understood; its use is thought to be attended
with favoritism. "There has always been a feud
between the railways and a section or sections of the
community whom they serve, in respect to real or
supposed inequality of treatment, as between different districts and different individuals. The feud
is as unsettled and as keen to-day as it was in the
infancy of the system. It is found to prevail
wherever railways have been established. It has
everywhere presented similar, if not quite the same,
phases, and it has, in the great majority of cases,
been found incapable of solution or settlement.   .
. . Railway companies make no secret of the fact
that in the entire absence of competition they are
accustomed to charge higher rates than they usually
do when they have competition to meet.* Their
justification is, of course, that if they did not quote
lower competitive rates, in the latter case, they
would lose the traffic entirely. They deny that the
acquisition of such traffic by such differentiation is
an injustice to anyone. The ordinary trader would
not, they say, secure any lower rates, even if these
special rates were not quoted. Nay, they go still
further, and maintain the fact of their being able
thus to secure otherwise doubtful traffic by quoting
specially low rates is a positive advantage to the
regular traders, whose rates are normal, because the
greater the volume of traffic over which the working

* No well-informed railway owner or agent ever admitted that
the traffic of a railway was in any case free from the restraining
influences of competition. It is more intense in some instances than
in others. That is all the difference.—M. M. K.

cost is spread, the larger will be the amount of net revenue available for distribution—for creating additional facilities, for generally lowering rates, and for dividend purposes."*

Such are the beliefs of Englishmen. They are the same everywhere. The laws of England prohibit unjust discrimination. They provide that tolls shall be "at all times charged equally to all persons and after the same rate, whether per ton, per mile, or otherwise,"† and that "no reduction or advance in any such tolls shall be made, either directly or indirectly, in favor of or against any particular company or person."‡ But these laws, like all theoretical laws not in harmony with the good of mankind, are not enforced, are a dead letter. They are statutory monuments of ignorance and affected solicitude. "It is not pretended that these enactments have been scrupulously observed. On the contrary, they are broken every day, by nearly every railway company in the United Kingdom. Their strict observance has, in effect, been declared to be impossible even by commissions and committees appointed (by the government) to inquire into their operation. . . . It has been much the same on the continent of Europe. In March, 1887, the French Chamber of Deputies held fourteen different sittings on this question. . . . Many specific examples of the evil of discrimination were quoted. One of the most important was that of the transport of corn,

---

* J. S. Jeans, "Railway Problems."

† *Ibid.*

‡ *Ibid.*

which is carried from Dunkirk to Paris for eleven
francs, eighty-five centimes, although the charge
made for inland transport over the same distance—
from Chateauroux to Paris—was four and one-half
francs more. . . . The railways of Great Britain
are perhaps more liable to the sin of discrimination
than those of any other European country. Our
import trade is much larger and more varied. We
have a multitude of industrial and commercial
interests constantly pressing for consideration.
The number of rates is consequently legion. The
London & North-Western company alone are said
to have twenty millions of them. The avowed principle of railway traffic managers—to impose on the
traffic such rates as it will bear—is a principle of
discrimination. There is no pretence of charging
rates according to the cost of service."*

The experiences of England find an echo in America, in France, in every country where railroads exist. They represent the actualities of business, the
forces that animate commercial affairs, and without
which it would not be carried on. Those who condemn them are not so dishonest as ignorant, not so
malicious as foolish.

Objection to special rates frequently arises from a
belief that they do not enlarge or simplify business,
but complicate it; that in giving expression to
them, railroads are not animated so much by a desire to make money as public carriers, as by private
contrivance. In the main, however, those who object to them are the unsuccessful in business life—

* J. S. Jeans, "Railway Problems."

the ne'er-do-wells. In their jealousy we see the
specious demagogism of equality. They represent the craze for uniformity; that kind of uniformity that would disregard principles and reduce
everything to a common level; that places men and
things on an equality without regard to natural
conditions; that believes great interests should be
brought down to the level of small ones; that the
country is benefited by pulling men down to the
meanest level; that minimum ventures should be
made the standard; that mediocrity and commonplace are the real bases of affairs, the real main-
spring of a country's greatness.

There can be no doubt but that much of the misapprehension that has existed regarding discriminatory rates is due to maliciously inclined men—to
those who do business in a small way, or are jealous
of the wealth and enterprise of those about them.
The misrepresentations of these men have been
taken up seriously by the ignorant. Demagogues
have also made the subject a rallying cry. The Interstate Commerce Commission of the United States,
made up of as able and fair men as we have, was
deceived in its early history in regard to the scope
and value of special rates. "The public very well
understood that private arrangements were to be
had if the proper motives were presented. . . .
It was in the power of the general freight agent to
place a man or a community under an immense obligation by conceding a special rate on one day, and
to nullify the effect of it on the next by doing even
better by a competitor. . . . Special favors or

rebates to large dealers were not always given because of any profit which was anticipated from the business obtained by allowing them; there were other reasons to influence their allowance. It was early perceived that shares in railroad corporations were an enticing subject for speculation, and that the ease with which the hopes and expectations of buyers and holders could be operated upon, pointed out a possible road to speedy wealth for those who should have the management of the roads. For speculative purposes, an increase in the volume of business might be as useful as an increase in net returns; for it might easily be made to look, to those who knew nothing of its cause, like the beginning of great and increasing prosperity to the road. But a temporary increase was sometimes worked up for still other reasons—such as to render plausible some demand for an extension of line, or for some other great expenditure. . . . Whatever was the motive, the allowance of the special rate, or rebate, was essentially unjust and corrupting; it wronged the smaller dealer, oftentimes, to an extent that was ruinous." * I do not believe that, after actual acquaintance with the practices of railroads, and the needs of commerce, the Commission would re-assert this; that its present members believe to-day that personal reasons, or corrupt motives, influence, or ever have influenced, carriers in making special rates, or allowing drawbacks, to any appreciable degree. It was misinformed—was prejudiced. Its opinion was based on common rumor; on particular instances, not on general practices.

---

* Interstate Commerce Commission, Report 1887, page 6.

CHAPTER VII.

NECESSITY AND VALUE OF POOLS.

Railway critics delight to particularize; to exaggerate isolated occurrences. They make much of individual instances. The pictures they draw are repulsive, exaggerated, and untrue. Railway owners and managers are not different from other men. Nor can we reflect upon them as a class. If one of them does wrong, let him be punished. But let us not damn the whole railway world or uproot our commercial system, because a particular man goes astray. The trade of the world should not be crippled because one of its operatives is unfaithful. The detection and punishment of such acts afford a legitimate and proper field for the officials of the State. Here they may perform a service much more valuable to the community than sending traffic managers to jail because of over-zeal in behalf of their employers. Such acts do not merit so severe a punishment. They are, in the main, to be commended, because based on commendable traits, loyalty to their employers, business activity, commercial enterprise, progress, thrift. They are overgrown virtues, to be regulated, perhaps, but not punished. The arbitrary lines it is sought to draw around railway officials, and the disposition there is, to make offenses common to trade criminal, in their case, suggest

9 (129)

that the punishment meted out by public opinion and legislative enactment, is not evenly distributed. It is superficial and partial. It does not go back of the act. Thus, rate wars of carriers are attributed wholly to the instability of their managers; to their jealousy of each other; to the super-serviceable activity of subordinates. These are factors only, to be commended and encouraged. They animate every man in commercial life, and a people that does not possess them is wanting in business skill, and commercial enterprise is dead. They are part and parcel of trade, and add to its picturesqueness and piquancy. When they become obsolete or criminal, men will go out of business and commerce will die.

Much that is said against railroads is personal, the outgrowth of ignorance, pique, envy, jealousy, hatred. It is not easy to detect, however, because covered up by a pretence of fairness, a specious regard for the interests of the people, a desire to protect them.

Railway criticism is diversified. Much that is written is by honest but ignorant men; much by those who are prejudiced; much by stupid people; much by those who seek purposely to mislead. The right of railroad managers to make rates is, especially, an object of attack. Critics see in it the enslavement of the people, injustice, favoritism, corruption, the exercise of arbitrary power. There is no propriety or justice in such criticism. As well might we inveigh against merchants putting a price on their goods, or farmers saying what they will take for their products. No one whose interests are diversified receives a uniform price for his products. Profits are greater in some instances than in others. There is more made in raising one thing than another. Producers must sometimes sell at a loss. The law of supply and demand fixes the price. But if we were compelled to sell at a loss perpetually, production would cease. And so it is with railroads. The products they carry have a price fixed upon them by the free and harmonious action of the world—producer, consumer, middleman, and carrier. The price is governed by a law as immutable as that of gravitation. But everyone does not know this.

The acts of railroads are more often misunderstood than otherwise. Their wars are an instance. These exceptional incidents afford an inexhaustible theme. While deplorable, they have not been altogether bad. Out of them the community and the carrier have derived some good. They have served to illuminate and clear the sky. While temporarily disturbing values, the harm they have done has been partially offset by the benefits that have flowed from them. They are the outgrowth of a too exuberant life, a superabundant vitality; a plethora of energy, interest, and ambition. Such strife prevails wherever men barter, wherever they own property, wherever they trade. It is not permanently harmful. It quickens man's impulses, widens his observation, adds to his resources, makes him more adaptable. If anyone disbelieves this, let him compare the progress of railway industry in America with other countries, where a steady, plodding conservatism, unnatural to trade, governs railway operations.

What is abnormal in progressive railway enterprise to-day becomes normal to-morrow, if its effect is generally beneficial. Men, if left unimpeded, strive to attain that which is most generally desired. Railway owners and managers are no exception to this rule. The public demands a low rate and an efficient service. This is the goal carriers have before them. They will attain it if not handicapped; they will not attain it if they are. Personal responsibility animates them as it does other men; rob them of responsibility, and you destroy their ambition and interest, lose the fruits of their creative talent.

In the operation of railways, the tendency of rival companies is to share in common the duties and expenses of traffic agencies located off the line, to reduce the number of such agencies, to prevent undue strife for business because of over-zeal and the suspicions engendered by shippers and others, to economize. The spirit is worthy of recognition and encouragement.

It is important that carriers should receive, generally, a fair rate for their services. Every depression is more or less permanent, so that if, through strife or outside interference, abnormal action is taken, it becomes to a certain extent normal. If not regulated, therefore, it is only a question of time when properties thus affected will cease to be remunerative; when they will be bankrupted; when they will become a burden to the community. For

these and other reasons they should be encouraged
to form such combinations as may be necessary to
mitigate strife. One of these means is the practice
of pooling —the right of carriers to enter into traffic
agreements with each other. The exercise of the
right menaces no one. It is accorded every other
trader in the world. Business would not be done if
it were denied. It should not be withheld from
railroads. Wherever it is practical, consolidation
will follow, if the restriction cannot be evaded otherwise. To prevent railroads from entering into an
arrangement with each other to mitigate strife, is to
force them to amalgamate. It is the only resource
left them—their only escape from ruin. If, therefore, governments do not wish to have their railways consolidated, if there is any benefit in separate
organizations, as there is, this concession must not
be denied.

What the effect of the general consolidation of
railroad interests would be, no one can tell. It is
not probable that the interests of the people would
be menaced thereby, if not carried to the point of
monopolizing sources of supply; if not world-wide.
So long as this is not done, competitive markets will
influence the price of products and the rates of carriers. But not to the extent that they do at present. Should the railroads of a country be consolidated, it should be attended with carefully systema-
tized methods of administration, impersonal in their
nature and not dependent upon men or parties.
Organization should, in fact, in such cases be conducted practically upon the same lines as that of

a constitutional government. Otherwise there is danger of its lacking efficiency or becoming otherwise objectionable.

The processes of competition are so obscure and subtle as to elude effort to describe them in detail. Every case possesses features peculiar to itself that must be especially considered. No rule applies with the same force or to the same extent in any two cases. Adjustment attends every case to the extent necessary to secure the desired end. It is this feature that makes the arbitrary efforts of governments to regulate rates fatal to the material interests of a community. Its futility is especially apparent in the attempt to classify railroads, limiting each to a rate corresponding to its assumed necessities or the amount of its business. Nothing could be more fallacious. Competitive rates must be the same for neighboring properties, no matter what their necessities. To reduce a rate arbitrarily, on a well-established line, involves a corresponding or even greater reduction on the lines of its less fortunate neighbors. In fixing the rate for one line, we fix it for all competing lines.

Under competitive practices, rates are not based on the requirements of particular properties. This is why pooling the business common to two or more lines does not result in harm to the community. Without this device, the value of such traffic is greatly lessened to the carrier, while the resultant warfare greatly injures the shipper. The value of competitive traffic is, in many instances, wholly destroyed by the warfare it engenders. This warfare does not manifest itself alone in rate-cutting, but in the employment of unnecessary agents, in expenditures for advertising, undue multiplication of trains, and other expensive elaborations. The traffic, moreover, occupies oftentimes the equipment of railway companies to the exclusion of other and more valuable business. It also in many cases affects prices at the disturbed points so greatly and rapidly as to render it impossible for merchants and manufacturers to determine the market value of their goods in advance, making it impossible for them to meet the requirements of trade and the competition of other markets and industrial centers.

The pooling system, however crude, has been of great value to railway companies and the public. It will become more valuable as it is better understood and the machinery for governing it is perfected. In order to secure its highest utility, it should receive the protection of the government. The expediency or wisdom of throwing around it this protection is disputed in the United States. But that it, or some equally effective measure, must be adopted sooner or later, there can be no doubt, if the necessities of the country, rather than its imaginary or romantic wants, are to be considered.

The theory and practice of the railway pool is right in principle and beneficent in practice. Its benefits greatly outweigh its disadvantages. These latter are not inherent. They grow out of uncertainties in regard to the duration of pools (when not sanctioned by the State), and the ability of managers to break them at will, coupled with the desire of carriers to build up a fictitious business upon which to predicate further claims.

As I have already stated, pools do not increase the rate, nor render an unfair rate possible. They simply add to the permanency of such rate as a business warrants, and prevent the product of the rate from being wasted in unnecessary expenses. Undue reduction of rates has been largely occasioned in the United States by excessive railway construction. Where one property would have answered, two or more have been built. Under such conditions, if carriers are not allowed to make an equitable division of traffic, they will covertly cut under each other, in order to obtain what they term their share. In the strife thus engendered, the modicum of profit the business should afford, is frittered away.

Wherever railroads are controlled by the government, rate-cutting is prohibited. In Russia, where the government guarantees the interest on the money invested in railways, competition is prohibited. When traffic is competitive, rates must be the same on all railroads or the business must be divided. The pool which we prohibit they enforce. And here we see the difference between theory and practice. It is the difference between spending your own money and your neighbor's. Wherever the government owns a railroad, it is more rapacious than the most grasping individual. Where it exercises a supervision, it is more unreasonable than the most exacting shipper.

The value of a stable rate is generally recognized. Commercial affairs require definiteness; ability to

forecast the future. "Rate wars are as unsettling
to the business of the country as they are mischievous to the carriers."* An unfortunate feature of
rate-cutting is the disposition of governments to
make such rates nominal, to base tariffs thereon, to
act arbitrarily in the matter. "No carrier has any
ground for just complaint if its published rates are
reduced by the authorities to the standard of the
average it accepts."† I am loth to believe that this
will be the guiding principle of our great commission; that exceptions are to be made the rule; that
the mistakes of carriers are to be made the standard
of their government; that the good that grows
out of their rivalry is not to mitigate against their
indiscretions.

The instincts of carriers are those of traders; such
as the strife of men engenders. They should not be
punished or judged too severely. Business men can
not be gauged by the standard of interest clerks, but
by the spirit of enterprise and progressiveness inherent in men who achieve great ends. "During the
summer last past, the commission had occasion to
make inquiries into the proper charge to be made
by the carriers of the northwest for the transportation of food products in that section of the country,
and in doing so it endeavored, amongst other things,
to ascertain what the carriers were actually receiving; that is to say, not merely what the rate sheets
showed, but what they collected from shippers.

---

* "Fourth Annual Report Interstate Commerce Commission,"
page 21.

† *Ibid*, page 31.

Those members of the commission who conducted
the investigation, became satisfied that the published rate sheets were not adhered to, and it made
a decision reducing the nominal rates." *

This decision was more specious than fair. It was
unfortunate. It made the exception of the moment
the standard of the general rule. How long, I
ask, would the progressive spirit, the enterprise
and ambition of carriers, to whom we owe our magnificent railway system, be kept up, if arbitrary
interference of this kind upon the part of the government was to be the rule? If men's mistakes and
weaknesses were to be made the basis of their lives,
the fulfillment of their fortunes? Men will not do
business on such basis; will not invest money under
such conditions. The government must be neutral;
must be fair and frank. The claim that "the rates
that are now being charged by railroad managements are, for the most part, such as have been
fixed by the roads themselves, under the stress of
severe competition, and if they are less remunerative than the roads desire, or deem necessary for
just compensation, the responsibility for the situation rests mainly upon themselves,"† does not excuse arbitrary and unjust lowering of rates by the
government. If the strife of carriers result permanently in lower rates, the hardship is self-inflicted,
and, therefore, not altogether unjust. It is in
accordance with the evolutions of trade—its vicissi-

---

* "Fourth Annual Report Interstate Commerce Commission,"
page 23.

† *Ibid*, page 28.

tudes—at once natural and consequential. It is
vastly different from arbitrary acts of interference
by the government, carrried on without reference
to the natural and necessary processes of adjustment that attend similar action upon the part of
the railroads themselves.*

The tendency of rates in the United States, where
pools have existed, has been steadily downward.
This has been demonstrated time and again. It
arises partly from the fact that railroads are progressive, and partly from the fluctuations of commerce. The latter fix the rate here, as in other
cases. This truth is not generally known, or is
ignored.

If the principles upon which competitive rates are
based could be made clear to the community, the
apprehension with which it views railway pools
would die out.

Pools prevent unjust discrimination as between
individuals, because they lessen the motive of the
carrier to draw business away from his rival by
undue concessions. They also prevent wide and
sudden fluctuations in prices. The ethics of government require that laws to prevent wrong, should
remove, so far as possible, the incentive thereto.
The pool does this. It is both a protective and a
preventive measure. Equitable rates can not be
maintained under certain circumstances without it.

---

*Since the action of the Interstate Commerce Commission, in
1890, its personnel has changed. Moreover, its action at that time
was suggested by the law. The law requires overhauling. It
attempts too much. While admirable in some respects, it is defective
in others.

It represents the adjustment of a part to the whole; the principle of equal distribution and harmonious adaptation. It is based on equality and justice. "The governments of Central Europe have given up trying to procure obedience to these principles by simple prohibitory laws, such as are occasionally proposed in Congress. To secure obedience, they take away the temptation to violate it. This they have found can only be done by pooling. This is, accordingly, legalized and enforced. It is carried on to an extent undreamed of in America. They have both traffic pools and money pools. There are pools between State roads and private roads, between railroads and water routes. It is regarded as a perfectly legal thing that one road should pay another a stated sum of money, in consideration of the fact that the latter abstain from competing for the through traffic of the former. . . . With all the police power that the German government controls—a power a hundredfold greater than anything we have in this country—and with all its dread of irresponsible combinations, it sees that pools are not a thing that can be prevented; that the only way to control them is to recognize them as legal, and then hold them responsible for any evils which may arise under their management. The sooner we reach the same conclusion in America, the better for all parties concerned. The attempt to bury the difficulties by thrusting our own heads into the sand, has already lasted too long. We must face the inevitable as inevitable, and do the best we can to regulate it. To meet the difficul-

ties successfully will be a hard problem. But to
evade them has been an impossible one."*

Pooling is a well-recognized procedure of business
in England, valuable alike to the carrier and the
State. Its operations are most prolix, penetrating
every incident of local competitive practice. Let us
take an example: "We will suppose that there is
a certain traffic to be conveyed between two towns
or districts, and that there are two or more railway
companies, each having a route of its own by which
it is enabled to compete for the traffic. An agreement is come to that the receipts derived from the
whole of the traffic, carried by all routes, shall be
thrown into a common fund, and that each company
shall be entitled to a certain percentage of the
whole, say, for example, fifty per cent. to the company having the best route, thirty per cent. to the
second, and twenty per cent. to the third. The percentages are usually adjusted on the basis of past
actual carryings, but in settling the terms of the
agreement, due weight is accorded to any prospective advantages which may entitle one company to
claim a larger proportion than it has carried in the
past. An agreed allowance for working expenses is
made."†

Man is suspicious — a creature of experiences.
He lives much in the past. He is always trying to
trace analogies between what is and what has been.
Thus, he compares the pools of to-day with the

---

*A. T. Hadley, "Railroad Transportation," pages 249 and 81.
†Colonel George Findlay, "The Working and Management of
an English Railway."

monopolies of past centuries; with the guilds of the
Middle Ages, the outgrowth of favoritism and the
creatures of oppression. The comparison, however,
is purely fanciful. They are not alike, either in
cause or effect. The pool is not a monopoly. It
does not prevent competition, but perpetuates it
and adds to its value. The benefits that the people
of the United States would derive from the establishment and legalization of pools at common points
are multifarious. "It would allow the proprietors
of the railroads to manage their own affairs, . . .
and at the same time would restrict the operation of
each individual road under the legalized coöperative
system, to the extent that it is necessary, in order to
carry out the intent and spirit of the law which regulates the conduct of common carriers in their capacity as public servants. . . It brings unity in
the management of railroads, as far as that is desirable or necessary; and, at the same time, it pre-
serves the individuality of each road, and reserves
to it the management of all its local affairs, in which
it and the country through which it passes are alone
concerned. Coöperation of the roads is only required in so far as the interest of the whole system
of roads and the public interest requires it—no farther. . . . It makes the separate individual existence of these roads possible, and puts a check
upon consolidation. . . . It secures all the advantages of consolidation, without its disadvantages.
Instead of conferring upon and concentrating great
power in the hands of a few, it has the contrary

effect—it will leave that power distributed among a great many."*

Pooling, while it does not prevent competition, modifies its personalities; renders consolidation unnecessary by removing the incentive; makes the strife between carriers less intense, without destroying the rivalry that is so advantageous to a country.

The practices that attend pooling are such as circumstances require. They are mere matters of detail, of no particular interest to any one except the carriers themselves. In some instances a division of the business is made on the basis of gross receipts; in others on the basis of the tonnage. Sometimes particular roads are allowed to charge less than others, because of the disadvantages of route, lack of facilities, etc. Such rates are called differential rates. Their use "presents one of the anomalies of railroad practice, which is that the poorest and weakest roads—those least able to furnish cheap transportation—do, in fact, carry the competitive traffic at the lowest charges, and to a certain extent determine the charges which their stronger rivals shall impose."† No more striking instance of the difference between theory and practice can be found than this, in commercial experience. "It is not uncommon to find that a road is able to compete for an important business, but is at a disadvantage in the competition by reason of greater length of line, or heavier grades, or of other

---

* Argument of Albert Fink before Committee of Commerce on the Reagan bill, January, 1880, pages 22, 23.

† W. D. Dabney, "The Public Regulation of Railways," page 148.

unfavorable circumstances, and that in consequence
it is unable to obtain what it deems a fair share of
business in open competition with rivals who offer
the same rates at every competing point. It is
therefore compelled, if it would share the business,
to make lower rates, and the rivals recognize this
necessity, and allow an agreed division of business
between all competitors to be effected, by giving the
carriers thus unfavorably circumstanced the right
to make rates sufficiently below those which are
charged by the others to attract a reasonable proportion of the business."* This is what may be
called natural adjustment; fixing the rates charged
by the several roads so as to afford each its share of
the business. Thus, particular lines abstain from
making a rate which will deprive less favored competitors of their portion of the traffic. If they did
so, a war of rates would follow, instituted on the
part of the weaker lines to compel the more favored
companies to divide the business. Thus the strong
lines permit the weak to make a rate sufficiently
low to attract some share of the business.†

The use of differential rates suggests the resources
of business men. They are at once simple and efficacious, such as the practical features of the situation require. They are a means of ameliorating the
destructive strife of competition. They are an ac-

---

* "Fourth Annual Report Interstate Commerce Commission,"
pages 22, 23.

† The Grand Trunk Railway of Canada is allowed to make a
lower rate to and from Boston than the more direct east and west
lines. Yet with this advantage it is only able to secure a small
percentage of the business.

cessory of pooling. No one questions the justness and desirability of pooling, who is familiar with its purpose and working. "Pooling, so long as the agreements can be fairly maintained, manifestly tends to remove one of the principal causes of local as well as personal discrimination. . . . The public benefit derived from the pooling system seems greatly to outweigh the danger of public detriment from its existence."[*] Not only is pooling unattended with injury to the public, but its effect is generally beneficial. It makes sure what without it is only conjecture. It encourages trade by making its basis secure, by enabling it to forecast the future. " In the unregulated and unreasoning strife between railroad companies, rate-cutting is not only carried on to an extent that is ruinous to the companies themselves, but it becomes a disturbing factor in all commerce, and it is perfectly correct for the railroad companies to say. as they do when defending pooling, that unjust indiscriminations are a necessary result. . . . Nothing can be plainer than the desirability that reasonable rates should be maintained with general uniformity, so that they may be calculated upon in the making of contracts and purchases, and so that small shippers as well as large, the man who merely sends his household goods as well as the speculator in grain and provisions, may have the benefit of them."[†] Pooling, moreover, is necessary

[*] W. D. Dabney, "The Public Regulation of Railways," pages 151, 153.

[†] Judge T. M. Cooley, Chairman Interstate Commerce Commission, *Railway Review*, January 8, 1887.

10

to the financial standing of railroads, to the maintenance of their credit; to the preservation of their
revenues; to the keeping up of their properties; to
enable them to furnish needed facilities, to pay their
employes living wages. "It can not possibly be
for the interest of any country, that so large a
portion of the invested capital should be wasted or
unremunerative. . . . What the country needs
is that they shall be made useful; not that they
shall be crippled or bankrupted."* August Schoon-
maker, for many years a member of the Interstate
Commerce Commission of the United States, suggests that the making of rates should be entrusted
to a federation of railway officials, the government
exercising a supervisory power: "Federation for
common purposes and to promote the common good,
is a plan approved by the experience of mankind
for centuries. It is especially the mode among
races endowed, like the Anglo-Saxon, with a genius
for government by lawful and peaceful means, and
is illustrated in its grandest form in the structure of
our own national government."

Federation is nothing more or less than pooling;
concerted action where it is necessary, independent
action where it is not. Federation, while it might
cover all traffic, would practically be enforced only
in regard to competitive rates. Carriers would, in
all other cases, make such rates as they pleased.
Indeed, the carrier practically makes such rates as
the business requires where pooling exists. But the

---

*Judge T. M. Cooley, Chairman Interstate Commerce Commis-
sion, *Railway Review*, January 8, 1887.

pool deprives him of the ability to take unfair advantage of his competitors. Thus their suspicions
and jealousies are allayed and rate wars avoided.*

Railways are constructed to make money. In
order to make money, they must do business. In
order to do business, they must meet the wants of
the community; must harmonize their interests
with those they serve. This they do. This natural
sequence of events, however, is only understood by
the few. It is doubted by the many. These last
are simply ignorant. They view with suspicion
everything that emanates from railroads, their
measures and policies—among other things pooling.
They think they see in it a means of undue ex-
action, a combination to oppress the public. They
therefore favor its prohibition. A law prohibiting
water from seeking its level would, however, be just
as sensible, just as effective. Wherever carriers are
prohibited from pooling, they will find a substitute
therefor, or, failing in this, will consolidate their
properties. Rate wars, it should be understood, do
not arise from any improper motive, are not dishonest. They are the outgrowth of instincts inherent in every trader—acquisitiveness, suspicion,
craft; a desire to over-reach his competitor; an unwarranted belief in his own superior resources.
"The greatest difficulty encountered in the attempt
to solve the railroad problem is the enforcement of
the tariffs after they have been mutually agreed
upon. It is owing to the spirit of competition that

---

* Aldace F. Walker, formerly an Interstate Commerce Commissioner, also heartily favors pooling.

exists between railroads; each company endeavoring
to secure the largest amount of business, to increase
its tonnage by taking the business from some other
road."*   The business interests of a country require
that this difficulty, this hindrance to its healthy
progress, should be eliminated.   This can only be
accomplished in one way, that is by combination,
by harmonious action, by mutual agreement, by
what has been found so efficacious in other countries
—legalized pooling.   Public interest and policy
require that this should be done in the United
States, not at some indefinite period in the future,
but at the earliest practicable moment.

* Albert Fink, argument before Committee of Commerce, February, 1882.

CHAPTER VIII.

RAILWAY RATES AND GOVERNMENT CONTROL—RATES
MAY BE TOO LOW, THEY CAN NOT BE TOO HIGH—
RAILWAY ENTERPRISE — UNNECESSARY RAIL-
ROADS: EFFECT THEREOF—PROPER SCOPE OF
GOVERNMENTAL SUPERVISION.

The sudden and vast growth of our railway system has had the effect to bewilder the public mind,
to prevent its problems being rightly understood.
The subject, in all its details, is too vast to be com-
prehended readily. Time is required for the acquisition of this knowledge and the assimilation of the
new industry with surrounding enterprises. The
liberal commercial spirit that animates railways has
not been understood, and, because of this, public
sympathy has been denied them.

The baneful effect that attends warfare on private
interests is generally recognized, but because of the
magnitude of railway enterprise and its impersonal
character, it has been thought to be an exception,
rendering it not only practicable but politic to
deny its owners the right to manage their property
in their own way, but to hold up their acts to public reprobation. The sooner this impression is dis-
sipated, the better it will be for the country. The
sooner the people learn that to deprive carriers of
any portion of their just earnings, to injure their

credit or the good repute of those who own or manage them, is to injure the country, the better it will be for all concerned.

The enormous wealth and power of the railway companies excite apprehension and jealousy, and the subtleties and apparent inconsistencies that characterize their operations, the result of environment, have bred a disposition to surround them with hasty and ill-advised acts of legislation. The railway system of the United States is inherently and grossly artificial, and the efforts of owners to adjust their affairs to these conditions and the necessities and the comities of business, have subjected them to many unjust charges. These accusations have their origin in ignorance, and will continue to find expression so long as the conditions that engender them exist and the public mind remains uninformed.

The questions of public interest surrounding the railway system are too great to be fully considered within the space of a single volume. Only the more important peculiarities of its growth and operation can be noticed. The situation in the United States is anomalous. Nowhere else is free construction known. Its effect has not been what was expected. Its benefits far outstrip its disadvantages. However, while the community thought that the multiplication of railways under all circumstances would prove a public blessing, their construction, under certain conditions, is found to be a public calamity; overproduction, here as elsewhere, entails disaster proportionate to the cause.

Free railway construction stimulates the ambition of railroad owners and managers to the utmost. It leads them to build and operate economically; to construct according to the work to be done, and to eagerly adopt every device that will improve the service, or lessen its cost.

Some of the mistakes that we have made in regard to railroads are quite apparent to us now. We know that, where free railway construction is permitted, monopoly is impossible. I think it may also be assumed, that while railroads are thought to disregard the interests of the community, they are exceptionally sensitive to their obligations in this direction; that while legislatures claim the right to fix rates, the anomalous conditions under which the railway system has grown up and its chaotic nature render the exercise of such power fraught with the greatest danger to the community; that while it is assumed by many that rates may be fixed arbitrarily, they are, on the contrary, the result of natural causes.

The vast territory of the United States renders railroads especially valuable in its development. Without them centuries would have been required to accomplish what they have made possible in a decade. They have everywhere vitalized business, opened new and productive sources of supply, built up industries that would not have been possible under other conditions. They have brought the centers of commerce, separated by vast distances, into active and continuous competition, and, under their benign influence, districts remote from water-

courses enjoy the same facilities, and in many cases
the same prices, that the most favored possess. They
have made the impossibilities of yesterday the
possibilities of to-day. Upon their beaten tracks
the poorest citizen travels in greater splendor than
the monarch of olden times. Distance is no longer
an element. The traveler that leaves us at dusk to-
day, after the lapse of twenty-four hours, we
discover pursuing his journey a thousand miles
away, carefully watched over, warmly housed, com-
fortably fed, serene, and happy. Such is the railway
system. It affects more nearly and vitally the prosperity and comfort of a community than any other
interest, than indeed the government itself. Super-
seding other forms of inland conveyance, it determines the location of business centers and vitalizes
by its presence or blasts by its absence. Upon the
care and skill exercised in maintaining and operating it depend the safety and comfort of those who
travel. If extravagantly or unwisely managed, the
waste is lost to the community. If injudicious
economy is exercised, the same community suffers
through the disasters that follow or the lack of
necessary and proper facilities. In order to compass
the results expected of them, the income of these
gigantic highways should be sufficient to afford the
peculiar labor and abundant supplies required in
their operation and maintenance. This income
should also be sufficient to meet the interest on the
capital expended in construction. If deficient in
either respect, the community suffers, not only in
the common conveniences of transportation, but in

the depressing influence that capital sunken in unproductive enterprises entails upon surrounding industries.

In order to obtain the highest possible results, both from the standpoint of the community and the carrier, railways should be wisely located.

Only such lines should be built as afford reasonable proof of profitable employment.

It is an industrial axiom that a man who causes two blades of grass to grow where but one grew before is a public benefactor. It should be equally an axiom in our day that the construction of two railways where one suffices is a public misfortune. It does not matter that the inherent vigor of a country, abundance of cheap land, a favorable climate, and attractive political institutions may enable it to push forward in spite of these conditions; they are none the less unfortunate. Such a country may excite our admiration, but while admiring we can not forget how much its commercial greatness might have been enhanced under a more beneficent state of affairs.

There can be no escape from the general proposition that, if the business falling to the lot of a particular railroad is only sufficient to pay its legitimate expenses and interest, the construction and operation of an additional line under such circumstances adds to the financial burden of a country. If rates could be advanced, at will, this burden might be distributed. But they can not. The effect, moreover, is to restrict the general usefulness of carriers, for the reason that no rate can be made that does

not at least pay the cost of operation and maintenance. Within this limit such rate may be made as
the conditions of business require. The importance
of this limitation is apparent, when we remember
that the profits of carriers are largely dependent
upon the amount of traffic handled; that a diminution
of business, by dividing it between two or more roads,
adds to the cost and lessens the ability of the carrier to handle it. Our aim should be to build up
the business of existing roads, to wisely locate new
ones; to prevent undue multiplication of lines.
Any one may, however, build a railroad in the
United States who can raise the money. "Authority to construct comes in the main from the legislation of the States and Territories; and if we examine
these we shall find that apparently the most important objects in the minds of the law-makers, in granting charters of incorporation for railroads, or in
passing general laws which shall stand in the place
of such charters, have been to invite and secure the
construction; to invite capitalists, or others who
can secure capital, by whatever means, for the purpose, to expend it to that end; and that with this
object in view they have been far more anxious to
make their legislation satisfactory to the promoters
of roads, than they have been to take care to satisfy
themselves that the building of a particular road is
important on public grounds, or that the road when
constructed will, in the service it will perform, meet
a public demand."* A similar state of affairs does

---

* Judge Thomas M. Cooley, Chairman Interstate Commerce Commission.

not exist elsewhere. Abroad no railway can be
built until the location has been approved by the
government, and this approval is only given after
hearing all the parties in interest. In England the
projectors must first define with minute precision
the location and character of the proposed line, the
necessities that exist for it, and the encouragement
that it has received. Afterwards the objections
of rival lines, communities, and individuals are
listened to and considered. The result of these minute inquiries is to determine beforehand whether
the property is likely to be profitable or not, or
whether there exists a necessity for it. The
rights of individual property owners are thus protected from unwarranted seizure, a reasonable and
wise precaution is taken to prevent capital from
being sunk in worthless enterprises, and existing
lines are protected in the business that belongs to
them and that is necessary to their wants. That
the exercise of this precaution is generally wise and
beneficial, no reasonable person can doubt. For a
time, no injury resulted from the lack of proper
supervision and restriction in the United States.
The first lines constructed were wisely located to
meet actual and prospective needs, and a reference
to them upon our maps shows that their projectors
anticipated every want of the country they traversed. In studying the location of these great
enterprises, one can but be impressed with the far-
seeing sagacity and wisdom displayed. If the
territory thus occupied had been protected from
invasion by rival companies, its traffic to-day would

be sufficient to afford the maximum of haul with the minimum of cost; in other words, the public would enjoy the low rates that attend an abundant and generally profitable business. This is assuming, however, that the lines would have been managed as efficiently as at present. But this is at least doubtful. Rivalry is beneficial. The necessities of competitive companies make them inventive, alert, economical, progressive, anxious to please; while, on the other hand, monopoly induces indifference, undue conservatism.

In every country except the United States, railroads are protected in their territory. But they nowhere afford the public equal, or as cheap, accommodation as they do in the United States. This seems to prove that our efficiency in some measure is due to the rivalry of carriers, and the responsibility we have put upon them. What else can it be? We are not smarter than others.

If railroads could be allotted a given territory without lessening their inventiveness and enthusiasm, their desire to please; if we could combine the advantages of monopoly with the fruits of competition, the acme of good would be attained. It is possible that such results might be secured if governments would abstain from meddling; if they would leave the responsibility with the carrier—where it belongs; if they would stimulate him by criticisms and comparisons, rather than handicap him with cumbersome rules and regulations. The experiment has never been tried.

The superior advantages offered by American

railroads; their cheapness, the low rates they afford, are undoubtedly due to active competition; to the fact that they have been allowed free exercise in every direction. The moment this condition of affairs is changed, either by government interference or otherwise, our progress will be less rapid, our facilities less ample, our charges less favorable. Responsibility will be lost. What was before freely accorded will be evaded or lessened.

A reason of the special misfortunes that attend excessive railroad building is the permanent character of these properties. But while it is undoubtedly true that railroads can not be moved or capital withdrawn from them when once invested, still, if we leave the owners free to adjust their affairs to conform to actual conditions, they will do so with the least possible injury to the community and themselves. The profit may be little or nothing for awhile, but a modicum may be realized over the cost of operating. But this will be dependent upon natural adjustment.

The cause of the great prosperity of the United States has been attributed to free railway construction.* This is not wholly true. The glamor of our institutions, the extent and boundless fertility of our soil, our mineral resources, and the sturdy and enterprising character of our people, have also had much to do with this prosperity. But all these

---

* "Many reasons . . . have been given as the cause of the prosperity of the United States, but the real cause has been the law allowing free railroad construction."—E. Bates Dorsey, Member Am. Soc. C. E., in *Railway Review.*

would have been in vain, had it not been for the
boundless capacity of those who own and operate
our railways; had it not been for the ambition that
has caused them to build largely and to exercise
their talent to its utmost to construct and operate
effectively and cheaply. This ambition has been
the result largely of emulation, of competitive influence. To these we owe our magnificent railway
system.

We have pitted the owners and managers of railroads against each other from the start; have placed
them on their mettle, so to speak. The effect has
been to create a class of men whose business and
inventive talent amounts to genius.

In order to secure minimum rates, carriers must
be afforded the maximum amount of business and
the greatest possible latitude of operations. The
average rate charged by a railroad, taking the property as a whole, ought to afford an income equal to
the cost of working and a reasonable return on the
capital invested. This is the most favorable condition; the most happy conjunction of circumstances.
Wherever properties are denied this income, there
is a shrinkage in the value of their securities, occa-
sioning loss to owners and sympathetic depression
elsewhere. Unproductive properties are also apt to
lack proper facilities, to be poorly maintained, to
lack the conservative instincts and responsibilities
that they should possess.

While more or less distress has attended the construction of railroads in advance of their need in
the United States, no remedy is possible in the case

of existing properties. Moreover, having been built under natural conditions, so far as the government is concerned, like conditions should generally attend their operation.

Wherever railroads are encouraged in advance of the wants of a country, the community must suffer the losses resulting therefrom, until such time as the natural growth of population and wealth corrects the evil. But while a government can not cure the evils that attend too many railways already built, it may, by preventing the construction of unnecessary roads in the future, prevent further injury. There is, however, no general public sentiment or instinct in the United States demanding interference of this kind. The people do not believe that in permitting the construction of two or more lines, where one can do the business, they have thus created so many more mouths to feed; that they increase their outlay without increasing their income. Not only is there no general opposition to the construction of new and unnecessary lines, but the reverse of this is and has been the case. Construction is everywhere openly encouraged, and credulous citizens are ever found to buy the securities of such enterprises. The question was not, "Is a road necessary? Will it pay?" but, "Can the money be raised for its construction?" In order to secure this, cities gave free entrance; railroads were aided by public and private subscriptions; every device likely to aid in accomplishing the end sought was resorted to. In the temporary benefits that attended expenditures for construction, the community forgot the results

likely to follow when expenditures should cease
and the depression that follows the unwise placing
of capital should begin.

Several causes contribute to intensify the interest
of a new community in the construction of railways.
First, the enormous enhancement of the value of
land. Second, the opening up of a market. Third,
the competition that ensues. Fourth, the money
brought into the community. The fact that a road
infringes upon the right of an existing line cuts no
figure. The possibility of having two mouths to
feed instead of one is forgotten. The people are
everywhere greedy to realize present advancement
without reference to future contingencies. In the
United States they acted more wisely than they
knew. However, they were not entitled to any
credit for it. The genius of others rescued them from
the difficulties of the situation. The skill of those
who owned and operated both the old and the new
railroads served to compensate, in a measure, for the
scarcity of business that the undue multiplication of
railways engendered.

Wherever two or more roads occupy the same
territory, competition is active and more or less artificial. This, coming upon the heels of a depleted
business, is peculiarly oppressive to the carrier. To
save himself, he has recourse to every device—combination, ingenuity, economy. Had it not been for
the skill of railway managers, the policy of the
United States would have forever prevented efficient
management or low rates. The people sought it in
the multiplication of roads without reference to their

necessity. The farther they traverse this course, the more mischievous the consequences to them, unless, indeed, it is attended with the entire freedom of the carrier, with his right to do what the situation requires, his right to adapt himself to circumstances, to avail himself of his boundless experience, all the devices of business to lessen cost and increase receipts. Undue multiplication of railroads, under other circumstances, can not but be fatal to a country. Competition between such roads can not be otherwise than injurious. It saps the foundation of values and disturbs everywhere the equilibrium of trade. It may, indeed, seemingly benefit some isolated community, some fragmentary district, but the result to the people, as a whole, will be deplorable, and the temporary advantages of particular sections will be offset by general harm.

No problem of commercial or financial life is at the present time of more vital concern to the community than that involved in the question of transportation. It affects everything we have; it determines the price of bread stuffs, the cost of our wearing apparel, the price of fuel, the cost of our houses—everything, in fact. In order to secure favorable rates without injury to the carrier, to procure the necessities of life at the minimum cost, railroads should be wisely located and judiciously managed. The competition of traders and the rivalry of markets will do the rest.

A railway is a fixture, as permanent as a watercourse, as the eternal seas ; but differing from these in this, that its maintenance involves an enormous

11

expense that never ceases for a moment, day or night. Other manufacturers can and do, when business is unprofitable, discharge their operatives and close their establishments until times are more propitious; announcements of this description follow each other in quick succession. It is not unusual to read that the closing of this or that establishment has thrown five, ten, or twenty thousand men out of employment. This heroic remedy, this immediate adjustment of outlay to income, is impossible in the case of railroads. They must go on and on, and in doing so can make little diminution in their outlay. To this extent, therefore, the natural law based on supply and demand is sensibly modified in their case. They must continue to produce, whether there is a profitable demand for their product or not. Other carriers may, when competition becomes too active or business is unproductive, seek more promising fields of industry. But this is denied to railways. If there is a healthy demand for their services, well and good; if not, the properties must still be maintained. But whenever business is unprofitable, expenses are curtailed and properties run down. Another evil is engendered, namely, the effect on capital. The owners of such property are no longer able to fulfill the normal conditions of life; their economies engender distress in other directions, and so the calamity widens until it becomes universal.

. Where the location of railroads is determined by the government, and the extent and number of such lines is restricted to the actual needs of the country they traverse, the government may supplement its grants by supervision and restriction more or less careful. I do not say it should. A line having thus an exclusive privilege accorded it, while not a monopoly, is less amenable to public opinion and interest than where competition is more active. For railroads thus instituted, the government may fix the limit of their income, according to the measure of cost. Having given them existence and surrounded them with exclusive advantages, the duty of seeing that these benefits are not abused may follow as a matter of course. But the acts of the government must be uniform and consistent, must follow each other in due sequence from the start. It is not proper to apply to railroads built under the stimulant of artificial devices (without reference to their productiveness or necessity), obligations that belong to semi-monopolies. Where a community has permitted and encouraged the construction of unnecessary railroads, in order to derive an indirect benefit from their construction, it cannot expect to supplement this benefit with all those that would attend more legitimate enterprises.

It is a common mistake to call railroads monopolies. It is a misnomer. It is especially so in the United States. Monopoly implies the exercise of a privilege denied to others, the possession of an exclusive and valuable franchise or right. No such right is, as a matter of fact, guaranteed or indeed exercised by railroads, except perhaps in isolated instances. So long as the great rivers, lakes, and seas of a country remain, the railroads clearly have not unrestricted control of transportation. If the

railroads of the United States were one homogenous
system, under the control of one management,
owned by one man, they would still not be a monopoly. As a matter of fact, they are divided under
many managements and owned by many men.
Every line has practically been paralleled. The
strife for business is incessant.*

Not only have we encouraged the construction of
railways in advance of their need in new and undeveloped regions, but wherever a line existed, and
through careful management and the growth of the
country had built up a productive business, other
companies were not only permitted, but encouraged,
to enter the territory thus occupied and strive for
a share of the traffic. Companies operating under
these conditions, and subject to invasions of this
character, are the farthest possible remove from
monopolies. The only monopoly they possess is
their name, and this is practically filched from them,
in many instances, by the ingenious devices of
younger and rival companies.

An apple-stand is a monopoly up to the point
where it begins to pay. To this extent our railways
may be said to be monopolies. Up to the point
where the business of a road becomes remunerative,
or is fairly established, the great cost of undertak-
ings of this character affords incidental protection.
The right, however, up to this period is valueless.
But at the point where business becomes fairly
remunerative and might be of value to the com-

* There is, practically, not a station in the United States that is not
affected by the business of some other station on a rival line.

munity, at the point where a steady, uniform, and constantly increasing reduction of rates might be expected to follow, a new line is permitted to invade the territory thus occupied. The effect is to divide the traffic, and in doing so destroy hope of a general or uniform reduction in rates, based on a plethora of business, until such time as the growth of the country justifies the presence of the second line. But at this period it is probable the mistake made in the first instance will be repeated. And thus the multiplication of unnecessary railroads goes on, and the community is deprived of opportunity to derive benefit from the presence in its midst of a carrier whose business is ample for his support, and affords a constantly increasing margin of profit, which he may divide with the people in the way of reduced rates and increased facilities.

If a field affords sufficient income for two or more roads, they will not suffer, because of the duplication, but the community will. Under the most favorable conditions, railroads are only allowed a reasonable return on the capital invested, whether there be one or many companies, so that a particular line is not necessarily injured by the construction of an additional road, if there is business enough to render a return on each. The loss the people suffer is the increased expense of operating two or more enterprises where one would do; also the amount of interest paid on the cost of the superfluous property. A remedy for the waste is in the prevention of unnecessary roads; in restricting them to actual wants.

The object to be sought in the United States, at the present time, is the prevention of further duplication of railroads and the preservation of the spirit of rivalry, of competition, that we now have and that has been engendered by free construction and untrammeled operation.

The railways of the United States in their location have neither method nor coherency. Their supervision or management, as a whole, is altogether beyond any man, or corps of men.

The evils that attend indiscriminate construction find amelioration, if not absolute cure, with the lapse of time and the growth of a country. But having once secured an adequate system, no new roads should be permitted without permission of the government, based on actual needs. The granting of these valuable franchises should thereafter be jealously guarded. Instead of permitting the free construction of railroads, thereby inviting the building of lines not needed, built perhaps for the money that is to be made out of construction or capitalization, the right to construct should not be easily obtained, and should be impossible where conditions do not warrant. The withholding by the government of the right to build a railroad, except after investigation, while it would not, perhaps, prevent, in every case, the construction of railroads that ought not to be built, would give to existing railroads likely to be injured, an opportunity to be heard. The community through which the road proposed to pass would also be afforded an opportunity to express itself. Of course such direction and control, to be valuable, should be exercised with honesty and reasonable intelligence. No body of men should be accorded the power, if they have the disposition, to grant charters under corrupt influences, or in a hidden or surreptitious way, or without such prolonged and public notice and discussion as would serve to attract the attention of all concerned.

The future government of the railroads of the United States should conform to their construction; to the methods under which they were built; to the peculiar conditions that surround each property. The railway system, having been allowed to grow up under the theory that the community derived its *quid pro quo* from the general enhancement of values, added facilities, and cheap service, must be left to the government of its owners, in harmony with its environment and the requirements of the several properties. Having permitted and encouraged the excessive growth of railroads, certain hardships that attend thereon can not now be avoided. But they may be modified by assisting railroad owners in their efforts, through pools and otherwise, to adjust the load to be borne.

There can be no escape from the proposition that the railway system must be placed on a paying basis before a country of which it forms a vital part can enjoy general or prolonged prosperity. In the accomplishment of this end, the owners of such properties should take the lead. The nature of the business requires this practical, common-sense course. The government's part should be a minor one. The railway system is too vast, and the peculiar circumstances of its construction and operation involve too many intricate and abstruse questions, to render its government possible except in minutest detail and with special reference to its requirements in particular cases. Having been constructed with a view to its operation in detail, it can not respond, except disastrously, to any general or fixed law that disregards these conditions.

Free railroad construction brings in its train, as has been shown, advantages unknown to monopolies. The strife engendered by rival enterprises deepens and broadens the intelligence and patriotic instincts of owners and operators. This last is apparent in the marked disposition of the railroads of the United States to adapt themselves to the slightest wish of the community. It is discoverable in the introduction by them of new appliances, and in the betterment of those already in use; in the introduction of means for comfortable and even luxurious travel; in the construction of ornate buildings, of palatial cars, of picturesque roadbeds, multiplied trains, and ingenious devices to avoid irritating or discommoding the public.

Rivalry between railway corporations engenders better service and heightened intelligence. But competition between them for a common traffic, based on undue reduction of rates and multiplied expenses, is injurious. Competition that arises between communities and countries, based on their respective wants, benefits mankind; that between railroads for a common trade does not, except within carefully prescribed limits. The former is governed by natural laws and is conservative in its action; the latter is largely artificial and erratic. One originates in the wants and capacities of great multitudes of people; the other, in misrepresentation and jealousy. One benefits mankind—is the Creator's method of adjustment; the other serves only to disturb, or temporarily benefit a petty district, at the expense of the general good. One enriches a country; the other impoverishes it. Under the operation of one, communities far apart are made to contribute to the common good; under the other, values are everywhere undermined to secure an unnatural aim.

Competition between railroads, when restricted to actual wants and carried on impersonally, is both proper and beneficial. But that which results in doing business at a loss, or in frittering away natural advantages, is neither proper nor beneficial.

Whenever a country stimulates the construction of railroads by gifts of valuable franchises, right of way, free entrance to cities, public subscriptions, private aid, donations of land, loaning of the public credit, and other devices, it must not afterward complain if the consequences have not been altogether foreseen. Acts of agrarian legislation and foolish manifestations of disappointment and hate will only intensify the situation. Having stimulated the construction of railways by every possible device, a country can not afterward refuse them its protection. Having invited capitalists to invest in railroads under unnatural conditions, it can not justly deprive them of their property, or the right of management.

It is a wise maxim in law that a man can not take advantage of his own mistakes. The rule applies with equal force to communities. It finds application in the railway problem. Having encouraged indiscriminate railway construction, to weaken or destroy the property afterward by restrictive legislation is unjust, and can not but result disastrously to a country that permits it. The construction of unnecessary lines was encouraged in the United States because of the real or supposed benefit the community derived therefrom at the time, without reference to the effect on those who furnished the capital. The community is, therefore, estopped from attempting to evade its share of responsibility. It is also prevented from exercising a restrictive influence over such properties, inconsistent with the conditions under which they grew up. Having encouraged and fostered a system based on the hypothesis that under it rates should be left to the competitive forces of trade, it can not afterward come forward and presume to treat them as monopolies.

The immediate advantages a community derives from the construction of a railway are numerous. It is benefited by the enhancement of local values, the introduction of new capital, and frequently by reductions of rates. But the loss it suffers from the construction of unnecessary roads, like the losses that follow over-production in other directions, are so complicated that they are not traced to their real source. But in the exact proportion that railways are built in advance of their wants, in that proportion will the community be injured ; depression will follow to just the extent construction is unwarranted.

Free construction of railways should be carried on under the same conditions that other business enterprises are. Whatever a company needs, it should pay for, to the utmost limit of bargain and sale. If it is allowed to occupy or cross a street, or piece of public or private ground, it should pay the same price for such privilege that a manufacturing establishment would for a corresponding amount of property of equal value. It should pay the full value of its right of way, and no benefits, rights, privileges, immunities, grants, or assistance should be extended to it that are not extended to private parties. Under such conditions, free railway building would be measurably deprived of objectionable features, for the reason that the cost of construction would be just so much greater, and in so far as it was greater, to that extent unnecessary properties would not be built, and those already in existence would be protected. But a railroad built under such conditions would, it is manifest, be entitled to the same immunities and privileges enjoyed by other manufacturers. The authority of the government could not extend beyond the supervision necessary to the protection of its citizens. Competition under such conditions would be conservative, because it would arise more from natural causes.

If we could conceive of such a thing as a railway monopoly, we might, it is probable, devise a system for formulating its tariffs, or we might conceive that it would be possible for an intelligent and experi-

enced commission to do so. But where railroads
have been built without reference to the rights or
necessities of existing lines, and have been allowed
to parallel, cross, and recross each other, at pleasure,
forming a conglomerate mass impossible to follow
or understand, except in minutest detail, any
attempt to formulate a law governing such a system, or to require a board of commission to exercise
such a power (except in an extremely limited and
conservative sense), can not but result disastrously.

The question is asked again and again, how far
does the law of political economy apply to railroads?
How far does the law of supply and demand govern?
In the end, absolutely. But for the moment it may
be modified, to the extent that railroads are built
in advance of their needs, because of donations of
money, lands, credits, rights, privileges, immunities, franchises, or otherwise.* The rule that a thing
will not be created until it is needed, or beyond
its need, does not apply in such cases. Wherever
artificial stimulants are applied, artificial enterprises will grow up. It is to the aid extended that
we owe largely over-production in railroads.
Wherever special inducements are held out, they
are certain to encourage enterprises in advance of
their needs. And in so far as this is the case, the
law of trade, that the supply of a thing will be
based on the demand, is modified. The abeyance
is only momentary, however. Railroads quickly

---

* Under the last-named head I embrace the use of surplus revenue of one line to build lines that would not otherwise be constructed.

adjust themselves to normal conditions, and, thereafter, are governed by its laws.

Over-production in railroads engenders over-production in other directions. It superinduces speculation—the frittering away of needed reserves.
Wherever free construction is permitted, bounties
should be prohibited. Those who build railways
should be compelled to pay for the property they
use. Thus capital will not be lured into unprofitable and unnecessary ventures.

It is hardly probable that the free construction of
railways will ever be forbidden in the United States.
We may, therefore, expect to see sudden and wide
fluctuations of prices, wherever the law of supply
and demand is transgressed—seasons of great prosperity and wild speculation, followed by periods of
depression. While undue duplication of railways
can not but be attended with more or less hardship,
nevertheless I think that if freedom to construct is
attended with freedom to operate, with freedom to
the owner to adapt himself to his environment, the
danger will not be great. The building of unnecessary roads is not nearly so injurious, not fraught
with nearly so much danger, as taking the responsibility and control of railroads out of the hands of
their owners and vesting it in the government. Not
that I question the value of government supervision,
if wisely exercised. But it should be merely supervisory; should not enter into the practical details of
business, such as the making of rates, the running of
trains, and kindred matters. Under these restrictions it tends to allay public irritation and suspicion,
and is, consequently, a valuable auxiliary.

Over-production, with its attendant hardships, is
accompanied under all forms of popular government,
by the growth of communistic ideas and the enactment of agrarian laws. Where the ignorant and the
enlightened, the educated and the uneducated, the
self-reliant and the dependent, the good and the bad,
the amiable and the vicious, the rich and the poor,
have a common voice in governing, the rabble will
avail itself of every excuse to pass laws that would,
under other circumstances, be called robberies. The
railway interest especially invites the attention of
this class. Being at once the greatest and the
least understood, and apparently that with which
the people have the least in common, it is the first
to be singled out for attack. However, other
industries are attacked in their turn. Robbers do
not respect persons. They may set out determined
to mulct only the rich, but they soon cease to discriminate, robbing all alike. So it is with the agrarian classes. They may set out to rob railroads
only, but it will not be long before the newspaper,
banker, merchant, and manufacturer will be called
upon to share their fate. It will not then avail to
say to this class that such laws are pernicious, that
they react upon those who make them. Those who
seek relief in enforced levies of this kind, do so
under a belief that by a master-stroke, values may
be transferred from one class of the community to
another, without subsequent embarrassment to the
parties securing them. They are intent upon acquiring something for nothing, and in the vicious
struggle, regard neither principles nor methods.

They overwhelm all in common ruin. Such agitation is characterized as communism in France; in America it is called the protection of the masses against the exactions of grasping monopolies. It is based on the theory that parts of a community may have interests permanently distinct from other parts, or from the country as a whole. That the provident may, by legislative enactment, be made to labor for the benefit of the improvident.

Wherever hardship is entailed by over-production, whether of railroads or wheat, we see it reflected, according to the intelligence and character of a people, in their newspapers and public assemblies. In Paris it manifests itself in a cry for the overthrow of the government; in the United States for railway regulation; for a reduction of rates. The latter offers, apparently, an easy opportunity to escape some portion of the shrinkage in prices, be it of coal or grain. It has, moreover, the merit of not offending any large portion of the community. It is not a matter, seemingly, in which the latter is interested, except in a vague way. However, reduction in the rates of railroads, beyond the point necessary to enable them to meet their obligations and render a return on the original investment, injures them, and through them the community. It is from this standpoint that the country must consider the question.

The magnitude and peculiar nature of railway property, and the necessity of its being operated at all times and under all conditions of business, render it impossible, as I have pointed out elsewhere, to effect any great or sudden saving in expenses. Such savings are possible through diminution of force, and the introduction of improved appliances and better organization. But this requires time. It is impossible that any instantaneous or effective measure should be carried out upon the spur of the moment to meet reductions in rates. Hence the hardship that attends such measures. Business depression or shrinkage in values, no matter how slight, reflects itself in the affairs of carriers. If trade is depressed, it affects their traffic. They could not, if they would, avoid the calamities that overtake those about them. It manifests itself in lessened number of passengers and in the falling off of tonnage, in loss of revenue. Frequently the depression of the carrier precedes that of the community; in some cases it is co-existent; sometimes it follows, but it exists in every instance in exact proportion to that of the community, and by no adroitness or subterfuge can it be evaded. It makes but little difference to the carrier, in operating and maintaining his property, whether times are prosperous or otherwise; his road-bed and equipment, with all their appliances, must be kept up to the maximum standard; taxes must be paid; men familiar with the geography of the road and the details of its traffic, and acquainted with the minutiae of its business and schooled in the operation of its trains, station and yard work, must be employed whether rates are high or low, whether business is productive or unproductive. It does not require a man experienced in railway affairs to understand these truths. They are self-evident. If carriers, then, must share in the hardships of their neighbors when times are bad, ought they not equally to be allowed to share in their prosperity when times are propitious?

The world occupies common ground, and the interests of men are never divergent. The disasters and hardships of mankind react upon each other. The millionaire and the laborer suffer proportionately. Every business disaster that occurs affects (according to its extent), every other industry; it may, indeed, not be perceptible to every one, but it exists, nevertheless; all classes, from the richest to the poorest, must bear their proportion of the burden. In the case of labor, the loss may not reflect itself in a reduction of the rate of wages, but may find expression in the purchasing power of such wages, or in enforced idleness. The result is always the same. If one interest is affected by extraordinary causes, all other interests will be affected in like manner, in the proportion that each bears to the other. Whenever an industry derives unfair advantage from the misfortunes of another, in so far as it does so at one time, it will react correspondingly at another time. There can be no escape from this law of natural adjustment. "As ye sow, so shall ye reap." Such is God's fiat, and it applies as strongly to the commercial and financial affairs of nations as it does to men.

The interests of a country do not lie in enforced reduction of rates of carriers, where sharp competition exists, but in strengthening their hands in their efforts to maintain them. I do not maintain

12

that every railroad can be made productive, or that it should be. The general law of adjustment applies to them, the same as to other manufacturers. But they should not be crippled by extraneous action. They should be left unhampered to work out their destiny, the same as other business enterprises.

Generally speaking, the productiveness of railroads should be uniform and steady, and their prosperity should afford the community the same gratification that the prosperity of agricultural, manufacturing, or mining industries affords them; a prosperity it participates in.

Under normal conditions, rates adjust themselves naturally and according to fixed principles. But with undue multiplication of facilities and other artificial processes, abnormal conditions intervene; strife usurps the place of order, intrigue of frankness; equivocation becomes an art; cunning takes the place of ability; the fundamental maxim in commercial life—that you shall do as you agree—is not always regarded, and honest practice and truthful statement, and the faithful execution of contracts and agreements, become problematical. Such are the fruits of artificial competition, if not practically regulated and controlled. Every one is interested in seeing that it is so regulated and controlled in the case of railroads. It can only be brought about by upholding the hands of owners and managers. Up to this time, the most efficacious means found for accomplishing this result is pooling, or, failing that, consolidation.

In railway administration, the strong companies protect and foster the weak; to break them down would be to entail hardships impossible to calculate in advance. Bankrupt properties are not governed by the conservative instincts of business men, or the equities of commercial affairs. Irresponsible and lawless action takes the place of order and concerted method in their affairs, and thus the productiveness of surrounding properties is weakened, if not destroyed. The conditions are the same with railroads as with merchants or manufacturers; a merchant or manufacturer can not expect to receive the maximum profit from his business, if other merchants or manufacturers are doing an unprofitable business. The unfortunate enterprises destroy the calculations of those more fortunate. The same rule applies to railroads; the average condition must be good. Therefore, wherever a weak property exists in competitive enterprise, we find the strong desirous of aiding it; willing to pool their revenues in order to secure peace and order. And in so far as they are willing to do this, their efforts should be encouraged, not thwarted. Every agreement of this kind should, after judicious investigation, if found equitable, receive the approval and support of the government. It is only in this way that warfare between lines competing for a common business can be controlled. It can never be wholly prevented.

In legislating for railways, their peculiarities and differences must be remembered. No rule or procedure can prove satisfactory that seeks to make rates for them. as a whole, or that binds them to

uniform methods of business. Conditions preclude
this. As soon might we attempt to maintain the
standard of a nation by giving to each person a
given quantity of food, air, water, physical exercise, mental labor. Men require nourishment according to their capacity. The commerce of a country and its system of transportation is but a reflex
of man's characteristics in this respect.

The duty of determining the rates of a railroad is
an exceedingly complicated and delicate task; one
requiring extended knowledge and study. It can
not be determined abstractly, or in advance of the
wants of business, but must be adjusted from day to
day to conform to its fluctuations. The force thus
engaged is very large. Its duty is to aid in pushing
business forward; to make it possible and profitable.
It is made up of experienced and talented men, familiar with the commerce of the country, and educated to respond to its requirements. Such a body
of men is not to be found in a rotative service.
They are bred, reared, and educated slowly and
laboriously, little by little. Each day adds something to their knowledge, to their usefulness. Such
a body has been slowly growing up in the railway
service since the first railway was constructed. The
skill of its members is still far from being perfect, but the progress they have made is as great as
could be expected. It must be remembered, that
they were called upon to meet new conditions, interests, prejudices, and passions; a work that no similar body of men in the world had ever been called
upon to deal with before. These facts should be

remembered in judging them, and in estimating the danger that will attend a transfer of their duties to others.

While everyone familiar with the working of railroads can not but doubt the advisability of governmental interference with their rates, they will hail with pleasure such reasonable and proper supervision of their affairs as may be necessary to satisfy the public of their equitable working, or that may be necessary to secure the just accountability of owners and managers ; that will secure due and equitable capitalization, and economical and faithful management. *Bona fide* disbursements should be the limit of capitalization, and similar expenditure the measure of operations. Here is a field for the government, at once broad and useful.

In railway operations, capitalization should go hand in hand with expenditure, but should not in any case precede it. To offer a bonus for the construction or capitalization of a railroad, should be a legal impossibility—an unlawful act. Supervision of this kind comes within the natural and legitimate province of governments. But it is less likely to receive attention than other matters not so beneficial, but about which public agitation and misrepresentation clamor. We shall ever see less disposition to restrict the number of railroads to actual needs than to control their rates ; less disposition to prevent undue capitalization than to award sufficient income afterwards ; less disposition to attend to the modest and practical duties of government than to attain the impossible.

The advisability of governmental supervision is generally recognized. It is indispensable to a correct understanding between the railroads and the people. It is valuable in cases of dispute, and facilitates a better understanding of the railway problem upon the part of the people; as a means of disseminating trustworthy information; as a means of correcting popular mistakes in regard to such properties. In this field its value can not be overestimated. The public believes the statements of its agents; it looks with suspicion upon those made by the owners and managers of railroads. Public supervision affords, therefore, an invaluable means of intercommunication. The railways desire only that the truth shall be told of them. They have nothing to conceal.

An impartial and responsible commission of government officers is thus valuable to the railroad companies, as well as to the public. But it is essential that it should be impartial, and that its duties and responsibilities should be confined within practical limits. It should not be a creative body. While possessing the right to inquire into all matters of public concern, its inquiries should be conducted in a spirit of fairness and with reference to the interests of the people as a whole, and not of a class or section. The relations between carriers and the people are always strained. Differences continually arise between them, and acts upon the part of carriers, that arise from natural and unavoidable causes, are often ascribed to sinister purposes. The public are both curious and uneasy. Their disposition to criticise does not arise from malevolence, but from want of proper understanding of the subject—from jealousy and fear, born of misapprehension. This is not strange. The magnitude and power of a railroad are so great that the individual voice seems powerless to make itself heard. Such is the public belief, however mistaken. An impartial tribunal has it in its power to correct all this. It is, therefore, at once a social and commercial necessity.

The imaginary evils of mankind are quite as hard to bear as those that really exist. The great bulk of the grievances of the public against railways are wholly imaginary, but none the less real on that account. For that reason, it is of the greatest importance that they should be cleared away; that the disposition of the people to attach real effects to imaginary causes, to distort petty grievances into great public calamities, to separate the interests of one class from another, to foster agrarian laws, should cease. This may all be brought about by officials of the government acting without prejudice.

The prime duty of the government, in regard to railroads, is to see that the laws are not violated, to inquire into complaints regarding excessive rates, unjust discrimination, lack of adequate facilities— to be a conservator, in fact, in the general interest; not having power to create conditions, but to ameliorate by investigation and suggestion; not having the power to relieve the owners and operatives of railways of responsibility to the public for the safety and convenience of travel and the necessities of business, but the right to investigate complaints and pass judgment thereon.

Too great care can not be exercised in giving extraneous bodies authority over railway property. Nothing should be allowed to come between the owner and the public. This association of interest and identity is necessary to the public good. No one can supply the owner's place. He should not be allowed to hide himself behind a commission. He should be directly amenable to public opinion for the manner in which he carries on his business. He is abnormally sensitive in this respect; more so than the officials of the government. The latter habitually shield themselves behind customs and formalities to which they ascribe the force of principles and necessities. They envelop themselves in their prerogative, as in a shell, in which they are as inaccessible to attack or criticism as if denizens of another world. It is the same in every country. As the representatives of the people, its agents and protectors, they are the creatures of form, the apostles of precedence, the slaves of precedent. Their safety, convenience, dignity, interest, and prejudice are the measure of their duty. Theirs is not a divided allegiance. They look at the country, as a whole; never to the individual. The latter is their natural enemy. They shield themselves behind impersonal laws. The delay of business, the convenience of the people, is as if it were not.

Railways lose half their usefulness when managed by public servants. The value of such property is so largely dependent upon the estimation in

which it is held by the people, that private owners
are compelled to listen attentively to every complaint, be it reasonable or not, and to act promptly
in providing a remedy. The government is not, for
these reasons, a fit substitute. It is too impersonal.
But a commission before which individuals may lay
their complaints; a board whose duty it shall be to
explain the principles of transportation, however
individual interests may be affected; a board whose
duty it shall be to consult with owners and operatives of railroads in regard to the real necessities of
trade; a board whose duty it shall be to enforce
such regulations as are necessary to the common
good and in accord with the usages and necessities
of business; a board that is honestly bent upon ful-
filling the office of an impartial arbiter, is desirable
from every point of view. Correct principles and
necessary conditions must, however, be observed in
its formation.

Such a board must not be based upon provincial
ideas or imaginary situations. Its influence and mem-
bership must not be apportioned between the railways
and the public, according to the measure of their influence or respective wealth, or upon any other assumed
basis, but must be at once general, dignified, and
honorable. It must be formed with the single purpose of accomplishing whatever measure of public
good its necessarily restricted office renders possible.
It must be a board favorable to the railroads, as a
whole, and equally favorable to the rights and privileges of other interests; a board that recognizes
that railways are and must be operated in harmony

with general principles of business; a board that recognizes that railroads must adjust themselves to the conditions of trade from day to day, according to the exigencies of business, as they arise.

Such a board would possess great value, and would be worthy of the intelligence and integrity of a great people. Its conclusions would be authoritative. It would exercise a peculiarly conservative influence, and under its protection the rights and privileges of railway property would be more fully assured. This great public service and agreeable duty, in the United States, falls naturally to the Interstate Commerce Commission and the various State commissions.

A country whose railways are unproductive, or unjustly harassed in their operations, is like a man whose legs are paralyzed. He may, indeed, move about, and continue, for a while, to eat and drink; but his days are as the grass. The affliction that first manifests itself in his extremities, soon spreads to his vital organs, and he languishes and dies. All the peculiarities of men's lives are reproduced in the trade they create. We see it in the inception, growth, development, and decay of business enterprises. Abnormal conditions affect the trade of a country exactly as they affect man. In order to realize the highest possible condition, the parts that go to make up the whole must be healthful and harmonious. No particular class, or industrial interest, can be permanently built up at the expense of others. The granger agitation in the United States aptly illustrates this. At that time, the agricultural limit had been extended beyond the just bounds of prudence or public need. Prices were greatly depressed in consequence. The afflicted people sought to transfer their burden to the railway companies by arbitrary reductions of rates. Laws were passed with this object, without reference to the necessities of carriers or the equities of vested rights. The railroads were crippled, and their earning capacity diminished. Their ability to meet necessary expenditures and interest was impaired. This affected their credit. The alarm spread to other interests, upon which ensued all the conditions of a financial crisis. This was followed by long-continued depression, until, through natural growth, the railway companies were compensated by increased business for the losses they had suffered, and capital was induced once more (by repeal of the obnoxious measures) to seek investment in the district where the agitation originated.

As I have pointed out, the construction of a parallel road does not involve immediate hardship. Directly the reverse. Money is plentiful ; prices advance ; no increase of rates follows. Quite likely rates are lowered, temporarily at least, in the strife that ensues. The people have, moreover, two lines instead of one, and henceforth may exercise some choice as to which they will patronize. Accommodation has for the moment been increased. Superficially viewed, therefore, they are the gainers. This is as far as they care to pursue the subject. But if the new road had been excluded, the existing line would have been able, sooner or later, to reduce rates because of a superabundant revenue. Thus its

prosperity would have been a source of saving to
the community. But with two roads reduction is
impossible. The people do not stop to trace the
cause. They have a vague feeling that rates ought
to be reduced. Their desire finds expression in the
acts of legislatures, in the voice of newspapers, in
public agitation, in private petition, and general discontent. What is the remedy? Manifestly the
prohibition of duplicate roads. When, therefore,
proposal is made hereafter to parallel an existing
line or build into its territory, let the government say,
through its commissioners, "This line is unnecessary; competition is assured; the present company
is abundantly able to afford the accommodation
needed; the new line will, moreover, retard reductions in rates; will prevent the existing line from
affording the abundant and cheap service that it
ultimately may if allowed the whole business."

The agents of governments may also be made con-
servators in another direction. They may prevent
the construction of lines in advance of their need.
When it is proposed to build a railroad that manifestly will not pay, that is not needed, that is in
advance of its time, let the government say: "Stop!
There is no demand for this road; it is purely speculative; its construction will have the effect to draw
capital from active employment to be locked up in
unproductive enterprise; when there is need for a
line let it be built; let supply go hand in hand with
demand." *

---

* The exercise of this power will prove especially valuable in the
case of railroads built largely by public and private aid. Such
properties are always more or less artificial.

From whatever standpoint the subject is viewed,
over-production in railroads is a hardship to the
people. We can not remedy what is past. The
water that has gone over the dam has been lost.
But the remedy for existing evils does not lie in
legislative enactments, in enforced levies; but in
patient forbearance until such time as the country
grows up to the needs of existing lines. There is
no other course.

Railways, like other manufacturers, sympathize
with those to whom they look for business. No
power can keep rates higher than circumstances
justify. They are the result, as has been shown, of
natural laws. They must be equitable. When they
cease to be so, production ceases.

The interests of the railroads and the country are
identical. No one understands this better than the
owners of railroads, and when I speak of them, I do
not refer to great capitalists. They own, at best,
but a part. They are leaders because of their great
talents and wealth. Their interest is not relatively
large, when we consider gross values. The real
owners of railways, and those to whom we are indebted for our great strides in commerce and trade,
are small holders.

Those who own railroads alone possess the administrative ability to manage them; they alone
possess the ability to discern where capital may be
used advantageously. They form the advance guard
of every great enterprise, an integral part of the
country, a valuable element without which its
natural resources would avail little. Their motives

should not be impugned, nor should we doubt the amiability of their desires more than those of other men. Unjust or intemperate abuse, whether bestowed upon the interest they represent collectively or upon them as individuals, can not but react disastrously on the community practicing it.

Wherever railroads do not furnish adequate or safe accomodation, or their methods are improper, it is a legitimate subject of criticism. But such criticism is vastly different from an attack upon capital. One is beneficial; the other ruinous. Under the granger agitation, already referred to, railway values were depreciated to an enormous extent, partly through loss of revenue and partly from nervous apprehension. The effect was perceptible for many years afterwards in every department of industry, and it was only when capitalists found that the conservative class had overcome the aggressors, that business revived and men were found courageous enough to invest in existing railroads, or provide means for the construction of new ones.

The sovereignty of the people, about which so much is said, and very properly, too, is not to be questioned; but a people can not transgress, any more than individuals, the natural laws that govern commercial and financial affairs. No class or aggregation of classes, however numerous or powerful, can conspire to oppress others, without destroying the basis and underlying principle of commercial life, without precipitating their own ruin with that of the interests they attack. These truths, however self-evident they may be to economists, can not be too frequently reiterated. The railway companies of the United States have, in every stage of their existence, shown a disposition to meet every legitimate responsibility. They have been superior to the harsh judgment that has been passed upon them. We can not trace their experiences except with wonderment; great newspapers have assailed them with unbridled fury; politicians have sought to undermine them with the people; juries have denied them justice; legislatures have openly impugned their motives and questioned their methods; the public has refused to give them its confidence or sympathy; every species of folly, every device of malice, the impossible requirements of ignorance, the selfish cunning of personal interest, the ravings of demagogues, the disappointments, jealousies, prejudices, and hatreds of mankind have each, in turn and in unison, assailed them. Denied every virtue, no accusation has been too monstrous to find believers.

CHAPTER IX.

The railway system of the United States, as it
exists to-day, is an afterthought, a makeshift,
fragmentary, illy conceived, incongruous. In the
beginning, railroads were located with reference to
local traffic only, with regard to their profitableness as short lines. Through business was a remote
contingency, something uncertain and vague, too
purely speculative to merit more than a passing
thought. It, however, grew apace, and with increase of wealth, and knowledge of manipulation,
the process of amalgamating petty interests began.
At first, only continuous lines were consolidated.
Then diverging lines were absorbed; afterward,
competitive interests. Isolated roads were bought
and consolidated, in many cases, to meet contingent
possibilities. The consolidation of roads having
little or nothing in common rendered it necessary to
construct connecting links to weld them together.
In the course of time, the necessity of connecting the great enterprises thus formed with distant
markets not considered in the original scheme,

13   (193)

forced itself on the attention of owners. This involved further building, the paralleling of existing lines, and other incongruous acts. In this "piecing out" process, this attempt to derive order out of chaos, primary conditions were reversed, and local traffic, from being a prime factor, became of secondary importance. Not only this, but the new lines, in many instances, by dividing the local business, destroyed its profitableness.

The railway situation was further aggravated by the presence of many roads built for purely speculative purposes, or to satisfy the sentiments of petty districts. The process of evolution is still going on, but becomes each day more and more simple.

Under the policy of giving bounties, the region east of the Missouri has been honeycombed with roads not contemplated in the original scheme. Many of them would not have been allowed, had permission from an impartial government board been required. Our railway system, having thus grown up under anomalous conditions, requires anomalous treatment. It is distinctively competitive. It is not homogeneous.

The weakness of the railway system of the United States has found frequent expression in the destructive warfare of rival companies. The introduction of pools (whereby business common to two or more lines is equitably apportioned), was the remedy whereby railway owners and managers sought to mitigate the evil. Unfortunately, however, the remedy could only be partially applied without the protection of the government—without the power to control those who transgressed its requirements. This protection the government not only refused, but finally passed a law prohibiting carriers from entering into any kind of pooling arrangement whatsoever. No other country in the world so greatly needs the aid of this device as the United States, because of the chaotic nature of its railway system, and yet the United States is the only country where it is denied to carriers. The law referred to was in keeping with public sentiment—with the desire to outlaw railway property. The people had long been told that railway companies were extortioners, public robbers, to be placed under the surveillance of the police. They did not, therefore, care to protect them. Ignorance and demagogism had full sway. Legislation intended to weaken the hands of managers, or cut down rates, everywhere elicited approval. There was nowhere a disposition to aid in preventing rate wars. Directly the reverse. Laws were passed permeated with the false doctrine that the direct intervention of the government was necessary to prevent the community from being injured by excessively high rates.

It was sought to inculcate the belief that we should look to the government, rather than to the owners of railway property, for honesty and wisdom; to a perfunctory service, rather than a discerning and intelligent one. In framing tariffs, economic laws were no longer to be regarded. The law of supply and demand was no longer to be considered. The belief was general that rates were excessive. Nowhere was the governing principle recognized that, while rates may be too low, the equities of trade prevent their being too high. The owners of railways were scoffed at. The selfish interest they have in protecting and fostering the traffic tributary to their lines, was ignored or disputed. They were to be regulated arbitrarily. Everyone was to be protected, save the carrier. Uniformly fair rates were to give place to uniformly low rates. Artificial competition was to be general, instead of exceptional. The statute books were filled with penalties against discrimination. These enactments, savoring of the blue laws of Connecticut, were an invocation to the discontented, a theme and justification for agrarian agitators. They covertly branded the owners and managers of railways as knaves or fools. They taught that associated capital was robbery; that it was unjust and overreaching. Those who criticised railroads alone were honest. The disposition was general to cater to the prejudices of the people, rather than the wants of trade. The accomplishment of political rather than business ends was sought. The aggrandizement of parties and the fulfilment of personal ambitions, rather than the good of the country, became the ruling idea. Laws were based on the theory that the railway problem was a special one, exempt from economic conditions governing other industries; that the law of competition did not apply to carriers; that their duties and responsibilities might be measured as we measure grain. The subtleties of trade that can not be disregarded, that characterize the traffic of railways as much as that of other manufacturers, were ignored.

Railway administration was to be brought down to the comprehension of school children. Public opinion was perverted; it utterly failed to comprehend the situation. It sought, in the enactment of agrarian laws against railroads, relief that should have been looked for in other directions.*

The equities of railroad traffic are variable and fortuitous. We can not describe them. As well might we attempt to teach the art of violin-playing by descriptive writing, to fathom the subtleties of men's minds, to comprehend their purposes, or measure their energies. They must be studied to be understood. The operation of railroads requires practical business experience, boundless patience, a desire to please, promptitude, knowledge of detail,

---

* In criticising the ill-advised, imperfect, and hastily-considered laws that have been passed, and the indefensible acts that have characterized their enforcement, I do not by any means wish to be understood as asserting or believing that all who advocated or voted for such laws were lacking in wisdom or sincerity. Far from it. I do not believe, for instance, that the Senate and House of Representatives were actuated by other than the most patriotic motives in passing the Interstate Commerce act. Nor did they act hastily. If the law is grossly defective in some respects, it is because the needs of the situation were not fully understood. And in this connection I wish to excuse myself if what I have written has the appearance of prejudice or undue vehemence. The matter is one about which I have thought much. My opportunities for thirty-five years have been especially favorable for observing and understanding the methods, policies, and motives of railway companies. I know them to be generally good, such as the country needs, at once business-like, sagacious and honorable. I know, also, that as a rule, those who criticise them are not nearly so patriotic, wise, or unselfish, as the owners of railroads; not nearly such good citizens; do not contribute nearly so much as they to aggrandize the country.

ubiquity. Wherever governments interfere, their
interference must contemplate similar labors and
experiences. They are manifestly unequal to the
task. To invest government with the authority to
make rates, or actively interfere with other business
matters, is to make the creative, aggressive genius
of a nation conform to the contracted sphere of
mechanical action. Such a course is destructive.
The agents of government should be endowed with
great power; with the authority of arbitrators and
judges in the disputes that arise between carrier and
patron. But acts upon which they pass should be
specific, carefully particularized; should not extend
to an adjudication of economic conditions or
methods.

Nothing illustrates the prejudices and passions of
mankind more aptly than its treatment of railways in the United States. These properties have,
in their progress, been made the subject of every
condition; of romantic enactments, imaginary necessities, undue expectation, misconception, public dec-
lamation, and general clamor. Their owners, from
being the recipients of personal and civic attention,
have reached a level where their high intelligence,
their courage, their enterprise, their honesty, are,
one and all, denied, or forgotten.

The people are disposed to question the fact that
the railway business is governed by the same
principles as other business, and does not invite the
initiative or intervention of the government, any
more than the business of raising corn. A law-
maker who should assume it to be his duty to fix

the price of agricultural implements, lumber, cattle, machinery, calico, or tea, would be hooted out of the community as unfit to be trusted. And yet that is exactly what is proposed for railroads. One is as reasonable as the other. The thought is provincial, restricted, narrow. It weighs the welfare of an empire in the balance against the interests of a particular person or market.

Many of the embarrassments and misconceptions that attend the operations of railways in the United States, grow out of the indiscriminate construction of such properties that we have encouraged. The situation is a perplexing one, but not such as to excite uneasiness or distrust. Its solution is simple. In the matter of rates, about which the public is most concerned, what is required is a law that recognizes that, like other prices, they are based on economic conditions; that they can not be too high, because competitive influences forbid; but that they may be too low, owing to the strife of local carriers. What is required is a law that will modify the latter; that will prevent competitive rates from being disturbed, except upon economic grounds. A law, in fact, that shall not forbid pooling; that shall distinctly recognize its equity. This right is not withheld, or its rightfulness questioned, anywhere else.

Our laws prevent excessive rates, but we have none that insures reasonable rates; we are carefully guarded from an impossible evil, but left exposed to one that is real.

The railway situation in the United States suggests a law designed to prevent wastage of the

resources of railways—a law that will prevent
internecine wars. But in devising this relief, the
responsibility of those who own railroads must not
be destroyed. It may be regulated. They alone
are equal to the emergency of management; they
alone understand the constantly changing requirements of commerce; they alone have the means to
meet them. The situation requires legislation that
will afford railroads protection and encouragement
without crippling them, or through them, the
country.*

---

*This chapter was written in 1886. I merely revise it. While
there has been much legislation since that time, I do not see wherein
I can change what I then wrote. It was true then. It is true now.
Railroad wants are still the same. The mistake that the public
and public servants make, is in treating exceptions in railway
practice as conditions; in mistaking surface indications for fundamental principles; in treating local distempers as constitutional
maladies; in applying the surgeon's knife when a mild poultice is all
that is required; in acting hastily, and oftentimes not upon experience
or wise counsel. The railway situation requires the strengthening
of the hands of owners.

Per contra, what I wrote in regard to railway rates, I find, upon
further study and reflection, to be lacking in adequate comprehension
of the subject. So greatly have I been impressed with this fact, that
everything I have published on the subject heretofore I have, so far
as possible, withdrawn and destroyed. I ascribed undue importance
to the cost of a property; also to the discretion of carriers. The
cost of a property practically cuts no figure in fixing the rate, while
the discretion of the carrier is so limited—applies to only so small
a part of the traffic he handles—that when we consider the business
as a whole, we find he has, practically, no discretion whatever.
It is like that of a merchant, who may put up the price a little on an
odd article, but on the great bulk of his goods—on everything of
consequence to the community—the price is determined for him by
influences that he has no control over whatever.—M. M. K.

The untrammeled operation of railroads is necessary to the freedom of trade, the interchange of commodities, the prosperity of business, the growth of a country. We can not wrap them in the cerements of mummies, or chain them to arbitrary conditions, and expect them to fulfill the vital and active functions of their office. If untrammeled, they will effect the widest possible interchange of traffic between the markets of a country. We cannot fix the rates they shall charge in accomplishing this end, in the mechanical manner that we measure lumber, or count the telegraph poles that line our public highways. They must be determined as exigencies arise, according to the equities of trade. The question is an economic one, and must be so treated by governments. Wherever governments meddle in such affairs, their action (if designed to benefit mankind) will be exceedingly moderate. It will be suggestive rather than mandatory. Government agents empowered to supervise railway affairs should not be accorded too much power. It can not be used safely or wisely. This will be especially true at first. Afterward, as practical experience suggests, the power may be enlarged. But experience will hardly invite this. The necessity for governmental regulation of railroads will ever be found to be more imaginary than real. Needed legislation, here as elsewhere, is that which attracts the least attention, about which there is the least clamor. Legislation designed to prevent undue multiplication of railroads, to stop railroad wars, will never greatly interest the people, but they will

clamor incessantly for protection against purely
ideal dangers. The law-making power must notice
these sentimental cravings doubtless, but in doing
so need not injure any real interest.

Laws regulating railroads should be generally of
a judicial character. They should empower the
officers of government to listen to the complaints of
carriers and shippers, and to investigate the causes
thereof and the remedies therefor; to prevent unjust discrimination, if found to exist; to make sug-
gestions where the railroads or the public are in
the wrong, or peace and good government may be
advanced thereby; to see that necessary police
regulations are enforced and that reasonable facilities are furnished; to investigate accidents and
make inquiries connected therewith; to collect and
publish the returns of railroads; to inquire into the
traffic agreements, contracts, and understandings of
carriers, and to legalize and enforce such agreements,
when not inconsistent with the public good, and,
finally, to prevent the construction of unnecessary
railroads. They should not be creative, but supervisory merely. Such laws are practical, safe, and
needed. They will not in any way restrict industrial freedom; will not create conditions, but ameliorate them; will not destroy the individuality
of the citizen, but intensify it. The railway system
and the interests it affects are too vital to the well-
being of a country to be made the subjects of arbitrary, ill-tempered, or hasty action. Interference
must be circumscribed and guarded. An industry
that requires the uninterrupted labor of an army of

experienced and able men, in shaping its policy and adjusting its affairs, cannot intelligently or safely be subjected to the arbitrary interference of men less in number or experience ; cannot be safely taken out of the hands of owners and transferred to the hands of those whose interests are merely perfunctory.

CHAPTER X.

When anything goes wrong in the world, or seems to go wrong, the ignorant and thoughtless everywhere, rise up and call upon the government to interfere, as if a perfunctory body, made up of agents, loosely selected at best, was more trustworthy than the masses, from which it derives life. Government interference is the *sine qua non* of young people, the hopeful, confiding, and simple. It is the panacea of cranks and schemers. It is never fully adequate. It lacks in intelligent interest, energy, and adaptability. It, moreover, has the effect to weaken personal interest and individual effort. Its substitution for private effort is to trade off the practical experience and enthusiasm of a nation for the service of hired men. But in questioning the ability of governments to carry on affairs effectively and economically, the basis of objection should not be misunderstood. It is not that the subordinate officials of a government, those who really do its work, are not able and trustworthy, but that they lack the peculiar kind of executive and administrative talent that is needed.

The carrying on of government is a business in which the government employe performs duties

somewhat analagous to those of a merchant, manufacturer, or banker. He both originates and directs.
He is not fitted for such duties. His genius lies in
another direction. He lacks the self-reliance, the
aggressiveness, the foresight, the instinct of trade,
the amiability, that the merchant possesses. If he
had these qualities, he would not be working for the
government; he would be a trader, manufacturer,
banker, or capitalist. Moreover, the incentive of
personal gain, the propelling force of the world, is
lacking. Thus essential qualities, necessary to carry
on any kind of business successfully, are wanting.
Their absence is fatal. This is why everything a
government does is poorly done compared with the
achievements of private individuals.

Nothing that the industry, ingenuity, or enterprise of a people leads them to do on their own
account, should be undertaken by a government.

The intervention of governments in the affairs of
business emasculates men, dulls their inventive
genius, chills their ardor, robs them of their independence, lessens their patriotic instincts, reduces
their sense of personal obligation. It takes the
affairs of a nation (so far as the intervention ex-
tends) out of the hands of natural leaders, and puts
them into the hands of clerks; it is to substitute
mediocrity for talent, mechanical effort for creative
genius, perfunctory service for interested effort.
The few men of wise judgment and great experience, who have charge of the great departments and
bureaus of a government, are not sufficient in number
to relieve the service of this just criticism. Thus,

our Interstate Commerce Commission, and the Board of Trade, of England, with their staffs, while made up of men of great ability, are as a drop in the bucket. They are, in fact, only equal in number to the practical men that every railroad finds it necessary to employ for its own use.

Governmental management lacks spirit, alertness, and a desire to please. It is at once meddlesome, slow, cumbersome, and bumptious. The absence of gain robs it of energy and a desire to please. Its acts are lacking in promptness and natural adjustment. It is slow to make changes; is loth to run counter to established practices, even when the interests of a country demand it. It is governed by precedent, instead of practical needs; by formulas, instead of principles; by the adaptations of theorists, instead of business men. It lacks commercial shrewdness. Under it, circumlocution, instead of being a mere incident of business, becomes a ruling principle, impossible to overcome or mitigate, because carried out ostensibly in the interests of the people.

In the ratio that corporate service falls below the high standard of private endeavor, so does governmental service fall below that of private corporations. It lacks the vitalizing force infused into corporate life by the owner; it lacks his directing energy and intelligence, his genius and self-interest, his personal concern, and supervisory usefulness. It is mechanical and plodding. Thus in no instance has the train-service of railroads managed by governments kept pace with that of lines operated by

14

private corporations, either as regards safety or efficiency.

Under every form of government, the methods of the operative are all-important. Public convenience is secondary with him, although he is unconscious of the fact. As the representative of the people, he is not to be lightly disturbed. Invention and innovation are synonymous terms with him. Change and betterment do not add to his comfort or fortune. But they do add to his labor. Moreover, they may occasion criticism. Under him, complexity gradually usurps the place of simplicity; it adds to his importance, and affords him a screen behind which he can hide. Clericalism envelops everything he does. Obsolete tools are his favorite utensils. He is familiar with them. He makes up in metaphysical dissertation what he lacks in practical sense and usefulness. The railroads he constructs are such as the engineer wants, rather than the trader. In operating them, cost is in the inverse ratio to efficiency. His tariffs are based on mathematical formulas, rather than the needs of trade. In everything he is a stickler for uniformity. It saves mental labor. In railway practice, it is his desire to base rates on expenses and interest, rather than on quality of service or value.* The picture is not exaggerated.

No kind of business can be carried on by govern-

---

* And when we remember how greatly cost of operation is heightened by his inefficiency and cumbersome methods, we may form some estimate of what his tariffs are, so far as he can control them.

ment, whether it be the operation of a railway, or
the carriage of express or mails, so economically or
effectively as by individual effort. The government
servant lacks in fertility of resource—in inventiveness. Hired to serve, he is superior to his employers in everything but energy, intelligence, and
experience. He is a hard master instead of a docile
creature. There are, of course, exceptions. The
government service has produced many men of
exalted wisdom and unselfishness, with a genius
almost godlike. It possesses many others of lesser
talent, who are capable and obliging, the equals of
the best. But they do not form any appreciable
number of the whole. The conditions are not such
as to engender them.

Governmental management is nowhere the equal
of private effort. It is objectionable, because of the
excessive cost that attends its operation, because of
its lack of facility, its lack of public spirit, its un-
approachableness, the high prices it engenders. A
government monopoly is the most objectionable
monopoly in the world, because, however baneful,
it is superior to assault, because carried on ostensibly in the interest of the public. It points to its
performances as creditable, without the people having the ability to judge by comparison whether they
are so or not.

Men who are themselves failures, or who do not
discern the certainty with which mankind achieve
great commercial ends when left to themselves, turn
to the government just as a child learning to walk
turns to its mother, with tears in its eyes, when it

14

falls. But a wise mother does not, because of this, take up the child and carry it. She encourages it to try again.

Government management of commercial affairs is never expedient, never wise, never fruitful. It is unnecessary. Competitive effort may always be depended upon to protect a people from the machinations of interested parties, if left free in its operations. But nothing can protect a people from government monopoly, from the stupidity, arrogance, and ambitious ends of governmental servants.

Those who advocate government interference in matters of business, do so from selfish reasons or from lack of knowledge. To the latter, a spot on their spectacles is greater than the luminous sun. Personal injuries, individual acts of injustice, are greater to them than the common good. They see in the railway system an engine of oppression, because some one has been wronged, because some one has been dishonest or foolish. They would destroy established methods of the greatest good, because, forsooth, some one has been oppressed, some one has derived unfair advantage therefrom. Unhappy the country where such men are listened to. They do not look beyond speculative endeavor. Their horizon is a sheet of paper, their object the utopia of the dreamer. They are unstable as water, the prophets of the simple, discontented, ungrateful, and vicious of society.*

* Among those who advocate government ownership of railroads, we may also include the owners of bankrupt and semi-bankrupt railroads. Other men, ignorant of the cause, hail this advocacy as an

Government ownership and management every-where means the same thing: lax responsibility, great outlay. It means the substitution of the operative's convenience for the public good. In the management of private corporations, a deficit is a serious matter, to be scrutinized with sharpness. In the operation of governments it is only an incident, to be looked upon with patriotic indulgence.

The owners of railroads find it difficult to super-vise their properties through the managers they employ, although constantly on the watch, although one and all are animated by the fear of personal loss. How much more difficult, then, must it be for the people to do so, who have neither direct interest nor influence!

Wherever governmental management is contem-plated, it should be preceded and attended by an effective civil service; a service founded upon fixed-ness of employment, loyalty, intelligence, business knowledge, and skill in the duties of carriers. It must be conducted on the same lines as private enterprise. Thus organized, it will still lack in

---

omen. It is, however, simply the interested effort of a seller; the voice of an impecunious, improvident, or slothful man, who has something on his hands that nobody but the government can be induced to buy. Such men will go to any length to attain their end. I have in mind a railway manager of this kind, who not only advo-cates the ownership of railways by the government, but, meanwhile, wants the latter to take possession of railways that do not observe the requirements of a particular law. The pointedness of this last sug-gestion was rendered more apparent by the fact that an officer of his company was at that time under indictment by a grand jury for dis-obeying the statute in question.

efficiency, because wanting in the supervisory intelligence and interest of the owner. And right here is where government control always fails. It lacks the incentive of ownership; lacks the wise advice and direction of practical business men, whose fortunes and the fortunes of others depend upon the wisdom of what they do.

For these and other reasons, government ownership or management of railroads is impracticable. It is especially so in the United States. The latter has the most extended system in the world, with a civil service the most lax. " When our politics are purified, so as to exclude from them selfish ends and improper means, it may be possible to bring the railways under political control without making. them a source of general corruption." * Without making' them a source of corruption, yes. But we can never make such a service as efficient or economical as one managed by private enterprise, because constructive and administrative ability will be lacking.

Not only is the government of the United States illy adapted to assume the ownership or management of railways, but the railway system itself is not in a position for so radical a change. It must work out its own destiny in its own way. "No comprehensive solution of the American railroad problem need, however, now or at any time, be anticipated from the action of the government. The statesman, no matter how sagacious he may be, can but build with the materials he finds ready for his

* J. F. Hudson, " The Railways and the Republic," page 337.

hand. He can not call things into existence, nor indeed, can he greatly hasten their growth. If he is to succeed, he must have the conditions necessary to success. So far as the railroad system of this country is concerned, in its relations to the government, everything is as yet clearly in the formative condition. Nothing is ripe. That system is now, with far greater force and activity than ever before, itself shaping all the social, political, and economical conditions which surround it. The final result is probably yet quite remote, and will be reached only by degrees. When it comes, also, it will assuredly work itself out; probably in a very commonplace way." *

But while we may question the utility of government ownership or control, we can not doubt the value of governmental supervision, wisely and honestly exercised. No harm can accompany it; it may correct many misapprehensions, may greatly allay public irritation, may prove a wise counselor. Wherever a demagogical spirit prevails, it may in this way be silenced, or rendered innocuous; where ignorance prevails, it may thus be enlightened. The responsibility of the office and the gravity of the situation will superinduce calmness and impartiality upon the part of those who fill it. In this simple and practical way a government will secure every good that could possibly flow from active interference, while the fatal evils that attend intermeddling with commercial affairs may be happily avoided.

---

* C. F. Adams.

CHAPTER XI.

GOVERNMENT SUPERVISION AND CONTROL: ITS LIMI-
TATIONS — THE VALUE OF PRIVATE OWNERSHIP
— FURTHER REFERENCE TO RATES: PRINCIPLES
UNDERLYING THEM.

Nations commercially great delegate to their governments only such functions of a business nature
as individual citizens can not be induced to take up.
It has been the same in every age. Witness the
practices of Great Britain in our time.* This, the
greatest nation that ever existed, not only accords
individuals the preference in every case, but carefully abstains from any interference with them
likely to dampen their ardor or restrict their achievements. Its policy, moreover, is applied fairly and
unreservedly to all; to railroads as well as to producers of corn and iron. It respects the property
rights of the rich, as well as the rights of the poor.

In some respects, the people of the United States
fall far short of England.

We are much given to loose talk about those who
are rich; about those who own railroads, banks, and
other great interests. It is a species of hysteria.

---

* "The people of England, proud of their commercial ability and
jealous of their commercial liberties, spurn the idea of governmental
ownership or management of the railroads."—Joseph Nimmo, Jr.

We do not always stop to inquire whether the purposes of the rich are beneficent or not.

We love to hold up to public scorn particular instances of wrong-doing.

We are much inclined to self-righteousness.

Many of our laws discriminate unjustly and oppressively against corporate industries.

We are more than half disposed to put the owners of such properties in the hands of the police and turn over their affairs to the government.

In reference to railroads, that form of government supervision that will best serve to quiet the apprehensions of the people, and will least interfere with the skill and purposes of owners and managers, is the best. It is not a material subject, but a sentimental one. There is really no need of any supervision whatever. But, because of public suspicion and misapprehension, it is both necessary and beneficial.

Public opinion and association of interest of carrier and patron will ever be sufficient to insure efficiency and prevent injustice. Of course, individual acts of wrong-doing will occur. But wherever one of these is prevented by government supervision, a dozen will creep in under cover of such interference. Government commissioners will be useful, so far as their talent, experience, and integrity enable them to throw new light on the subject. But they must be just and impartial. Otherwise they will be a curse to a nation.

Government interference, whether local or general, like all extraneous influences, must be such as to invite the confidence of those it concerns; in the case of railways, of those who own them. It must be wisely exercised. If it is not, capital will abandon interests thus afflicted. Undue interference in the affairs of railroads, however necessary, is harmful, because it lessens private interest by dividing the responsibility. It chills the ardor of those to whom we must look in matters of this kind. Its effect is to retard improvements, to prevent new enterprises, to lessen the interest of owner and manager in the comforts and conveniences of the people. Government interference, unless exercised with great moderation, blasts every interest it espouses, every industry it attempts to supervise.

Arbitrary action in business matters must always be circumscribed by the interests of surrounding industries. Those who own and manage railroads have little or no discretion, except in facilitating public wants and in adjusting tariffs to meet the ever varying needs of commerce. They must act, whether they will or no. Any attempt upon their part to evade the just responsibilities and duties of their office, is met with loss of business and merciless criticism. They must respond to every need, quickly and effectively. Business can not be carried on otherwise. A railway operated on any other basis would be so cumbersome, so illy adapted to the needs of trade, that business would quickly forsake its lines. It is no disparagement to government officials, no reflection on their intelligence or interest, to say that they cannot thus respond to the needs of commerce. In everything they do they must conform to some law or precedent. It is thus the people protect themselves against those who govern them. There is no other way. The result is, the government servant is disqualified from filling any office requiring the exercise of discretion— any office requiring its incumbent to adapt himself from day to day to constantly changing needs.

The servant of a government is like a blind man, when not governed by law or precedent. He requires these to substantiate his good name, to shield him from attack. In every situation and experience, consequently, he hedges himself about with rules and regulations. The more minute and exhaustive they are, the better. He can not, if he will, vary them to meet practical needs or the interests of in- dividual citizens. He is autocratic. In guarding the interests of the people, he looks jealously after his own prerogatives and interests. The power he exercises and the general limitations of his office, all combine to make him a prosecutor, instead of a con- servator, of those so unfortunate as to have relations of a business nature with him. The fault is not his, but that of the system of which he is a part.

In considering the subject, three reasons may be assigned for State ownership of railroads: (1) Avoidance of abuses incident to private manage- ment. (2) Lack of private enterprise. (3) Increase of political influence of the government.*

Government ownership in the United States and England is advocated for the first-named reason.

---

* A. T. Hadley, "Railroad Transportation," page 238.

The last two are, generally, the incentives else-where. In every country, save England and America, the State owns more or less railroads; it is also more or less active in operating them. But wherever State and private management have been pitted against each other, the superior skill of the latter has been marked. In Germany and Belgium, private competition was found to be so intolerable that the State proceeded to buy up the private railroads. State ownership in Europe is simply another form of exercising political influence; another form of strengthening the governing class.

Wherever railroads have been managed by the State, it has been sought to base rates on cost of property and operation. This was to be expected. It is in accordance with the conservative instincts of governments, their mania for uniformity. They have no commercial sense. Their operations are either mechanical or theoretical. In framing a tariff, they proceed in the most direct way to ascertain the cost of terminal charges, expense of movement, interest, and taxes, and having done so, to base the rate thereon.* The result is what might be expected. Such a rate, while theoretically perfect, is not practicable in actual operation. If progressive, it will estop trading in distant markets, while for short distances the terminal charge will be so large as to send business by other conveyances, or prohibit it entirely.

* Thus, the rate in Germany, " on any class of goods, consisted of a fixed charge to cover terminal expenses, independent of distance, plus a rate per mile to cover movement expenses."—A. T. Hadley.

Rates based on relative cost retard traffic, except within exceedingly circumscribed limits. This theory falls to the ground with actual practice. "There was never a more mistaken idea than the idea that rates would be reduced if they were based upon cost of service. The principle keeps rates up. If it is strictly applied, it makes it necessary that each item of business should pay its share of the fixed charges. A great deal of business which would pay much less than its share of the fixed charges (though still giving a slight profit above train and station expenses), is thus lost. This is bad for the railroads, bad for the shipper, and bad for the prospect of low average rates. It makes the business of the roads so much smaller that the share of fixed charges which each piece of business has to pay (under this system), becomes higher, while the profit does not increase, and the inducement to new construction is lessened. These things are not mere theory, but are matters of history. The great reductions of rates, whether in the United States, Belgium, or elsewhere, have taken place under the stimulus of competition, even if it was only temporary. They have been made at the very periods when the principle of basing rates upon cost of service was most systematically violated. It is the countries which have passed through such periods that enjoy the lowest rates." *

A tariff based on cost is practically impossible. Wherever sought to be introduced, its use is attended

---

* A. T. Hadley, " Railroad Transportation," page 250.

with countless exceptions, special rates, concessions, avoidances, sliding scales, and other makeshifts designed to harmonize it with actual needs ; to make it fit the wants of commerce, rather than the theories of empires and politicians. Austria, like Germany, attempted to base rates on cost, but unsuccessfully. The effort, however, was fertile with suggestion. Thus, it sought to make middle distance traffic pay relatively more profit than the long or short distance. Rates finally were based on what the traffic would bear, but the government sought to make it appear as if they were based on cost of service.* Governmental-like, after deluding the people into the belief that cost formed the proper basis, it avoided it in actual practice, without acknowledging the deception.

The belief that every rate should bear its share of cost and interest is theoretically perfect. Technically it is right. Practically it is absurd. The necessities of trade can not be made to conform to any such cut-and-dried rule, to any such political delusion or prejudice. It must be handled for the profit there is in it. Traders understand this, and act accordingly. No one else does or can.

Happy the country whose commercial and industrial affairs are left to the control of traders ; to those who alone are imbued with the instinct of trade, or possess the adaptive talent to conform to its needs.

In some respects the business methods of Europe are more straightforward and practical than ours. If Europeans do not possess greater commercial

* A. T. Hadley, " Railroad Transportation," page 247.

wisdom than we, they are more courageous in enforcing the ideas they have. Thus, while we appreciate
as highly as they the value of stable rates, of rates
that shall conform generally to the laws of trade,
that shall be generally uniform, we deny carriers the
power to enforce them.   We refuse even to consider
the subject, but fly incontinently, like children, before the ignorant and demagogical cry that the
people are injured by combinations having such
objects in view.   The suggestion that they are
trusts, that they are monopolistic, destroys the
courage of our law-makers.   In other countries the
law-makers are less timid.   They not only recognize the necessity of carriers combining, but encourage them to do so.   They have found that where
railroads are in active competition, nothing can
preserve the stability of rates except granting them
permission to divide the business—to pool it, in fact.
European governments not only recognize the necessity and equity of pools, but legalize and enforce
them.   They carry them "to an extent undreamed
of in America.   They have both traffic pools and
money pools.   There are pools between State roads
and private roads, between railroads and water
routes.   It is regarded as a perfectly legal thing that
one road should pay another a stated sum of money,
in consideration of the fact that the latter abstains
from competing for the through traffic of the
former."*   The experiences of European roads are

---

* A. T. Hadley, "Railroad Transportation," page 249.   This
exposition is so graphic that I can not refrain from quoting it a
second time.—M. M. K.

not peculiar. The needs of railroads are the same everywhere. They are everywhere governed by natural laws, if left to themselves, and are valuable to a community in just so far as they conform to such laws.

Government management of railroads is never based solely on commercial and social requirements, but upon personal and political needs as well. It is made up in about equal parts of business and politics, trade and theory, frankness and evasion, knowledge and ignorance, industry and sloth. A country thus afflicted can not compete with others more favorably situated in the trade and commerce of the world. It is too heavily handicapped.

Wherever State management has been tried, it has been found lacking in effectiveness, in ability to compete with private endeavor. However, we must not look to see governments generally acknowledge this fact. That would be expecting too much. Here, as elsewhere, self-interest clouds men's intelligence quite as much as their ambition disinclines them to relinquish power. Instances are not wanting, however, where the shortcomings of government management have been so glaring as to compel recognition. This was so in Italy. The case was exceptional. The financial situation of the country was critical. The government felt unwilling to take the responsibility longer. It accordingly turned over its roads to private parties. In relinquishing control, it summed up the case against itself as follows: "It is a mistake to expect lower rates or better facilities from government than from private companies. The actual results are just the reverse. The State is more apt to tax industry than to foster it; and when it attempts to tax industry, it is even less responsible than a private company. State management is more costly than private management. Much capital is thus wasted. State management is demoralizing, both to legitimate business and politics."*

The Italian government did not speak or act hastily. Its experiences had been varied and exhaustive. "Italy has had more experience of different methods of railway management than any other country on the face of the globe. It has tried State ownership and private ownership; it has tried allotting a district to a company, as in France; and it has held an investigation into the whole subject unparalleled, both in extent and minuteness. It has laid under contribution the railway experience gathered in the course of fifty years by every nation in the world."† Its action, therefore, was conclusive, so far as the commercial needs and experiences of Italy were concerned. That these were not noticeably different from those of other countries, we know from the analogies of trade.

Government management of railways is practiced more or less in many countries. Not because the people thought it the best way, but because government aid was necessary in the first instance to build the roads.

---

* W. M. Acworth, M. A., "The Railways and the Traders," page 164.

† *Ibid.*

No people who possess commercial sense and business shrewdness accept government management as the best. It does not solve a single problem of business. Directly the contrary. It is not more selfish, perhaps, than private ownership, but it is less intelligent, less discriminating, less sensitive to the necessity of co-operative effort. Its power enables it to make its selfishness effective. It crowds out private capital, stifles private enterprise, prevents competition. It is both greedy and narrow. It is the most vicious and the least amenable to reason of any monopoly in the world, because founded ostensibly on the public good.

In France, the obligations of the railroads were guaranteed by the government; at the expiration of a hundred years, the properties were to revert to it absolutely. In locating the different lines, each was made a monopoly, so far as possible. The profits that have attended their operation are not due so much to successful management, to economical construction and operation, as to the absence of healthful competition. Their rates are much higher than those of the United States, while their service is in every way less effective. Government control, here, as elsewhere, is very conservative, i. e., is loth to do anything. While extremely anxious to satisfy every expectation, it has made little progress. It is too prolix, too circumstantial, is lacking in virility, inventiveness, business skill, ability to adapt itself immediately to the wants of the community. Its operations are those of a bureau, rather than those of business men.

15

The Belgian system of government railroads has been esteemed from the first the highest pattern of this form of management. Its initiative was admirable. It thundered loudly in the index, but has not kept up with expectation. Its "early arrangements were admirable for the time in which they were devised. But they were not changed to keep pace with progress elsewhere. The Belgian system of reports and statistics, when first adopted, was the best in the world; a generation later it was the worst. In their engineering arrangements, machine shops, etc., what was at first admirable precision soon became intolerable old fogeyism." * However, characterizations of this nature do not apply to the Belgian system alone. They apply to government management everywhere. Government officials are the same in their dispositions and methods in every country. They cling to that which they know. Their changes are mainly mechanical, clerical; the adoption of new checks and safeguards; of new designs, to keep the people in order and at a respectful distance.

All government service is generically alike in its disposition to multiply offices, to magnify details. Its opportunities afford no adequate incentive to industry; it does not regard economy; the wages it pays are excessive; its hours are short; its vacations are long; its supplies are bought, not with reference to their needs, but with a view to stimulate tastes and industries. It is extravagant. The losses it

_____

* A. T. Hadley.

entails, however, are so covered up and diffused in the annual budget that they are not generally known or appreciated. The inefficiency and extravagance of government management is not recognized, for lack of something better to compare it with. Every form of government is alike in its desire and ability to hide its shortcomings. The exception to this, so far as we know, is the case of Italy. But the experiences of that country were particularly disastrous. One of its provinces, Lombardy, found it necessary at one time to suspend her freight service, because of lack of ability of those in charge to handle it. But this was an extreme case. Under private management, the roads of Lombardy had been vigorous, economical, and effective.

Government interference in commercial affairs increases the influence of those in power. This is as true of republics as it is of monarchies. If the government is not a despotic one, it is debased by the contact. It corrupts the law-making power and weakens the executive. Thus, to cite an instance, the Belgian government found it necessary, at one time, in order to conciliate a particular class, to make rates without reference to the needs of business, simply to secure a political end. The case was not peculiar. Under State control ministers, legislators, office-holders, and judges become the arbiters of trade. Could anything be more absurd? The injury a country suffers from such contact is not alone pecuniary, it is also moral. Not that official corruption is necessarily implied. This may perhaps be avoided. But temptation is constant and

extreme. In Australia, where railroads are domi-
nated by the government, it is said not to be an unusual occurrence for legislators to make investments
in a particular district, and then proceed to obtain
the construction of a road thereto, either by the
government or under its bounty.

It does not require a fertile imagination to picture
the advantages corrupt legislators may take wherever railroads are built or operated by the State.
The incentive to make such properties the medium
of personal aggrandizement will be constant and
irresistible, but so insidious and hidden, so covered
up, by one specious pretence or another, that the
acts of the demagogue and rogue can not be distin-
guished from those of the upright legislator.

The government ownership and management of
railways in Australia has been both curious and
instructive. There is little in it to encourage those
who favor government interference in such matters.
"Construction of railroads in Australia failed as
a private enterprise. Then each one of the five col-
onies took the matter up separately as governmental
enterprises. . . . Their construction has been
a source of grave charges of dishonesty, and their
management a subject of popular complaint, especially among the farmers. Freight charges are
much higher on the Australian railroads than on
our American roads. The governments have been
obliged to place their roads in the hands of commissioners, or 'general managers,' as we would call
them, independent of parliamentary control. So that
the Australian system is really one of quasi-govern-

mental management.''* While the railroads of Australia were located with the express view to avoid competition, they have yielded little or no profit. The experience of Cape Colony, South Africa, has been the same.

In the management of railways, economy of operation and low rates usually go hand in hand. There is no cut-and-dried formula, like cost of service, mileage, or value of property, for determining the rate. It is based on the value of the thing handled; on the value of the service. There is no other way. Arbitrary rates ought not to be possible under a government, any more than under individuals. A government rate that is too low entails hardship through the deficiency it engenders in the budget; if too high, it prevents business.

No material interest can be benefited by government management of railways. Every stable interest lies in the contrary direction. It is only a matter of minor concern to a government, whether the railways it manages are operated economically and efficiently or not; it is everything to the private owner. Governments may shield themselves behind prerogatives and rules of procedure; private owners can not. The interests of the latter and those to whom they look for business are identical. They are compelled, therefore, to foster the interests of their patrons to the utmost. Herein lies their profit. Under private management, every resource of capital is taxed to its utmost to attain mutually satisfactory

* Joseph Nimmo, Jr.

results. Every economy is practiced that a desire
of gain and an alert and versatile talent can
suggest ; the individual shipper is the unit of the
service ; his complaints are heard, his wishes grati-
fied whenever possible. On the other hand, the
government considers the patron only in a general
way ; his identity is lost ; he becomes mixed up
with the good of the nation as a whole. Problems
of far greater political importance crowd him out,
and thus the concrete good of a people is frittered
away in the attainment of general or governmental
aims or in the gratification of ideal dreams.

Public management of railroads is hampered by
the effort to adjust public needs to private wants ;
by the fear that some existing arrangement may be
disturbed ; lest some one will be injured ; lest the
government be misunderstood ; lest it be accused of
favoritism or improper motive. Thus, individual
enterprise is hampered and progress blocked.

In the affairs of government, extraneous influences
are ever quite as potent as those immediately concerned; political ends as great as material necessities. In this spirit, governments build railroads
without reference to their needs, and operate them
without reference to their profitableness. "All that
can be said in favor of government ownership or
control of railways is, that it can regulate the
freight charges and prevent excessive rates that
would interfere with the industries of the country.
Practically, it has no such effect. The result of the
writer's experience and observation is that the
highest railroad freight rates in the world are

where the railroads are either owned or controlled by the government; and the lowest rates are those in the United States, where there is free railway construction. . . . If the English freight rates were in force in Eastern Tennessee, the iron and coal interest, that is being so extensively worked under our low railway rates, could not exist; and in place of the busy mines and furnaces, there would be only a few farmers raising enough food for their own support, shipping, perhaps, a little cotton, for nothing else could stand the heavy freight rates to the seaports. In English South Africa, all the railroads are owned by the government, and the evil effects of the State ownership can be readily seen. In order to get the necessary votes in the assembly to pass a bill authorizing the construction of meritorious lines, it has been necessary to build other lines that were not required and will not pay. . . . As the government and railroad officers wish to make a good financial showing, they are obliged to charge high freight rates on the good lines, to make up for the loss on the poor ones. This has caused such high freight rates as to be nearly prohibitory to farming, except near the sea-coast. Diamond and gold mining, sheep and ostrich farming, are the only industries developed in the interior that can stand the high freight charges. The government will not grant permission to construct private lines, for fear of competing with and injuring the public lines." *
The experiences of the Cape Colony are not peculiar.

---

* E. Bates Dorsey, at annual convention of the American Society of Civil Engineers, May, 1891.

Government management is the same everywhere
—arbitrary, contracted, expensive, lacking in both
business acumen and adaptability.

No commercial people, no people fond of affairs,
have ever been benefited by government interference in business matters, least of all with railways. Trade is self-adjustive; conforms to its own
laws and customs. Governments are not thus
adaptive. They lack flexibility, the desire to meet
the wants of a community that is born of a love of
gain. Their management is everywhere attended
with the same drawbacks—restricted competition,
high rates, antiquated machinery, distrust of capital, absence of private endeavor. Government management of railroads is advocated as a means of
redressing wrongs, of preventing unfair advantage,
of securing reduced rates. It does not accomplish
any of these things. Whatever was bad before
it makes worse.*

A means of securing equitable rates is to restrict
the profits of owners; to determine in advance the
maximum amount they shall receive in the shape of
interest and dividends. The purpose is not objectionable in itself, but commendable. But, like all
interference with economic laws, its results are not
what we expect. Far from it. Money thus diverted does not revert to the community in the

---

* The highest good that can attach to government intervention in
a country whose people possess commercial spirit or enterprise, is to
be found in a merely supervisory body, such as the Board of Trade
of Great Britain, or the Interstate Commerce Commission of the
United States.

shape of reduced rates, but is wasted in extravagances; in undue multiplication of employes, in
excessive wages, in costly improvements, in luxurious appointments. Every dollar thus withheld
from the owners of a property is frittered away in
unnecessary improvements, or divided up among
employes, or those who furnish supplies. The surplus of a railway adjusts itself naturally, whether
much or little. The attempt to limit it is sentimental; is not based on correct principles or good
sense. The owner should be encouraged to earn all
he can. He will thus be led to economize, to operate
prudently. Every dollar he gets we may be assured
he will use wisely—will wisely re-invest. Every
dollar improperly withheld from him, we may be
sure will be wasted. An official for many years
connected with the government of England, referring to this subject, says:* "The principle of limitation of dividend is in itself faulty. So long as the
charge is not too high, the public have no interest
in the reduction of dividend. Their interest is in
the reduction of price, which is a totally different
thing. The fallacy lies in supposing that what is
taken from the shareholders necessarily goes into
the pocket of the consumer. It does no such thing;
it is probably wasted in extravagances, which the
company have no motive whatever in reducing.
Indeed, one of the worst consequences of the system
is, that it takes away inducements to economy. It
leads not only to extravagance in current expenses,

---

* Sir Thomas Farrer.

but to an extravagant waste of capital. In fact, in this parliamentary limitation of dividend and capital, we have gone on a perfectly wrong track, and have involved ourselves in a maze of absurdities."

Much dissatisfaction, at one time and another, has been expressed, both at home and abroad, in regard to the management of the railroads of the United States. Many of the criticisms have been justified. But the fact remains that the management of these roads has been the most effective in the world; they have been prudently constructed and economically worked ; the rates they charge are abnormally low ; their service reasonably safe and effective. This is now generally recognized. Reductions in rates have gone hand in hand with economizations in construction and operation. Similar conditions do not attend arbitrary reductions in rates ; they manifest themselves in fewer and slower trains, in poorly maintained properties, in lack of general interest and concern. Americans do not want low rates on such terms. Their commercial prosperity and supremacy depend, not in curtailing facilities, but in constantly increasing them. These are to be obtained, not by harassing the owners of railroads, but by protecting and encouraging them. They have given us the lowest rates in the world. If left unhampered, we may be assured that they will further reduce them as opportunity offers. Nothing is to be gained by interference. Directly the contrary. The owners of railroads do not need any such spur.

In no instance has State ownership of railroads answered the expectation of those who advocated it from a belief that rates would be cheapened and facilities bettered thereby. But nowhere, it is probable, has public expectation been so grievously disappointed in this respect as in Germany: that country of exact ways, honest methods, and, comparatively, efficient public service. The German advocates of government ownership believed that the State would operate railways for the general good, that there would be low tariffs and better service. This expectation has not been realized. The State, because of the increasing financial importance of its railways, has gradually come to look upon them as a source of power and revenue, not as public institutions that should be administered so as to lessen the cost as much as possible of everything to the community. It is found that the State is quite as greedy as private owners were, while it is less economical and efficient; lacks the administrative genius they possessed. Its power enables it to defy public opinion, to refuse reductions of rates, to refuse facilities that are needed, to refuse to keep pace with the mechanical appliances of roads elsewhere. Frequent accidents make it apparent that no added security has been attained in this direction, while lack of facilities manifests a want of comprehension of the needs of trade that is distressing. For these reasons, State ownership in Germany has, from the standpoint of the people, proven a burden. From the government standpoint, however, it is esteemed a success, because it has added greatly to the power of the government.*

---

* I glean these facts in regard to German railroads from *Die Nation*, of July 25, 1891.

The question of government ownership and management of railroads has not been much discussed in the United States. There seems to be a tacit understanding among practical men that it would not be desirable. The government itself has studiously discouraged such reference.*

---

*Government ownership of railways has been tried in a limited way in the United States. Fifty years ago the State of Illinois constructed a road at a cost of one million dollars, but disposed of it later for one hundred thousand dollars. Indiana had a similar experience. Georgia owns a railroad, but has found it expedient to lease it to private persons. Pennsylvania constructed a railroad from Philadelphia to Columbia, but subsequently sold it, for the reason that the commonwealth, on reflection, believed that transportation was to be regarded as a private enterprise, and not as a public function. Massachusetts acquired the Troy and Greenfield line, but found it expedient to part with it. Michigan, in its early history, constructed and operated railroads, but within a decade found it advisable to dispose of them, and the people of that State, by provision of their constitution, subsequently forbade the State from participation in such work.

CHAPTER XII.

GOVERNMENTAL CONTROL VERSUS PRIVATE CONTROL
— WHEN GOVERNMENT CONTROL IS DESIRABLE
— WHEN UNDESIRABLE — ITS TENDENCIES.

Among other reasons assigned why governments should own and operate railroads, and one much applauded, is that it will take them out of the hands of rich men; that the latter already are too powerful. This is very much like advising the people on board a ship to throw the pilot overboard, because of his prominence and the prerogatives he exercises. The rich men, including the honestly-striving-to-be-rich, are the commercial pilots of a nation, sagacious, progressive, and conservative. They are not only its safest advisers, but the only ones who have ability to forecast the future. They alone have surplus capital to invest or the courage to make new improvements. A nation without such men to advise and lead, is like a school without a teacher. They represent its accumulated experience and wisdom. They alone know how to make money, how to preserve it, how to invest it. They are the storehouse of a nation, the reservoir from which the stream that animates its industries flows.

If I were asked when government ownership and management of railways would be advisable, I should reply, when the self-interest and experience of individuals cease to be safe guides for men to follow in commercial matters. Government control can never be justified on the ground of the greatest good to the greatest number, from the standpoint of effective and economical management, or material prosperity. Government control is advisable when private property is not accorded protection; when the spirit of a nation is agrarian; when it does not afford justice and fair treatment to the owners of railroads. Then, undoubtedly, State ownership is preferable. Security in such a country is, at best, precarious. Mob rule, if not present, is near. Under such circumstances, property is safer (if anything can be safe), under governmental supervision and control than under private management. In a country thus cursed, the owners of railroads should sell to the State, lest their whole investment be confiscated. Let them make the best terms they can, and with the proceeds seek a more favored land. Neither personal liberty nor property can long be safe in such a country. The subversion of both is only a question of time.

In a country, however, blessed with equitable laws and a law-abiding people, no government organization that we can conceive of, no matter how perfect, will ever prove a fit substitute for the management of an active and alert people. This is true, both of railways and other property.

The practices of countries differ, as I have shown, in regard to railroads. In England the lines are owned by private parties. And while the government service is as good as any in the world, at once

trustworthy, conservative, and wise, the people have
not encouraged it to acquire control of railroads or
to actively interfere. The question has been much
discussed, but always with the same result, namely,
that private management was best. Such a result
we might expect from so progressive a people. On
the continent of Europe, public and private management exist side by side. In some cases the government has leased its lines to private parties; in others
it operates them itself.

Lack of similarity between railroads prevents
accurate comparison of the results of State control
and private management. Under some circumstances it seems favorable to the former, under
others unfavorable; thus, expenses of administration
of traffic will be less in one instance, while they will
be more for maintenance in another. Such differences determine nothing, unless the conditions that
attend the operation of different properties are alike,
and this we know they are not. In France, the railroads operated by the State are generally branch
lines, while private parties manage the trunk lines.
The conditions, therefore, are unfavorable for the
State, and favorable for private management. In
Germany it is the reverse of this. Italy, after
attempting to manage her railroads, as I have
shown, has withdrawn from the business, leasing
them to private parties. Generally speaking, the
governments of Europe are exceptionally situated
for conducting affairs of this nature. Their civil
service is the best in the world. It is based on
fitness. It is lifelong. Politics has nothing to do

with appointments or dismissals. Faithfulness and capacity are the governing forces. It lacks, however, the instinct of trade that those engaged in commercial affairs should possess. This is its weakness. It lacks the advice and directing force given by the owner in the case of private management. It lacks his genius for business. No amount of mechanical skill can compensate for this loss. It is irreparable.

In France, in consideration of certain guarantees and favors, it was originally agreed that the railroads should revert to the State at the expiration of one hundred years. The agreement was that the reversion should be without cost. But it was expected that the sinking funds that would be laid aside by the companies, meanwhile, would be sufficient to pay off their capital. The money for these sinking funds was not to be furnished by those who leased the property, of course. It was to be added to rates during the ninety-nine years. It was thus to come out of the nation. Superficially viewed, the transaction seemed very favorable to the State, but it was not so in fact. The State was required to pay for all it got with usury. The people of this century were to pay for those of the next.

Companies operated under a limited tenure are not so favorably situated as if the tenure were perpetual. Their interest is always a qualified one, and they can not be expected to maintain the property at a high standard as the expiration of the lease draws near. Thus the owner gains nothing, while he loses the interest and skill that attach to proprietorship. The total cost of the French roads, it is apparent, was to be added to the expense of operating, during the one hundred years of the lease, in order to recoup those who furnished the money to build them. Such a burden could not but prove a great hardship to the nation, rendering it difficult, if not impossible, for it to compete with countries not thus handicapped.

The question of government supervision of railroads has been a subject of discussion ever since the first line was built. It has, however, few advocates in England or America. Men are too wise, too practical. They love, however, to coquette with the subject, to speculate upon it. But they show no disposition to embrace it. The risk is too great; too appalling. "It is not a question to be decided by an epigram or an analogy. It is a curious and intricate question, I might say, with more than two sides to it."*

One of the strongest reasons given for government ownership, is that the State can borrow money to build railroads at a less rate than private parties. This is, undoubtedly, true in the majority of cases. But whether it would remain true or not, if governments undertook to discharge great affairs of business, is doubtful. Their credit is good, simply because their transactions are limited and their resources great.

The greatest disadvantage, in my judgment, that attends State control of railroads is the loss of the

---

*Edward Everett Hale.

16

experience, interest, and skill of the private owner. No advantage can compensate for this loss.

In the case of State ownership, money raised to build railroads should not be merged with the general indebtedness of a nation. Such burdens should be borne by the districts benefited, and not by the general public. The interest on the cost of every railroad should be met by the district immediately benefited; also any attendant losses. In the case of government control, as in the case of private management, properties must be operated with a view, not only to paying expenses, but interest on cost. Their affairs can not be bulked with other concerns. In no other way can we determine whether a property is managed efficiently or not. Such separation is absolutely necessary to effective supervision. Without it, the grossest extravagance may characterize a management without the fact ever being known.

The success of governments in handling mails and other limited enterprises, has been cited as an evidence of their ability to handle railroads successfully. The comparison is hardly fair. Handling the mails is largely mechanical, while the other requires active and harmonious coöperation with mankind in all its commercial ventures and journeyings. The administration of the post office by the government of the United States has not been financially successful. Enormous deficits have characterized its management in every stage. Its failure, moreover, would have been much greater, would have been still more apparent, except for the enforced aid it has received from private citizens. It has never hesitated to claim coöperation and assistance at its own price ; to bully when it could not coax. Private capital and enterprise have provided the railroads and the trains in which the mails are carried, while a hard and fast leveling statute has determined the compensation that the railroad companies should receive for performing the service.* The spirit shown by the government, in recompensing the railroads for carrying the mails, has been that of master to slave.

There is no doubt but that the mails could to-day be handled more effectively and economically by private carriers than by the State. Coöperation is all that is required. Excuse for government intervention no longer exists. When the mail service was inaugurated, there was no transportation system. The government had to provide it. Now we have one at once effective, economical, and trustworthy. However, it is not probable that any change will be made. It is doubtful if a change would be wise.

Government control of great affairs, including railroads, is necessary and proper among a non-commercial people, like those of India. But the government should look forward to the day when it may safely relinquish control, encouraging its people, meanwhile, to fit themselves for such duties. Among a people who possess ingenuity, enthusiasm, executive talent, business capacity, ability to

---

* Joseph Nimmo, Jr.

manage, government control is degrading. It not only lacks in effectiveness, but teaches people to be dependent, timid, lacking in courage and commercial enterprise.

It has been claimed that government ability to manage railroads with reasonable success has been demonstrated in the United States, in the administration of receiverships appointed by the courts, and acting under their jurisdiction. Such cases, however, prove nothing. They are fallacious and misleading. In the majority of instances, the receivers know little or nothing about the practical operation of railways. They are frequently lawyers, more often politicians. They are merely fiduciary agents of the court—its representatives. The active management is entrusted to practical railroad men, who conduct the business as in other cases. Properties thus administered occupy a unique position, one exceedingly favorable for the manager. They have practically no creditors, no stockholders, no bondholders; there are no charges to provide for, except such as the court designates. They are thus freed from embarrassing circumstances, from local harassments and agreements, from past obligations. The situation is exceptional, and such as to suggest exceptional results. Only normal results, are, however, attained, and these would not be prolonged if the situation were continued indefinitely, or the arbitrary power of the court, which respects neither persons nor obligations, were withdrawn. The government, here as elsewhere, is bent on having its own way; on achieving results favorable to itself, no matter who suffers or how greatly material interests are crippled.*

Notwithstanding the phenomenal achievements of railway administration in the United States, the fact has not generally been recognized. It has been everywhere assailed as corrupt, untrustworthy, extravagant, disregardful of every interest but its own. Prof. R. T. Ely accuses it of being unscientific, un-business-like, wasteful; comprising one-eighth of the aggregate property of the country, he sees, in its parallel lines and active competition, a perpetual drain on the labor, land, and capital of the country.†

All this, he thinks, might have been avoided by harmonious, unified management of all parts acting as a whole; such measures, moreover, would, he believes, have given us a rational and economic system. Moreover, he sees in the situation of railroads a necessity of their seeking political power for private ends ! a necessity for defrauding thousands of people

---

* The late Justice Miller thus spoke of the receivers of railroads: "The appointment of receivers, as well as the powers conferred on them, and the duration of their office, has made a progress which, since it is wholly the work of courts of chancery and not of legislatures, may well suggest a pause for consideration. The receiver generally takes the property out of the hands of its owner, operates the road in his own way, with an occasional suggestion from the court, which he recognizes as a sort of partner in the business; sometimes, though very rarely, pays some money on the debts of the corporation, but quite as often adds to them, and injures prior creditors by creating a new and superior lien on the property pledged to them."—104 U. S. 137.

† The improvement of the service, the cheapened devices and low rates that we owe to the competition and strife of carriers, the Professor does not see at all.

of their property!! an opportunity and excuse for
owners and managers proving unfaithful to their
trusts!!!   On the other hand, he sees in government
ownership and management an opportunity for making many improvements. Under its benign influence,
the morals of railway administration would be purified, through the publicity that government ownership
entails; politeness would take the place of brusque-
ness on the part of officials; greater care for human
life would be observed, and diminution in the cost
of operation would be brought about.   He also believes that the effect would be to elevate the civil
service of the government, as private corporations
would no longer be able to attract to their service
the business talent of the land.

Observe his last reason.   It is a tacit admission of
the great talent of those who manage our railroads.
He wishes to see those managers in the service of
the government.   But in wishing this, he forgets
that their impulse and inspiration are derived from
those who employ them; from the owners of the
property.   In the service of the government, they
would not be different from other government servants.   Public writers and advocates generally overlook this fact.   The genius of the railroad manager
lies in those who employ him; in those who build
and own the properties; in the commercial leaders
and rulers who direct him.

As regards the morals of railway administration,
it is probable they will compare favorably with
those of our political administrations.   As for the
politeness of government officials, we need not dwell

on that. If railway employes are sometimes lacking in politeness, the fault is not general. Every owner is interested in correcting such an evil; it injures his property and lessens his income by driving trade from his line. The government has no such incentive. That greater care for human life would attend governmental management of railroads, it is not reasonable to believe. Private owners are not less amenable to the dictates of humanity than government officials, while they have the added incentive that attaches to direct personal loss in such cases. They are affected, moreover, by the odium that attaches to railroads known to be disregardful of the safety of property and persons. That diminution of cost of operation would be brought about by government intervention, is so improbable as not to merit argument. In reference to the desirability of improving the service, to deny its need is to deny the law of progress of which railways are the greatest exponents. But that such improvement would be facilitated by government management, is contrary to all the teachings of experience and the legitimate conclusions of every established principle I have laid down.

Perhaps the most strenuous argument advanced by those who favor government ownership, is that it would lessen the cost of operating railroads; that many expenses, now duplicated, would be avoided thereby. Particular items of expense might be lessened, it is possible, but, as a rule, the time of every man now employed by railroads is fully occupied, and the work he performs would not be dispensed with or lessened by government ownership. Station and office needs would not be less than they are to-day. Room must be had for clerks, supervising officials, and the movement of traffic. No reduction would be practicable here. More men are not now employed by railroads than would be needed if the government operated them. The forces engaged in handling traffic and supervising and managing could not be sensibly lessened, if efficiency was maintained. There is a limit to man's ability, and the consolidation of railways into a few great corporations has reached that limit for the present. There is to-day, practically, no duplication of labor occasioned by the separate operation of railways. Each man has his work to perform, which would scarcely be less if railways were consolidated. On the other hand, government ownership would add greatly to expenses, because the methods of governments are much more elaborate than those of individuals. Each office is tied down with innumerable rules and regulations, which only the department chief can change. The number of hours government employes work is generally less than that of private corporations, while their zeal is not nearly so great. They lack the inspiration imparted by the owner in the case of private companies The difference that this implies, is the difference between managing for one's self and for another. It is the difference between genius and mediocrity. Moreover, under such circumstances, a government seeks constantly, through artificial measures, to counteract natural advantages. In the operation of railroads, it would strive to stimulate languishing industries and trade centers by artificial processes; to put them on an equality with those more wisely managed or located. Its efforts would ever be directed to correcting the inequalities of nature, to remedying the handiwork of the Creator, to making the improvident man equal to the provident man. In doing this, it would not build up the weak, but pull down the strong. The burden of such endeavors, and the losses they engender, are borne by the country at large. That they greatly retard its progress, there can be no doubt. We can only restrict them by restricting the cause.

Aside from these objections to government control, however, there are others of a personal nature. The railway service, instead of being amenable to the public, instead of being the creature and the slave of public need, would become autocratic, dictatorial, and distasteful; would become its master. Mr. Chauncey M. Depew, referring to this feature of the case in his description of German railways, says: "To form any adequate idea of the autocratic manner in which the railways of continental Europe under government control are managed, it is necessary to personally observe the methods of their administration. To illustrate the character of this autocracy, I will relate an incident which I know to be authentic. A party of American students, traveling through Germany, reached a railway station in one of the large cities just as their train was pulling out. An official, seeing that they had started to run after the retreating train with the evident intention of getting aboard, called out to them not to attempt to get on the cars while they were in motion. As the cars were moving slowly, they paid no attention to this official warning, and clambered aboard the train. The result of their disobedience of the railroad man's command was, that at the next stop they were met by a guard of soldiers, and all marched off under arrest. At first the young Americans treated the whole affair as a huge joke, and inquired, with mock seriousness, when their trial for the heinous offense of jumping on a moving railway train would come off. But they changed their tone on being informed that, having deliberately violated an ordinance of the German Empire, they had been already tried, convicted, and sentenced to thirty days' imprisonment."* The experiences of Germany

---

* The experiences in Germany of the Hon. Shelby M. Cullom, United States Senator, while not so severe as those recounted by Mr. Depew, were, nevertheless, sufficient to greatly harrow up his feelings. The author of our Interstate Commerce act found government ownership and management of railroads there anything but agreeable. He discovered that it greatly increased the number of employes, and surrounded the service with tedious and harassing regulations. "There is," he said, "at each station a small army of uniformed employes, who make more fuss about the arrival or departure of a train than one sees in a year's travel in the United States. If American railroads were to employ such a number of men, and pay them the current American rates of wages, the lines could not earn enough to pay them, if traffic rates were doubled. Then, too, except at some points, the government-owned railroads are not as well managed as our American roads are. In this country you can get into a car, your baggage is safe without your bothering about it; you go right on to your destination, and the conductor and a couple of brakemen take care of everything. In Germany all is fuss and feathers. Every railway employe is a government official, and there is enough red tape to weary an American."—Chicago *Post*, Sept. 24, 1891.

are not peculiar. It is thus tyrannies are created or kept alive everywhere. An assumed necessity is the excuse for every act curtailing man's freedom, until in the end individual liberty is lost in the multitude of enactments laid down to protect him from himself. One of the chief duties of the government servant that he lays down for himself, and one in which he takes the greatest delight, is the formation of these rules. But what is most astonishing is, that he has no idea that anything but good to his fellow-man can come of his action.

CHAPTER XIII.

THE TENURE OF RAILROADS UNDER THE LAW—THE INTERSTATE COMMERCE LAW OF THE UNITED STATES—THE REQUIREMENTS OF THE ENGLISH LAW.

The railways of the United States are incorporated under general or special laws. Permission is first granted to subscribers to the capital stock to form a company. Thus incorporated, the personal responsibility of the owner is limited. Attached to incorporation is the right to sue and be sued; to acquire, by condemnation, land and property situated thereon; to charge for services performed; to enforce rules and regulations, and do other things that the business requires. The various States have, from the first, arrogated to themselves the right to enforce such regulations as seemed to be necessary to the convenience and safety of the people. The conditions under which capital was induced to subscribe to railway enterprises, have been generally respected by the government. Some of the notable exceptions to this rule I have noticed.

The inception of railway enterprise is so recent, and its development so great and unexpected, that it is unavoidable the government should not, in every case, have apprehended fully the situation of affairs; that it should not have always understood the reciprocal relations that exist between the people and the carrier, and the necessity of their being based on natural laws, and, because of this lack of comprehension, should have made mistakes. Such mistakes were not only to be expected, but were excusable. But when blindly adhered to, after having been demonstrated to be so, they become political crimes.

The legal incorporation of railroads is only a feature. Legislative action affects them in every direction. The provisions of the law reach, directly or indirectly, every nook and crevice of the service, take cognizance of every act. The government concerns itself, not only with the relation of the carrier to the public and the State, but also to his employes. It takes notice of the fiscal methods of railroads, and in many cases the price they shall charge for their services. It prescribes in certain directions the physical appliances they shall use. It imposes the duty of transporting persons and property, including the mails, and fixes the responsibilities and liabilities attached thereto.

Legislation affecting railroads divides itself under natural heads, such as taxation; the safety of the public and the employe; limitations of franchise; right to construct; property rights; the rates that shall be charged; the supervisory power of government. This volume refers to the last two. In reference to the others, they are so diffuse, vary so greatly in different States and countries, are so intertwined with the law-making power, the decisions of judges, the force of precedents and common practice, that to attempt a description of them in detail would confuse rather than enlighten. I shall, therefore, not attempt it. I shall, however, have occasion to refer to various aspects of the subject in several of my books.* The reference will, however, be incidental only, will be intended to afford those connected with the different branches of the service guidance, rather than instruction. Those who require a technical knowledge of legislation affecting railroads, their rights, limitations, and responsibilities, must go to the fountain-head to obtain it; to the statutes, the decisions of the courts, the rulings of the State, common practice, the advice of lawyers, etc., etc. They can not be embodied in any volume or series of volumes, because each day brings with it some withdrawal, addition, or modification of right, privilege, immunity, penalty, duty, or responsibility.

In all legislative supervision and practice, this fact in reference to commercial affairs should be borne in mind, namely, that no enterprise can or will be prosecuted successfully that does not remunerate all parties concerned; that does not pay the proprietor, as well as his patron and employe. In the case of railroads, we must not expect of them safe or adequate accommodation, if we deny them due compensation. The owner, like every other manufacturer,

---

* Notably, "Capitalization, Construction, and Maintenance," "Train Service," "Baggage, Express, and Mail Traffic and Accounts," "Passenger Traffic and Accounts," "Freight Traffic and Accounts," "Principles to be Observed in Collecting the Receipts of Carriers," "Railway Disbursments and Accounts," etc., etc.

expects and is entitled to a return proportionate to
the value of his property. His method of remuneration is through the right accorded him to charge
for his services. To qualify this right, or seriously
limit it, is to cripple him, and through him the State.
The interests of the two are co-existent. They can
not be separated. The unthinking and the vicious
may believe it possible, but experience will teach
them their mistake. In our time a nation is prosperous or otherwise according to the efficiency of its
railroads; according to the measure of their ade-
quacy and the cheapness of their service. Competition with other countries is possible or otherwise,
according to the measure of their prosperity and
efficiency. A nation advances or retrogrades, grows
rich or poor, as they are prosperous or otherwise.

Referring to this subject in connection with the
United States, the Interstate Commerce Commission,
in its fourth report, says: "The railroads have, in
fact, been the most important physical agency in
national recuperation since the great civil war, and
in giving wealth and prosperity to the country as a
whole. What they have done has been accomplished
because the railroad interest, as a whole, has been
prosperous, and whatever would unjustly destroy
or restrict their prosperity would be as mischievous
to the country at large as it would to their owners."

The greatest single blow corporations have ever
received, in this or any other country that professes
to respect law and property, was the decision of the
United States Supreme Court, instigated thereto by
a semi-political judge, that agreements entered into

between the State and the railway companies might
be altered or amended by the government at pleasure, the carrier, however, being held meanwhile to
a rigid accountability for what *he* had agreed to do.
The decision was misleading, superficial, and demagogical. It claimed to be in the interest of the
people, to be based on the necessity of curbing the
spirit of corporate power. It was purely political—
a blow at vested rights, at free institutions. Its
effect was to unsettle long-established practices, to
create distrust in the minds of capitalists, to coun-
tenance and encourage agrarianism, to intensify the
jealousy of the masses, to make the people and their
representatives less amenable to reason and justice.
It sought to offer up the owners of railways as a
vicarious sacrifice to the spirit of discontent abroad
in the land. The author of the innovation, it is
gratifying to know, only partially realized the
political distinction he hoped to gain from it. He
is now dead. He represented a class of judicial
parasites of which we have as yet but few, but of
which, owing to our peculiar methods, we stand in
constant dread. He was what might not improperly
be called a judicial hermaphrodite, politician, and
judge; a man, who, dying, left behind him an odor
that nothing can dispel.

In marked contrast to the agrarian spirit of this
decision, afterwards emphasized by legislative enactments, has been the steadfast course of Great
Britain in her observance of the rights, privileges,
and immunities granted to railways, under the acts
of Parliament creating them. Such changes as

17

she has made in these enactments have, in every
case, been mutually agreed upon by all parties in
interest in advance. They have been such as com-
mend them to honorable men. Each railroad of
Great Britain, it should be remembered, is created
by special act of Parliament; the government claims
and exercises the right of veto in the location of a
road; the right to inspect and accept it, before it
shall be opened for business; to see that necessary
measures are taken to secure the safety of the public;* to enforce proper and equal facilities for all;
to prevent discrimination in rates; to reduce rates
when the return on the property exceeds the percentage agreed upon; to require rates to be posted
at stations; to require all freight offered for transport to be received, unless it be dangerous; to
require railroads to allow the use of their tracks to
persons who wish to provide their own equipment
and motive power; to require at least one train a
day to be run each way; to require a uniform rate
to be charged to passengers, according to the accommodation furnished, allowing a given amount
of baggage free in each case; to require the adoption
of a standard gauge; to carry soldiers, police, public baggage, and government stores at fixed rates; to
run such mail trains as the postmaster general
shall require; the right to inspect the property and
equipment whenever thought proper; to make regulations for handling the traffic at junctions in a safe
manner; and, finally, to limit the return on the

* Railroads in the United Kingdom are liable, as in America, under
both common and special law, for injuries to persons and property.

capital invested to the amount agreed upon. In every case, such changes as have been made in the organic law of railroads have been mutually agreed upon by the government and the corporation. They have been a matter of barter. Where a company required some new right or privilege, the government, before granting it, has exacted such changes in the original act as seemed right and proper. This has been the extent of its coercion, if so strong a word can be used. The government has said: "We will give you the rights you ask, provided you will do so and so," leaving it optional with the railroad to accept or decline. On the other hand, the governing power in America has been both arbitrary and exacting; it has said to its railroads: "Reduce your rates and increase your facilities; we do not care about your rights, nor do we care whether you are able to do what we ask or not." The difference between the two is the difference between honest practice, give and take, and common robbery; between a government that respects the rights of all its citizens, and a government that respects only the rights of those having the greatest number of votes. While the spirit of the English government has been conciliatory and fair, it has not been lax or disregardful of its rights and duties. It has from the start exercised a most searching supervision over its railways; but not such as to lessen the responsibility of owners and managers, or to impair their efficiency in any way.

Any reference to the railroads of America, and the laws governing them, would be incomplete without a description of the supervisory power of the general government, as expressed in the act of Congress creating the Interstate Commerce Commission. The purpose of the act is to bring the administration of railroads under the eye of such commission. Previous to its becoming operative, in 1887, such governmental supervision as we had was exercised by the various States. But, as their powers did not extend to business passing from one State to another, their supervision was necessarily limited. The act in question was designed to cover this particular class of business which the general government alone has power to regulate. Probably no more important act of legislation affecting the internal commerce of a country was ever devised.

The Interstate Commerce Commission thus created is a semi-judicial tribunal, having most extended and important powers. The rates of carriers come within its notice and scope, in so far as it has power to decide whether a rate is reasonable and just, or not. But it has no power to fix rates. An important part of the act, known as the "long and short haul clause," is as follows:

"It shall be unlawful for any common carrier subject to the provisions of this act to charge or receive any greater compensation in the aggregate for the transportation of passengers, or of like kind of property, under substantially similar circumstances and conditions, for a shorter than for a longer distance over the same line in the same direction, the shorter being included within the longer distance; but this shall not be construed as authorizing any common carrier within the terms of this act to charge and receive as great compensation for a shorter as for a longer distance: Provided, however, that upon application to the commission appointed under the provisions of this act, such common carrier may, in special cases, after investigation by the commission, be authorized to charge less for longer than for shorter distances for the transportation of passengers or property; and the commission may from time to time prescribe the extent to which such designated common carrier may be relieved from the operation of this section of this act.''

The discretion here allowed the commission is of the greatest necessity and wisdom. It appears, however, too great to be exercised in a practical way by any human body, however capable or industrious it may be—and the Interstate Commerce Commission is both. The wording of the law suggests that the work is to be done in detail, not in the aggregate. This is a Herculean task, impossible of adequate fulfillment. Except for the right accorded railroads to carry long distances at a less rate relatively than for short distances, the act would have resulted in ruining our internal commerce, and disrupting our federal union. It would have destroyed the mutual dependence of one section upon another, consequent upon the interchange of products. It would have built up local centers of industry antagonistic to all others. This antagonism would at first have been slight, but would finally have culminated in hatred and war. Such would have been the effect of the enforcement of the rule preventing the great railways that traverse the continent from making rates that would have brought the most distant places into close relationship with each other, through the interests that attach to an interchange of business. But carriers exercise the right at a tremendous sacrifice—one they should never have been called upon to make. It was at first thought that refusal to allow carriers to charge less for a long than for a short haul would prevent unjust discrimination, and would otherwise result in great good to the community. But, like every other interference with the natural laws of trade and the common practices of traders, it is impracticable. The value of the concession in the law of the right to charge less for a greater than a shorter distance, is greatly lessened by the fact that it can only be applied in special cases, after investigation by the commission. The emergencies of business do not admit of such delay. The idea that it will wait until permission can be obtained from Washington, is absurd. Rates must be made on the moment, as the exigency arises. If they are found to be improper or unjust, the commission should have the right to change them. This would not weaken its power in any way, but would strengthen it, by making its practices conform to business needs.

The benefits that were expected to accrue from the long and short haul clause have never been realized. No single enactment ever devised by man, it is probable, has occasioned so much confusion as this. It upset at one blow every rate in the country, destroyed at one stroke the result of fifty years of experience and adjustment between carriers, communities, and persons. It disregarded alike the laws of trade and the customs of business. A former member of the commission,* referring to the act, says one of its effects upon railroads "has been the loss which it has entailed in continuing competition for through business over the routes longer than the most direct line to a given terminal. Many well-established routes of traffic are quite circuitous, and some that are in active use are nearly twice as long as the short line. Business for local points, upon routes of this character, would naturally be carried upon tariffs graded increasingly with the distance; but when a point is reached where the rate is as high as the rate by the short line to the distant terminal, the law forbids any further advance, and the road was given the alternative of reducing its intermediate rates or retiring from the competitive business. This condition is found in every part of the country; and the value of participation in the through business usually has been felt to require the acceptance of the sacrifice demanded by the law at local stations. The statute, in this respect also, favors the direct lines against those which have a greater mileage, by making it much more expensive for the latter to compete with the former. The operation of this rule has removed from many jobbing centers important advantages which they previously had, and has enabled interior communities, formerly of little apparent consequence, to deal directly with

* Aldace F. Walker.

distant markets. Interior manufacturing points
have also felt its blight. In other words, it has
worked to the advantage of the great points of im-
portation, production, and distribution, and to the
disadvantage of the minor cities and towns, which
had formerly been known as jobbing points or trade
centers, within the various States in the interior of
the country. This tendency soon became so marked
that the jobbers in some of the States labored for,
and in some instances were able to obtain, State
legislation which was designed, and which had the
effect, to partially nullify the principles of the interstate commerce law.''

The Interstate Commerce act may be briefly sum-
marized as follows. It is intended to apply to carriers engaged in the transportation of passengers
or property wholly by railroad, or partly by railroad and partly by water, when both are used,
under a common control, management, or arrangement, for a continuous carriage or shipment from one
State or Territory to any other State or Territory,
or from any place in the United States to an adjacent country, or through a foreign country to any
other place in the United States; it also applies to
the transportation of property shipped from any
place in the United States, to a foreign country, and
carried from such place to a port of transhipment,
or shipped from a foreign country to any place in
the United States, and carried to such place from
a port of entry, either in the United States or an
adjacent foreign country. The provisions of the
act do not apply to the transportation or handling

of property wholly within one State, and not shipped to or from a foreign country from or to any State or Territory. The term railroad includes all bridges and ferries used or operated in connection with any railroad, and also all the roads in use by the carrier, whether owned by him, or operated under lease, or otherwise. The term transportation includes all instrumentalities of shipment or carriage.

The act provides that charges shall be reasonable; it forbids unjust discrimination, undue or unjust preference, and requires that carriers shall afford reasonable and equal facilities for interchange of traffic; it enacts that carriers shall not receive any greater compensation in the aggregate for the transportation of passengers or property for a shorter than a longer distance, as already mentioned; it prohibits pooling; by its provisions carriers are required to keep printed schedules of their rates posted at stations, and no advance therein is allowed, except after ten days' public notice, nor may reductions be made, except after three days' notice; the act requires carriers to file with the commission copies of all their schedules of rates, and notify it of alterations therein; they must, also, file with the commission copies of all their contracts, agreements, or arrangements with other carriers; all joint tariffs must, also, be filed with the commission, and made public in such manner as the commission determines; advances and reductions in joint tariffs may be made only as in the case of ordinary tariffs. The law provides that carriers may charge no more or less

than published tariff rates; that continuous carriage of freight must not be unnecessarily inter-
rupted; that carriers contravening the act are liable
in damages, and that railway officials implicated
shall be compelled to testify and produce their companies' books, a claim that such testimony might
criminate the person giving it not being accepted as
an excuse. The law is highly penal. Punishment
for violation is fine, imprisonment, and, in some
cases, damages as well. It imposes penalties for
false billing, false classification, false weighing,
false representation of contents of packages, false
reports of weights by shippers, inducing carriers to
discriminate unjustly, etc. A commission of five
members is created by the act. It is known as the
Interstate Commerce Commission. The members
hold office for six years. This commission has
power to inquire into the management of the business of common carriers, subject to the act, to compel the attendance of witnesses, and production of
books and papers, to hear and adjudicate upon
complaints made against railroads. The law provides that the findings of the commission shall be
accepted as *prima facie* evidence, in judicial proceedings; that its reports of investigations shall be
of record ; that it may provide for the publication
of its reports and decisions, and that such publica-
tions shall be the evidence thereof. In case of the
violation of the act, or of any other law, by a
carrier, or, in case injury has been sustained by
any person in consequence of such violation, and
the commission is satisfied of the fact, it is required

to give the carrier interested notice, requiring it to
desist or make reparation, or both, within a specified
time; if within the time it appears that the carrier
has conformed to the commission's requirements,
the fact is recorded, and the carrier released from
liability. In the event of the refusal by a carrier to
comply with the requirements of the commission,
the latter is empowered to petition the courts authorized to hear and determine the matter, and if the
court decides that a lawful order of the commission
has been disobeyed, it is required to issue proper
process to enforce it.*

The commission is empowered to make rules for
the conduct of its own proceedings; parties may
appear before it, either in person or by attorney.
Every vote and official act of the commission is of
record; it has a seal which is judicially noticed, and
its members may administer oaths and affirmations,
and sign subpœnas. The principal office of the
commission is at Washington, but it may hold special sessions in any part of the United States, and
may prosecute any inquiry necessary to its duties
in any part of the Union. The commission is also
authorized to require annual reports from carriers
in such form as it may prescribe, and may prescribe
methods of bookkeeping. It makes an annual report to Congress, embodying such information and
data as it considers valuable, and also recommenda-
tions as to additional legislation. The law permits

---

* If the order of the court is disregarded, a fine of $500 per day
may be levied upon the offender. In cases involving over $2,000,
appeal may be had to the Supreme Court of the United States.

the carriage, storage, or handling of property without charge, for federal, State and municipal governments; also for charitable purposes, and for fairs and expositions. It allows the free carriage of destitute and homeless persons, the issuance of mileage, excursion, or commutation passenger tickets, reduced rates to ministers of religion, and free transportation to the officers and employes of railways. Finally, it gives jurisdiction to the courts to issue writs of mandamus, requiring the movement of interstate traffic and the furnishing of cars and other facilities.

The Interstate Commerce law is necessary and beneficial in many things, and this fact, coupled with the high character of the commission, entitles it to the greatest respect. The law, however, needs changing in several important particulars. In reference to its effect upon competitive practices, I do not know that I can do better than quote further what is said by Mr. Aldace F. Walker. "The operation of the law has intensified former conditions. . . . When the act took effect, railway rates in the United States, especially the long-distance freight rates on which interstate traffic is moved, had reached a plane so low as to be the wonder of the world. The forces which drove rates downward during the twenty years previous to the enactment of the statute have since continued in play, and other potent influences in the same direction have been added by the law. Whether this result is or is not of ultimate advantage to the public, may be open to question. It is undeniable that a point must at some time be reached where further rate reductions will seriously inconvenience the public by becoming the occasion of unwise, and perhaps fatal, reductions of expenditures in railway maintenance and service, as well as the cause of bankruptcies and the commercial disasters which follow in their train.   .   . .   .   When the law first went into operation, it was felt that a new era had arrived.   The statute demanded the undeviating and inflexible maintenance of the published tariff rates.   Rebates, drawbacks, and all other devices whereby a carrier should receive from one person greater or less compensation for any service rendered than from another for a like service, were expressly declared unlawful, and were punishable by a heavy fine.   This was just what conservative and influential railway managers desired.   It was not only just, but it protected their revenues.   The new rule was cheerfully accepted, and imperative orders were issued for its obedience. But toward the close of 1887, it began to be perceived that there were difficulties, which became much more serious in 1888.   On even rates the traffic naturally flowed to the direct lines, which could give the best service and make the best time.   Roads less direct, or of less capacity, roads with higher grades or less advantageous terminals, and roads otherwise at a disadvantage, found that business was leaving them. It was discovered that the law in this, its most essential feature, as well as in other respects, was practically a direct interference by the government in favor of the strong roads and against the weak. Dissatisfaction arose among officials of roads whose earnings were reduced, and which were often near the edge of insolvency. It had been customary for them to obtain business by rebates and other like devices, and they knew no other method. It presently became to some of them a case of desperation. There was nothing in the law specifically forbidding the payment of commissions, and it was found that the routing of business might be secured to a given line by a slight expenditure of that nature to a shipper's friend. Other kindred devices were suggested—some new, some old. . . . If the carriers had been left free to make arrangements among themselves, upon which each line might rely for eventually receiving, in some form, a fair share of competitive traffic, the temptation for secret rate-cutting would have been, in a great measure, removed, and the country would have been spared most of the traffic disturbances and illegitimate contrivances for buying business which have since been periodically rife."

Interference with the laws of trade and the practical necessities of business has resulted here, as it always does when governments interfere, in making matters worse instead of better. In preventing pooling, the government deprived the railroads of the right to protect themselves, and transferred to an army of middle-men, in the shape of commissions, revenues needed to maintain the property, provide facilities, and pay interest.

In addition to the Interstate Commerce Act described above, each State of the Federal Union is more or less actively engaged in supervising the

State business of railroads. Many of the States claim and exercise the right of making rates, regardless of owners or managers. The inexpediency of this, after what has been said on the subject, need not be further pointed out. The States exercise sole police powers over the railroads within their borders. They each and all require returns of receipts and expenditures and other details of operation. Their supervision is minute and searching. In some States it is arbitrary and tyrannical, in others not noticeably objectionable. The situation in several States is fraught with great peril. But time and sober second thought will, it is believed, bring relief.

CHAPTER XIV.

MUTUALITY OF INTEREST IN THE PROSPERITY OF RAILWAYS.

Having pointed out the more important principles that govern the affairs of railroads, and the conditions necessary to the economical and efficient management of such properties, it may be proper to say a word in regard to the concern the community has in their prosperity. It is special and perpetual. The multitude of details incident to the conduct of railroads, while embracing many things that are peculiar, are, in the main, common to every business and of general interest. So far as concerns the construction and keeping in order of the plant, it is not noticeably different from that of other manufacturers. They are liberal consumers of the products of others, and generous and continuous patrons of labor. Their disbursements cover an infinite number of things, and have three purposes in view: the construction of the property, and its successful maintenance and operation. These disbursements embrace every variety of object, from the purchasing of land for tracks, stations, and shops, to the payment of employes; from the erection of mammoth warehouses to the planting of shade-trees; from the purchasing of a locomotive to the procurement of a tin cup; from the purchasing of a cargo

18

of coal to the insertion of an advertisement in a newspaper; from the hiring of a scrub-woman, through all occupations, trades, and callings, to the employment of a constitutional lawyer. The disbursements of railways are general. They help to aggrandize every class of society, and are the life-blood of many important interests and trades. They may be likened unto the widespread branches of a great tree, under whose generous canopy widely separated industries find shelter and protection.

The industries, thus nurtured, animate in turn still others.

The disbursements of a railway company are of two kinds, permanent and incidental. Under the former may be embraced those of a preparatory nature, those connected with the building up of a property; under the latter, those incidental to its operation and maintenance. Permanent disbursements cover first cost, including rights, privileges, and franchises. Incidental expenditures include operating expenses, taxes, interest, and dividends.*

A very large and respectable class of people— indeed, I think I may say a majority—do not think of railroads except as common carriers, as real or semi-monopolies; as gigantic properties owned by non-resident stockholders, in the main illiberal in their tendency and short-sighted in policy; aliens, so to speak, having nothing in common with the people they serve; aggregations of capitalists leagued together for profit, without thought of the

---

* Particulars in regard to disbursements will be carefully elaborated in "Railway Disbursements and Accounts."

permanent interests of the communities they serve; short-sighted, selfish, and soulless. Nothing could be farther from the truth. The interests of railway companies and farmers, manufacturers, and merchants, occupying a common territory, are, as I have pointed out, identical and inseparable. Disaster can not overtake the latter without affecting the former. Nor can the carrier be prosperous if the others are not.

The railroad companies of a country are much more concerned in the well-being of farmers, merchants, and manufacturers, than a newspaper or lawyer can possibly be. Why? Because their prosperity is bound up forever with them. There is no escape; can never be any cessation of interest, any other resource; they rise or fall together.

The capital invested in railroads is so vast, and so fixed in perpetuity in the heart of a country, that owners must always be the first to apprehend any disaster to the people; the first to discountenance any act, the effect of which will be to injure or cripple them. They look to them for support, for a profitable business. Without it their property is valueless.

No other interest is so permanent and consistent as that of a railroad. It can not be moved, and has no value outside its immediate use. Carriers are, for this reason, peculiarly amenable to the good will of their patrons; are especially desirous of securing their confidence and support. Self-interest, if not inclination, compels them at all times to pursue an equitable policy towards their patrons, and self-interest of this nature, is the only interest that never

changes, is never fickle, is always loyal, alert, and
intelligent. All others are transitory, selfish, and
short-sighted; quite as likely to injure as to benefit.

Much of the capital invested in railways has
never returned anything whatever to its owners.
The bulk of the earnings of a great mass of railway
property is paid out each month for wages, supplies,
and taxes, without leaving anything for the invest-
or.   It is estimated that sixty-four per cent. of earnings is expended as fast as it accrues, for operating
expenses.   The money never leaves the community
where it is earned—scarcely reaches the treasury of
the carrier.   In addition to this, more or less is disbursed each year for improvements and additions.
These expenditures will go on forever.   Under the
most favorable circumstances, the return on railway
investments is not such as would satisfy active business men or investors generally.   It is, at the best,
meagre and uncertain.

A large percentage of the expenses of a railroad
company is made up of wages paid employes.   They
represent a population five times their own number.
This enormous mass of people gives employment incidentally to another large class occupied in supplying its wants.*   Still another class is engaged in

---

* "One man out of every eighteen and a half men occupied in any
kind of work in this country, either mental or manual, was employed
in 1880 in connection with railroads, and since then the proportion
has been greater. . . . . For many years, more than one man
in every ten men employed in any kind of gainful occupation, aside
from agriculture, has been engaged either in constructing or operating railways."—Edward Atkinson, "The Distribution of Products,"
page 280.

preparing the material which railways need; another class is busied in ministering to the wants of the latter. These classes represent the most industrious and frugal element of society. They are one and all affected, in a marked manner, by the prosperity or otherwise of railroads.

If we should attempt to trace the beneficiaries of railroads, we should find them in every vocation of life; in every trade and calling; in our mercantile houses, in express and telegraph offices, in manufacturing establishments, work-shops, printing rooms, banks, the offices of lawyers and doctors; in stores of every kind; in our mines, in our forests, upon our farms, and in the employ of railroads. Our telegraph and express systems, with their great number of employes and dependent classes, are but appendages of the railway interest; are directly affected by it. If it is injured, they are correspondingly affected. This vast army, so widely separated, so diversified, yet so closely associated in interest, is vitally concerned in the prosperous and uninterrupted operation of railways; in seeing that no injustice is done them; in seeing that they are allowed to carry on their business according to its just needs, equitably and fairly. If we should attempt to trace the community of interest, we should find the line lengthened and broadened until it embraced every human being. We should find that there was no diversity anywhere — that injustice or harm to railroads reacted unfavorably on all.

Of the injurious effect on the individual and collective members of society, because of the warfare

that has been made on railroads in the United
States, those most affected have known nothing.
They have not only been indifferent, but have been
participants oftentimes. They have neither understood nor appreciated the community of interest
that existed. They looked on complacently. It
was somebody else's bull that was being gored. In
this they erred. Each one of them contributes
from his own veins some portion of the blood that
is being spilt; each one is robbed; each one is injured. They would discover this if they stopped to
trace the close relation that carriers in our day sus-
tain to every industry and calling; to trace cause
and effect. The employes of railroads, and those
engaged in the manufacture of railway supplies,
and all the classes dependent upon them, are, above
all others, especially and markedly concerned in
the prosperity of railways. In order to enable a
company to pay fair wages, to buy needed supplies,
and make necessary improvements and additions, it
must be accorded fair treatment and equitable rates.*

---

*No other capitalized industry, whether controlled by persons
acting as individuals or in a corporate capacity, purchases so largely
in the general markets of a country. These purchases give employment to vast numbers of people, directly and indirectly. Railroads
are also the largest single employers of common and professional
labor. Vast numbers of civil engineers and attorneys find steady or
occasional employment in their service, and many eminent doctors
and surgeons thus add largely to their income. Few indeed are the
professional men who live along the lines of our railroads, who have
not, at some period of their experience, found both profit and professional distinction in the, to them, fortuitous circumstances that
called them, either temporarily or permanently, into the service of
some railroad company.

The pocket of every individual is directly affected by any act of injustice to railroads. Herein lies the hope of everyone who wishes to see fair play. When the pocket is touched, we may be sure the conscience and intelligence of the individual will not long slumber. We may therefore, I think, safely leave the interests of railroads, so far as the community is concerned, to time and the reflections of mankind. Enlightenment is all that is required. When the public understand that the prosperity of railroads is necessary to their own prosperity ; that it must be continuous, not spasmodical ; that railroads must have an income sufficient to remunerate owners and meet necessary and reasonable expenses of operation and maintenance ; that the confidence of those who own railroads must be respected, they will accord them protection and regard. When this is generally understood, the people will frown upon unjust and demagogical acts affecting railway property with the same unanimity that they frown upon open or covert attacks upon financial institutions, mercantile houses, manufactories, and other interests necessary to the comfort and prosperity of society. Heretofore, the community of interest has appeared so distant, has been so illy defined, as not to be recognized. Hence the indifference of all classes, even of railway employes, to attacks upon railways. The indifference has been like that of a man who stood calmly by and watched the burning of his own house, under the impression that it was the house of an enemy.

In addition to those I have particularized as

directly affected by the disbursements of railways, there is another and constantly growing class, for which this phase of the subject possesses a vital interest. I refer to the owners of railway bonds and stocks. They are more or less dependent for their support upon the return their investment renders. Attacks on railroads not only endanger the returns on such securities, but endanger the principal as well. They certainly affect the selling price. The owners of these securities embrace representatives from every branch of society—capitalists, business men, clergymen, clerks, trustees of estates, managers of savings banks, widows, children, sewing women, and others. A default of interest or a reduction of a dividend means, to them (or the bulk of them, at least), something more than an incident or inconvenience. It means a sacrifice of property to meet present necessities. It foretells future anxiety, destitution, want. All these people are concerned in putting a stop to demagogical warfare on railroads. The number of those directly interested in the welfare of railways can not be computed. They comprise a large element, at least one-half, of the population ; the balance are also concerned, but not so directly.

CHAPTER XV.

Rates are affected much more sensibly by the
expense of working a railroad than by the cost of
constructing it. But in so far as the latter operates, it is, in the United States at least, generally
favorable to low rates. Cost is rarely, if ever, fully
capitalized.

Many people regard a railway as fully completed
when opened for business. To such, all stocks and
bonds issued after the opening are thought to be
fictitious. These people are as sincere as they are
ignorant. Others, however, make such charges maliciously. Every dollar thus added to the capital
of a railway, the latter represent as "water;" as
having a reality only in the desire of the proprietor
to make the community pay dividends thereon.
They seek to make it appear that the rates of railroads are higher than necessary to afford a reasonable return on the capital actually invested. As
proof of this charge, they cite isolated instances.

Some excuse has been afforded for these charges
in the general neglect of railway companies to
emphasize in their accounts the distinction between
construction and operating expenditures. Failure
to capitalize construction expenditures when made,

or otherwise definitely locate them in the records
and returns at the time, renders the public distrustful of claims subsequently put forward. When the
owner seeks to capitalize his investments, the community has ceased to remember the benefits they
conferred, and is loth to acknowledge its justice.
Much of the misapprehension of the public, in
regard to the cost of railroads and their capitalization, the companies themselves are thus responsible for. The neglect of owners to capitalize their
investments at the time, or particularize them in
their returns, does not presuppose wrong, nor has
any followed, except to the owners.

When the construction charges of a railroad are
embraced under the head of operating expenses, it
is because it is necessary to build up the property
in the confidence of owners and investors; to
strengthen it against the time when its resources
may be unduly taxed. It is a simple, practical way,
that every business man and investor understands.
Because of this necessity, many companies have not
thought it necessary to separate construction from
operating expenses in their reports. The returns of
the Interstate Commerce Commission requiring construction charges to be particularized, will remedy
this omission in the future.

Many weak companies have made it a practice
systematically to include the cost of additions and
improvements under the head of operating. If a
railroad was unproductive or in discredit, its owners
bolstered up its falling fortune by using net receipts
to add to property account, without thinking of sub-

sequent capitalization. Such a policy can have but one end. If the property should ever be able to earn a return on its full cost, it will quite likely be prevented from doing so, because of the difficulty of making the cost appear. The facts will not be known, or if known, public sentiment will forbid the capitalization; it will say to the owner: "Do you want to rob us? We know nothing about these old construction accounts you seek to revive. They are nothing but 'water.' You must not capitalize them or attempt to pay dividends thereon."

The instances where a company is obliged to discredit its future, by suppressing reference to its construction work, are not general. They will grow less frequent with the development of the country. As we grow in riches and acquire greater knowledge of financiering, capitalization and expenditure will go hand in hand. But there will always be more or less money spent for construction purposes that can not be capitalized. The limitations of accounts are such that the full cost of a property can never be made to appear on the books of a company or in its returns, no matter how desirous the owners may be that it should. The reason is well known to those familiar with such matters. The construction accounts of a railroad are peculiar. In many cases, the accountant can not separate that which comes under such head from that which comes under the head of operating. When this is so, the amount is charged to the latter, or mainly to that account. However, the rule is not universal. It is probable that items have been charged to construction that were known to belong to operation. But such cases have not been common or important. They are indefensible.

The accounts of railroads are incongruous. Thus, many items, that will ultimately represent great values, pass on to the books at merely nominal figures. Other amounts, again, that represent large expenditures, will prove to be, in the end, practically worthless. Subsequent adjustment, however, is impossible. A former railroad commission of Wisconsin, referring to the cost of railroads, says:* "The elements of cost often include exchanges of value under every possible form, and under all conceivable circumstances, with no record preserved, except of the nominal sums paid and received. In original railway construction, bonds and stocks are exchanged indifferently for labor or property; sometimes sold for money, hypothecated for loans, donated for contingent purposes, divided as interest on investment, or sacrificed wholly on sale and foreclosure. Oftentimes the record is itself wanting, and even nominal amounts of investment become the subject of speculative estimate." Practices such as these, coupled with a lack of knowledge of accounts, in the early history of railroads, render it impossible to-day, except upon a few railroads, to determine what they cost.

In the early days of railroads, no attempt was made to properly classify construction expenditures. Many petty items of construction are still largely

* "Wisconsin Railroad Commissioner's Report," 1874, page 19.

unprovided for in the returns, and will always remain so, because to notice them would be to greatly increase expenses. Money is saved by embracing them in operating expenses. Both principal and interest, if capitalized, would not equal the clerical expense that their separation from other expenditures would entail. Only items of considerable magnitude, such as the construction of buildings, sidings, new rolling stock, fences, platforms, yards, etc., are generally thought worthy of being embraced in the construction account. The regulations of railroads on this point are substantially alike. Sometimes these regulations are printed, oftentimes they are only verbal. Upon many lines, the policy of charging only large items to construction, has become a settled one. Thus, a great company * explains to its employes that it is its desire "that only important and permanent additions, materially increasing the value of the property, are to be charged to construction."

A separate account should be kept of all construction work that does not involve burdensome clerical labor.

A separation of construction accounts from operation is necessary as a check.

The poverty and unproductiveness of railway enterprises, and the risks attending their operation, suggested the idea of merging first cost with operating expenses. If a company was poor, or not able to earn a return on its capital, or was apprehensive

---

* The Atchison.

of the future, little regard was paid to keeping construction separate from ordinary working expenses.
Moreover, in early days, many of the accounting
officers of railways had only crude ideas of the distinction between permanent expenditures and cost
of working.   The result is apparent in the accounts
they compiled. Another reason was, and is, the
expense. Separation of construction expenditures
from cost of operating, although not great, is so
considerable as to deter accountants from attempting it in small matters, unless especial reasons exist
therefor.

Still another influence has operated to lessen
the apparent cost of railroads. Many of these
properties have been operated at one time or another by their bondholders. When this was so, the
temptation to use surplus income to better the
property, without capitalizing the amount, or otherwise allowing the holders of deferred securities any
return thereon, was oftentimes too strong to be
resisted.*

Another obstacle in the way of accurate accounting is the opening of new roads before they are fairly
completed. Construction and operating expenses
are, in such cases, mingled in one indistinguishable
mass. In the United States and other new countries, railroads are, as a rule, opened for business

---

* It is not to be inferred from this that the interests of such
holders eventually suffered. Quite the contrary. Such measures,
while dictated by purely selfish motives, were conservative, and in
the interest of the permanent good of every class of holders. Great
corporations are thus built up and maintained.

long before completion. The moment the track
permits the passage of trains at nominal rates of
speed, flaming advertisements announce the opening
of the line. Many influences contribute to this
haste. But the principal one is lack of capital; a
desire to make the property earn something. This
has caused the opening of many lines that otherwise
would have remained in the hands of the contractors
and builders. It has caused the acceptance of roads
with grades so abrupt as to render the property
worthless for many purposes to owner and public ;
the acceptance of tracks barren of ballast, laid perhaps on the unraised earth ; of light iron and poor
ties, where neither should have been used; of ditches,
the width, slope, and depth of which were ridicu-
lously inadequate ; of embankments so circumscribed and narrow as to barely preserve the equilibrium of trains ; of cuts through mountains and
hills hardly wide enough to admit the passage of
trains. It has caused the acceptance of pasteboard
bridges and culverts, giraffe-like trestles, inadequate
yards and incomplete platforms ; the opening up
of roads without sidings, fences, or signals, illy
equipped and more illy organized. Upon many lines
permanent buildings are at first unknown, abandoned cars and rudely constructed sheds serving as
offices and warehouses. Nor is systematic and effective effort made to clear the right of way from
trees, brush, and grass.

Such were and are the circumstances that attend
the opening of railroads in a new country, dependent
upon the resources of its citizens to provide the

means. In Europe more formality is observed.* But in any event the cost of a railroad, up to the time it is opened, is only partial. In a new country it is oftentimes merely nominal.

No greater misapprehension, it is probable, exists in the public mind upon any subject than that about the cost of railroads. Its effect, from an economic point of view, is likely to be very serious in the future, if systematic effort is not put forth to correct it. While a road is never completed, the community looks upon every line as practically finished. Legislation based on such premises can not but prove unfortunate, both to railroad companies and communities. A memorial to the Wisconsin legislature, designed to correct public opinion in regard to the cost of railroads, says: "When a road is graded, laid with iron, and declared open for business, the popular impression is that the work is finished, whereas it is only fairly begun. Considerable ballasting and surfacing are required, and a great many warehouses, elevators, and station buildings must be provided, together with a large amount of rolling stock and numerous other facilities, before much business can safely be done. Cuts

---

* Thus in Great Britain no "railway can be opened for the public conveyance of passengers until one month's notice of the intended opening shall have been given to the Board of Trade ; and if, in the opinion of their inspector, the opening would be attended with danger to the public, the Board may postpone the opening for one month. . . . The Board may go on postponing the opening from month to month until their inspector's requirements have been complied with."—Royal Com'n. on R'ys. Report, page xxviii. This is stated elsewhere.

have to be widened, sidings put in, bridges and culverts strengthened, fences built, renewals made, and many other improvements made which add to the cost of construction." Every defect or omission in construction must be made good afterwards. New needs must also be provided for. Oftentimes the credit of a company is such that these things must be deferred for many years. Its only resource, perhaps, is its net earnings. It has no standing or credit. Needed improvements must therefore be made from revenue, as opportunity offers. The incentive to keep a separate account of construction outlay is lacking in such instances, and without this incentive it will never be done. A company unable to earn a fair dividend on its stock, with nothing encouraging to look forward to, will more than likely discontinue further charges to construction. Such expenditures appear like a reflection on the management. "Why throw good money after bad?" the stockholder asks. On the other hand, the manager says, "Why make further charges to construction, when we are unable to pay on what we have? Why subject ourselves to criticism by further increasing our property account, so long as we can not capitalize present cost?" Such arguments, of course, ignore the fact that a time may come when the property will be able to pay a return on the whole, and, if preparation has been made, will be allowed to do so. But business men reason, and rightly, that the needs of to-day are more important than the possibilities of the future.

Few, if any, American railroads have earned a

19

fair return on cost. Some of them earn a return on their capital. But capital and cost travel far apart. Whether the railroads of the United States will ever be financially able to issue shares or other evidence of cost to cover unrepresented values, or whether they will be permitted to do so, if able, it is impossible now to tell.

Of all accounts, the construction account of a railroad is the most difficult to keep.* Only those familiar with such matters know how difficult it is to separate construction from ordinary working expenses. Trustworthy returns require circumstantiality and accuracy, and accuracy can not be expected, except approximately, as a large number of those whose duty it is to furnish the data, possess no knowledge whatever of their duty in this respect, nor aptitude in acquiring it.

In renewing and improving a property, many things enter into cost beside the principal items of labor and material. Thus, in replacing a temporary with a permanent structure, we must ascertain what is a reasonable charge for use of tools, value of implements lost or damaged, transportation, use of engines and cars, superintendence, accounting, etc., etc., and when the work is done, the cost of the structure replaced must be deducted from the whole. Many items entering into cost of construction are so mixed up with operating expenses that they can only be approximated. This requires careful analysis, and, in many instances, exhaustive

---

* This account will be referred to more at length and particularly in " Railway Disbursements and Accounts."

research, and an overhauling of returns, at once
tedious and unsatisfactory. The expense of keeping an accurate construction account is a severe tax
upon a wealthy company. To a poor corporation it
is a burden. And here in a nut-shell lies an explanation of the neglect to keep such an account in
many cases, except for costly improvements. And
even with these we frequently notice lack of accuracy in important particulars, such as a charge for
transportation, use of tools, compensation for equipment, superintendence, etc. Only important items
are picked out; the others are disregarded. A volume might be filled with explanations of the influences that lead corporations to suppress or omit a
part of the cost of their properties from their
accounts. One more must suffice. Those familiar
with the owners and managers know them to be extremely conservative. They are intent upon building up and strengthening their investment. Like
the farmer who digs a ditch or plows a field, they
know that every dollar judiciously expended is seed
wisely sown. The instinct of gain and caution inherent in them, and to which they owe what they
have, continually urges them to make improvements,
but to defer capitalization; to keep such expenditures as a reserve—a margin against contingencies.
In this way they are continually adding to the
security of their property and its productiveness,
without adding to its capital representation. Their
sagacity cannot be questioned.

There are instances where those who represent
railroads, are lacking in conservatism. There are

reckless men among this class, just as there are among bankers, manufacturers, merchants, and hack-drivers; men eaten up with the desire of immediate realization; men who can not await the processes of time, who want to become rich at once. But this class constitutes only an insignificant minority. Its antics have, however, created great distrust of railway enterprises generally; it is so much more daring and conspicuous than the better element, that it attracts attention where the other remains forever unnoticed. One is positive, the other negative. A drop of ink is sufficient to discolor a goblet of water, but a drop of water will occasion no change whatever in the aspect of a like quantity of ink. And so it is correspondingly with these classes. One unstable man will cast discredit over a railway enterprise employing fifty thousand men. Writers and others, to whom the public look for guidance, take advantage of these anomalies to throw discredit over the whole railroad world; to awaken and keep alive a feeling in the community that it is unworthy of trust. The result is mutual want of confidence. Nothing in the experience of men is more interesting and curious than the attitude the people and the railroad companies preserve toward each other. On the part of the former, it is one of aggression; of accusation, vituperation, abuse — volley on volley. On the part of the latter, it is that of deference, of explanation, of mild expostulation; they are noticeably careful to treat their traducers with forbearance and courtesy. Their policy is to temporize; to await the sober sense, the second thought of the people.

It is quite probable they have carried this policy too far; that they have been much too deferential to the demagogues who harass them; have offered too little resistance to acts of injustice and oppression. Indeed, their timidity has oftentimes been so marked that it has suggested attack—has invited interference and oppression.

CHAPTER XVI.

LOCAL AND THROUGH TRAFFIC—STATE *vs.* INTER-
STATE—IMPOSSIBILITY OF DISTINGUISHING ONE
FROM THE OTHER—EFFECT ON LEGISLATIVE
ACTION.

The accompanying reflections in regard to State
and interstate traffic are suggested by the divided
duty that attaches to national and local supervision
of railways, and the impossibility, in many instances,
of determining where the jurisdiction of one begins
and the other ends. The subject attaches to governmental supervision in America, and in other countries where federal and State authority exist side by
side. It also treats incidentally of the inter-road
traffic of railways. The theme is a practical one, of
interest to those connected with railroads or concerned in their affairs.

––––––––––

When Percy was told that Glendower could call
spirits from the vasty deep, he replied that he could
also call them, but would they come ? Legislation
that assumes that the traffic of railroads may be
classified upon the basis of State lines, excites in
those familiar with the subject a feeling of incredu-
lity akin to that which the boast of Glendower ex-
cited in the breast of Hotspur. It can not be done.

State traffic refers to business confined wholly within a State ; interstate business to that which passes from one State to another. The difference is simple enough. But the separation of the two is as idealistic as calling spirits from the vasty deep. The incorporeal spirits that hovered around the romantic Glendower were not more incapable of separate identity than State and interstate business in many cases.*

In considering legislative supervision of interstate traffic, it seems not to have occurred to those having the matter in charge that there would be any difficulty in distinguishing one from the other. But such is the case. The traffic of a country is homogeneous. It leaves no more connected or recognizable trace of its presence or methods than does the swallow in its flight or the vessel in its course; it takes no more account of State lines than the winds or clouds take account of them. It has no separate identity, except in the private practices of individuals.

The difficulty of classifying a thing so intertwined and indistinguishable as the traffic of a State, is experienced in all countries. It is an inherent difficulty, based on the idiosyncrasies of men, the accidents of business, the fluctuations and vagaries of trade. It is aggravated by the peculiarities of railway construction, location, extent, service, traffic,

---

* This indivisibility will, it is believed by many, have the effect to cement the relations existing between the officials of the general government and the State governments; will, in fact, ultimately render their consolidation necessary.

arrangements with surrounding lines, the talent, experience, and adaptability of those who operate them.

I will enumerate some of the things that prevent a separation of the traffic of a nation on imaginary or arbitrary lines. And first, in order to separate local from through traffic, it is essential that all business (including passenger as well as freight), shall be followed in the accounts, from the point of departure to the place of final destination. Whenever this is not done, or can not be done, the separation will be doubtful and at best only partial. A bag of potatoes consigned to a merchant at Syracuse, N. Y., shipped from Utica, N. Y., is presumably State traffic, but the passenger ticketed from Syracuse to New York City, while apparently local, may, in reality, be pursuing an uninterrupted journey to some remote State or Territory. Herein lies the difficulty in a nutshell.

The devices of railroads for handling their traffic are such as their necessities impose, coupled with the legitimate requirements of business. Each road is compelled to treat the bulk of its traffic as an entity; as if it originated and terminated upon its line. It is not practicable to do otherwise. In a country of restricted territory, like that of Great Britain, where the mileage of railroads is relatively small and communication between the most remote points requires but a few hours, it would seem as if traffic might be billed through without serious risk or expense to the carrier. But it can not. The exceptions are both general and marked. In the

United States, where distances are great, the routes to be followed complex, and the vicissitudes of tariffs uncertain, it is not practicable to bill either passengers or freight through, except over particular systems of roads located within restricted territories, or having intimate traffic arrangements. Business passing beyond terminal points is, as a rule, re-billed. In this process of re-billing, the original place of shipment is lost, or whether lost or not the effect is the same, as the traffic, from being interstate, perhaps becomes local, or vice versa. Nevertheless, its nature is not changed; from its place of departure to its final destination it is the same. The accounts may treat it differently, but this fact proves nothing except their lack of adaptability, their inutility. Perhaps the reader will say, "Change the methods of handling such business, then." Unfortunately, this can not be done. We can not follow the details of traffic, any more than we can trace a pedestrian upon our streets by the impress he leaves upon the granite sidewalk. Nothing would be more difficult than to ascertain the origin or destination of much of the business of a railroad. In the case of freight, a careful analysis of the records, laboriously following each shipment from one point of billing to another, and from one railroad to another (where there is any record of the transfer between the latter), would enable us, in the majority of cases, to finally ascertain its character. But this is no more practicable than it would be for us to hold our breath while the air about us was being analyzed to determine whether it was pure or not.

The freight traffic of railroads is exceedingly cumbersome to handle. The accounts are equally cumbersome. A car-load of freight going from Cincinnati, Ohio, to Cleveland, Ohio, may be billed through, or may be re-billed several times en route; with each re-billing it may apparently change its character. Moreover, it may not be made up wholly of one consignment, but of numerous consignments, partly local, partly interstate. In billing this freight no distinction is made. The whole is embodied upon one sheet. In order to separate it, we must examine the bill in detail. That which comes from or goes to points outside of Ohio, is, of course, interstate traffic; the other may be local, but not necessarily.

It frequently occurs, however, that the final destination of traffic is not given. Whenever this is so, its true character is, of course, not distinguishable. One case is sufficient to illustrate this: A car-load of horses, consigned to Cleveland, Ohio, may really be destined to a point in Montana; the final destination not being given, for the reason that the transfer at Cleveland is a matter that the owner intends looking after himself. He does not, consequently, esteem it necessary that he should notify the carrier of the ultimate destination. Cases of this kind are of constant occurrence. Instances will also occur where it is impossible to determine the origin of a business. It would be so in the case of the horses referred to, after they pass Cleveland. While apparently originating at that point, they perhaps came from Kentucky. In order to determine whether freight traffic is State or interstate, it is necessary to scrutinize each way-bill, item by item; to trace each shipment from point to point. This is impracticable, or, if performed, leaves the work still in doubt, from the impossibility of ascertaining the real origin or destination of the goods.

The difficulty of classifying passenger traffic is even more marked. A very large percentage of passengers is carried upon mileage tickets, that may be used in riding from station to station, or continuously over thousands of miles of road. Much of the property transported in express and baggage cars is also carried upon tickets of similar form and utility. It is impossible to separate business of this character.

In many cases, the point to which a traveler buys a ticket affords no clue whatever to his real destination. Thus, a person going from Chicago to New York, will, perhaps, buy a through ticket, but a passenger starting from some interior point in Illinois (at a place where through tickets are not for sale) for New York, will buy a ticket to Chicago only. Thus, he will appear as a State passenger for the first part of his journey, and as an interstate passenger for the last part of it. Yet the difference in the nature of the ticket he travels upon does not change his character at all, and neither the limitations of railway accounting nor legislative enactment can make him otherwise than what he is. If through tickets could be sold from every station and passengers could be made to buy them, it would simplify matters somewhat; but, unfortunately, passengers will not always buy tickets, and, even when they do, will not always buy the right ones. In a country, moreover, where there are thirty thousand widely separated ticket-offices, it is not practicable to keep tickets to all points for sale at each office; accommodation could not be provided for them, and the accounting involved would be of so voluminous and intricate a nature as to surpass the capacity of agents and the accommodation and financial ability of carriers. It is the general custom of railroads to ticket passengers between all the great centers, no matter how far apart, or how many lines must be traversed. This is all they can do. But this is not feasible with freight. In the latter case, it is only where the interchange of traffic is very great that property is billed through. In the majority of cases, it is re-billed at the terminal point of each line or system. To attempt to do otherwise would engender delay, create misunderstandings, occasion errors in rates, create confusion in the accounts, and add greatly to the expense of doing business. Present methods are the only practicable ones. No great change is possible.

Such are the mechanical difficulties of the situation. Much of the interstate traffic of a railway appears as State traffic; much of the interstate business can not be identified. No matter how conscientiously we may strive to make the separation, the most we can do is to guess at the nature of the business, in many cases, and while our guess may be of abstract interest, it is hardly suitable for any concrete purpose.

CHAPTER XVII.

MODERATION EXERCISED BY WISE GOVERNMENTS IN
MEDDLING WITH THE RATES OF RAILWAYS, AND
IN EXERCISING THEIR POLICE POWERS—THE
REASONS THEREFOR—THE STATUS OF RAILWAYS
IN ENGLAND, CANADA, AUSTRALIA, GERMANY,
FRANCE, AUSTRIA-HUNGARY, BELGIUM, SPAIN
AND PORTUGAL, ITALY, RUSSIA, AND JAPAN.

I do not know that I can bring this volume to a
close better than by giving a brief synopsis of the
legal status of railways in some of the principal
countries of the world, premising my statement by
saying, that while every government reserves more
or less arbitrary control over rates, the more enlightened have not, heretofore, as a matter of fact, meddled in such matters at all. They have left them
wholly to those who own and manage the properties.
This has also been true in regard to their police powers.
They have not interfered with rates, nor sought to
exercise their police rights, except in urgent cases.
They have not willingly interfered with carriers,
any more than with grocers. They have sometimes
found it necessary to do so, in order to quiet public
apprehension, or answer some specific case. Every
day emphasizes the fact that governmental interference with railroads lessens the interest and
responsibility of owners and managers, and in so

far as this is so, retards progress and lessens
efficiency.   No government, it is possible, has exercised such notable restraint as Great Britain.   An
exception to this rule, however, in her case, is the
sentimental efforts of the English government, aided
and abetted by the managers of many English railways, to throw around the railroad service of that
country a theoretical protection out of all proportion to its cost.   Enormous sums have been expended to render crossings, stations, and trains
ideally safe.   Protection here, as elsewhere, may be
carried too far.   It may have the effect to add so
much to the cost of working railroads as to prevent
them doing business that the commercial and social
good of a country demands.   It has, to a certain
extent, had this effect in Great Britain.*   Wherever
public opinion is allowed to dictate the protection

---

* When a pedestrian is injured or killed on the streets of a city,
we do not hear the cry raised that the roadway should be elevated or
depressed.   Such accidents are recognized as inevitable.   It is the
same with railways.   Efforts to make them absolutely safe are purely
sentimental ; as senseless as an effort to make our street traffic
absolutely safe.   It is too costly.   Cities and countries that indulge
in such practices can not compete with others where the ordinary
accidents of life are accepted philosophically.   Nor is travel likely
to be rendered more safe by the appointment of government agents
to pass upon the permanent way and appliances of railway companies.
The discredit entailed by an accident, and the bills for damages, are
quite sufficient to force a company to exercise every reasonable care
and precaution.   Carriers are much more likely to exercise this
precaution if the responsibility is left with them, than if taken away
and vested in a government supervisor, who may or may not attend
to his business.   Government supervisors are very well as a corollary,
as an advisory adjunct ; but the initiative and the responsibility
should be left with the railroad company.

that shall be thrown around the railway service, it will in every case magnify the duty; will be governed largely by romantic aspirations and needs. In its efforts to protect every one from harm, it will so add to the cost of doing business as to greatly restrict traffic, particularly the freight business. This last it will not see, and in the majority of instances will not consider at all. It will not remember, if it ever knew, that every dollar added to the cost of working railroads lessens, by just so much, their ability to do business; lessens, by just so much, the interchange of traffic; lessens, by just so much, the commercial and social development of a country; lessens production and increases cost. No business can be done that does not at least pay the expense of operating; consequently, every cent added to such expense increases the minimum rate, and in so far as this is so, decreases that much the limit within which rates may be made. Interference with the operations of railways, I may say in conclusion, while it may apparently be helpful, is really hurtful. A glance over the world emphasizes this fact, and it is superior to all contrary arguments; namely, that the countries wherein railways have been allowed the greatest freedom, have been meddled with the least by the government, have made the greatest strides in wealth, commercial greatness, and social happiness. The general laws of a country are quite as effective to protect a people from railway corporations as they are to protect them from merchants and manufacturers generally. There will be isolated cases of wrong-doing, just as there are cases

20

of merchants giving short weights and selling an inferior quality of goods. But such instances will not by any means be general, and will carry with them their own cure.

––––––

THE STATUS OF RAILWAYS IN ENGLAND.

The railway question has received the close study of English statesmen ever since railways became a recognized means of conveyance. In their early history, when railways were demonstrated to be practicable, there was a mania for their construction. The consequence was over-production, and, ultimately, a financial crisis. This was in 1847. After that date, the English Parliament exercised great caution in authorizing the construction of railways, requiring always in advance indisputable evidence of their need. This control of the government over the inception of new railroads is a marked distinction between the American and English railway systems. Before a railway can be constructed in England, the government requires that the scheme shall be submitted to Parliament, which examines it critically and in detail, and considers any objections presented by parties who may be affected thereby. The points upon which Parliament requires to be satisfied are, that the road is a public necessity, and will tend to develop and improve interests along the proposed route, and that the projectors are able to carry out their plan successfully. If Parliament concludes to allow the construction of the proposed road, a bill is passed,

which, in addition to authorizing the construction
of the road, gives the railway company specified
powers and imposes such restrictions and conditions
as may seem equitable. This bill incorporates the
company, provides for the limited liability of shareholders, prescribes the number and qualifications of
directors, the time within which the railroad shall
be completed, the tolls and maximum rates of
charges for passengers and freight, etc., etc.

Not only must specific authorization from Parliament be obtained before a railway can be constructed, but after the road has been built, it can
not be opened for business until sanction has been
given by the governmental department or bureau
known as the Board of Trade. Before permission
is granted, the board is required to be satisfied that
the opening of the road will not be attended with
danger to the public in using the same, by reason of
the incompleteness of the works or permanent way,
or the insufficiency of the establishment for working such railway.*

When once the sanction of Parliament for the
construction of a railway has been given, it must be
completed and operated, or the consent of Parliament procured to abandon it.

The Board of Trade, so called, of England, is really
a bureau of the general government. It possesses
certain supervisory powers over rates and the by-
laws of railways regarding the conduct of their
business.

---

* Railway Regulation Act, 1842.

The laws of England provide for the punishment of railway employes who are guilty of misconduct, and also of persons obstructing railway employes in their duties, or trespassing upon railway property.

In 1844, a law was passed which provided that, if the profits of any railway constructed after the law came into effect, divisible upon its paid-up capital stock, equalled or exceeded ten per cent., the government should have the power to revise such company's tariffs, so as to reduce the divisible profits to ten per cent. The company was, however, in the case of such revision, to be guaranteed its ten per cent., and revisions were not to be allowed, except with the company's consent, oftener than once in twenty-one years. This act also provided that the government should have the right to acquire any railroad constructed after its date by purchasing the same for a sum equal to twenty-five years' purchase of annual divisible profits, estimated on the average annual profits for the three years preceding the date of purchase. If, however, the average profits for such three years had been less than ten per cent., and the company thought the purchase price based thereon inadequate, because of the future prospects of the property, the matter was to be referred to arbitration. Under this law, however, the government was not empowered to take branches or extensions of old lines, constructed after the date of the act, unless it took the whole system, if the company required it to do so. This law, so far as it relates to the government acquisition of railroads, has never been acted upon. Twenty-three years later (in 1867), a commission appointed by the government to report on the subject stated: " We are of the opinion that it is inexpedient at present to subvert the policy which has hitherto been adopted, of leaving the construction and management of railways to the free enterprise of the people, under such conditions as Parliament may think best to impose for the general welfare of the public." The act of 1844 also required railways to keep their accounts open to inspection; that one cheap train should be run daily; that facilities should be granted for the transmission of mails and the conveyance of troops, etc.

With the growth of the railway system in England, and the necessity that arose for billing business through over two or more companies' lines, some of the railways formed an association among themselves to facilitate such interchange of traffic. It is called the railway clearing house. It was first formed in 1847. In 1850, it was recognized by Parliament and a legal existence given it. The act incorporating it enables the body to sue and be sued; provides that any railway company may join or retire from it at a month's notice; and that any company may be compelled to retire at the request of two-thirds of the associated companies. In it each company is represented by a delegate; the delegates constitute a committee for conducting its business; this committee is empowered to adjust all accounts between companies, and decisions by a plurality of votes of delegates respecting matters of accounts are final and conclusive; any balance due from a company is a debt to the committee, for the recovery of which a special remedy is conferred by the act. The committee is required to keep entries of all proceedings, which are received in evidence in any suit against a company which is a member of the association.

In 1854, Parliament enacted a law requiring railways to afford reasonable facilities for forwarding and delivering traffic, and prohibiting undue or unreasonable preference.

In 1868, a law was passed requiring railway companies to prepare and print half-yearly statements of account, and balance-sheets and estimates of proposed expenditures of capital for ensuing half-years. These are required to be filed with the Board of Trade, and copies are given on application to any person financially interested in the company to which they relate. Under this law, government inspectors must be allowed access to a railway company's books and documents, and such inspectors may examine officials and agents under oath. The law also requires passenger fares to be posted at stations.

In 1871, it was enacted that the Board of Trade should appoint inspectors to make inquiries respecting railways and their operations, and to investigate accidents. Such inspectors are empowered to examine a company's stations, works, buildings, offices, stock, plant, permanent way, machinery, etc.; they may examine officials and employes, and may require the production of any books, papers, and documents they think necessary. Notice of all accidents, attended with loss of life or personal injury, must be sent by the railways to the Board of Trade; also of collisions, in which a passenger train is involved; also of derailments; also of accidents of any kind, which have or may cause loss of life or personal injury. The Board of Trade is required to inquire into accidents, and make formal investigation thereof; the inquiry must be conducted publicly, and for this purpose the board possesses judicial powers. Its conclusions and reports thereon must be published.

In 1889, the Board of Trade was given authority to order passenger railways to adopt the block system;* to provide for the interlocking of switches and signals;† to use continuous automatic brakes.‡ To meet the expense of this, the board may authorize railway companies to issue debentures or debenture stock, bearing interest at a rate not exceeding five per cent.

Railway companies are required to furnish the Board of Trade periodical returns as to the persons in their employment, whose duty involves the safety of trains or passengers, who are employed for more than such number of hours at a time, as may be from time to time named by the board.

---

*In December, 1890, the percentage of double-track road used for passenger traffic, operated on the absolute block system, was 98½ in England and Wales, 100 in Scotland, and 35 in Ireland.

† The percentage of switches, grade crossings, etc., properly interlocked, was 95 in England and Wales, 87 in Scotland, and 65 in Ireland.

‡ The use of continuous automatic brakes on passenger trains has been made compulsory on practically every mile of road in Great Britain.

By the law of 1889, it was enacted that every passage ticket issued by a company should bear upon its face, in legible writing or in printed characters, the amount charged for fare; that every passenger should produce and deliver up to an officer or servant of the company his ticket, when called upon, or in default pay his fare from the place whence he started, or give his name and address. In default, he could be fined by a magistrate and the fare recovered by the company. A person traveling, or attempting to travel, without having previously paid his fare; or, having paid a fare, wilfully proceeding beyond the distance for which he had paid, with intent to avoid payment, or failing to pay his fare when requested, can be fined ten dollars by a magistrate in the first instance, and in the case of a second offense may be fined one hundred dollars, or, in the discretion of the court, imprisoned for a term not exceeding one month, in addition to which the company has the right to recover the fare.*

In addition to the control exercised over the English railways, as indicated in the foregoing, by the Board of Trade, an act of 1888 provided for the appointment of a commission consisting of two commissioners, one of whom must be experienced in the railway business, and three *ex officio* commissioners. This commission has jurisdiction to entertain and adjudicate upon complaints against railways of

---

* This law is by no means a dead letter. Its provisions are rigidly enforced by the railway companies, and prosecutions of would-be defrauders frequent.

anything done or omission made in violation of the
law requiring railway companies to receive and forward traffic without partiality or unreasonable delay,
and to grant equality of treatment where railways
operate steamships, etc. This commission is empowered to fix terminal charges; has control over
agreements between railway and canal companies,
etc. It also has power to direct that no higher
charge shall be made to any person for services, in
respect of merchandise carried over a less distance,
than is made to any other person for similar services,
in respect of the like description and quantity of
merchandise carried over a greater distance, on the
same line of railway.

THE STATUS OF RAILWAYS IN CANADA.

The present status of railroads in Canada is embodied substantially in two acts of Parliament, the
first in order of date having been passed in 1886,
having relation only to the sale of passenger tickets. The second, which is comprehensive, came into
operation in 1888. It was the result of conclusions
arrived at by a royal commission appointed to inquire into the subject. Its conclusions will be of
especial interest to the American reader, because it
had under consideration the Interstate Commerce
act of this country, which had at that time already
come into operation. In reporting to Parliament, the
commission in question thus stated its conclusions
in reference to legislation affecting tariffs. It said:
"The commission have carefully considered all the

information before them on this important subject, and believe the interests of commerce will be best served by leaving the arrangement of tariff rates for passengers and goods in the control of the several companies respectively, subject only to approval and revision of the maxima rates by an authorized tribunal." In regard to uniform mileage rates (i.e., the basing of rates on distance), the commission said: "This question has probably given rise to more discussion than almost any other point connected with railway management. It forms the subject of much of the evidence given before the commission, and the greatest diversity of opinion exists upon it. It has been the subject of repeated legislation, and in the celebrated 'granger' agitation in the West, uniformity of mileage rates was imposed upon the railways by State legislation. The subject has also received the greatest attention in connection with the Interstate Commerce bill, and the principle of uniformity of mileage rates was finally sanctioned by the act, reserving, however, to the railway commission power to suspend its operation on sufficient reason being shown. This power has since been exercised by the commission in certain cases, and it is not now imperative on all railways to establish uniform mileage rates, under like conditions and in the same direction, for long and short distances. The reasons given for the suspension of this section of the Interstate Commerce act have received the greatest attention by the commission. They can not lose sight of the fact that where conveyance by water comes into competition with railways, it is not in the public interest to compel railways to transport freight at uniform mileage rates, as it involves the establishment, either of such low rates as render the local traffic unremunerative, or such high rates as leave the through traffic between the competitive points wholly at the mercy of carriers by water. The public interest will be best served by permitting rates between such competitive points to be determined by the respective carriers. It is, moreover, manifest that the through traffic of Canada by railway, which the commission regard of the utmost importance, can not possibly be carried on except at such rates, in combination sometimes with navigation, but more generally with American railways, as would be utterly inadequate if applied to ordinary local traffic. While stating their opinion that the competition by water and rail, from almost every important business center in Canada, forbids the adoption of uniform mileage rates, the commission have not lost sight of the alleged unfair treatment of certain localities in Canada itself by railways. They believe, however, that such cases can be considered and relief obtained, under the powers which they hereafter recommend should be granted. They, therefore, recommend that it is inexpedient to adopt a rule of equal mileage rates, irrespective of distance and cost of service."

The act of 1888, based upon this commission's report, provides for the establishment of a "Railway Committee," which consists of the minister of railways and canals, the minister of justice, and two or more members of the privy council,

appointed by the governor. It will be noticed that
this body is made up entirely of politicians. The
commission, in recommending a body so constituted,
recognized the fact, and admitted that "serious
objection may be taken to it," because such a body
must "delegate to subordinates much of their important work," and because "they hold their office
by a political tenure and are liable to sudden change,
whereby the value of their experience is lost."
That they "could scarcely be regarded by the public as absolutely removed from personal or political
bias, as independent members of a permanent tribunal." But they pleaded that the body was
"necessarily tentative, and it seems undesirable, at
this time, to remove its operation, in its inception,
beyond the direct criticism and control of Parliament."

The Railway Committee thus constituted has
power to regulate and limit the speed of trains, and
exercise certain other police powers of a kindred
nature. It has power to inquire into, hear, and
determine any application, complaint, or dispute,
respecting right of way, changing location of lines,
construction of branch lines within certain limits;
the crossing of tracks, by different companies; the
alignment, arrangement, disposition, and location of
tracks; the use by one company of another company's facilities; the construction of works in navigable waters; the construction of railways on and
across highways; questions as to compensation for
property; tolls and rates for freight and passengers;
tolls and rates between companies; running powers,

or haulage; traffic arrangements; interchange of freight; unjust preferences, discrimination, and extortion, and any matters, acts, or things sanctioned, required to be done, or prohibited by the law.

Under the law, railway companies are authorized to fix and regulate rates, but it provides that they shall always, under the same circumstances, be charged equally to all persons. The rates for large quantities or long distances may be proportionately less than for small quantities or short distances, if such rates are under the same circumstances charged equally to all persons; but in regard to quantity of freight, no special rate is allowed for less than one car-load of at least ten tons. Railway companies are compelled to conform to any uniform classification of freight which is from time to time prescribed. Rates must be approved by the governor, and, with the order approving same, must be published in the official *Canada Gazette;* they may be revised by the governor. Railways must post rates in their offices and at places where they are collected. Unjust or partial discrimination is prohibited, but discrimination between localities, which, by reason of competition between water or railways, it is necessary to make in order to secure traffic, is expressly stated not to be unjust or partial. Secret special rates, rebates, drawbacks, and concessions are prohibited.

Arrangements between different companies for the interchange of traffic and for the division of rates, etc., for any term not exceeding twenty-one years, may be made by the companies interested, but they must be made with the consent of two-thirds of the stockholders, and are subject to the approval of the governor. Before the approval of the governor is given, the fact that he will be applied to therefor must be published in the *Canada Gazette* for two months.

Facilities for interchange of traffic are to be afforded by railroads to each other, and they are prohibited from exercising unreasonable preference in such matters.

Railways allowing express companies to operate over their lines, must grant equal facilities on equal terms to any other incorporated express company demanding the same.

Railways are forbidden to buy their own stock or the shares, bonds, or other securities of other railways in Canada.

Railways are required to make annual returns to the minister of railways in the form provided by the act. Each railway company must also each week prepare returns of its traffic for the preceding seven days, in the form provided in the act, and file one copy of same with the minister of railways, and post another copy thereof in some conspicuous place in the most public room in the head offices of the company, so that it can be perused by all persons.

Railway companies are prohibited from declaring dividends to be paid out of capital, or whereby the capital is in any degree reduced or impaired. They may, however, until the railway is completed and opened, pay interest not exceeding six per cent. on money subscribed.

THE STATUS OF RAILWAYS IN AUSTRALIA.

The railways of Australia are owned by the various colonial governments. Their management by the governments was very unsatisfactory, and in February, 1884, they were placed under the direct management of a commission of three members appointed by the government. These commissioners hold office for seven years and are eligible for reappointment. They can not be removed except by Parliament. In addition to management of existing roads, this commission has charge of the construction of new lines. The powers and duties of the commission are as follows: It must provide proper transportation facilities for freight and passengers; must see that the roads and the service thereon are properly maintained. It has extensive police powers over the railways, their property, and employes; it regulates the terms and conditions under which special trains are run; fixes charges for warehousing goods, parcels, and baggage; imposes conditions on which baggage will be carried; imposes differential and special rates and charges for the carriage of passengers or goods; establishes demurrage charges; makes agreements with shippers for insuring them against loss or damage on freight, and it may also insure the government against such liability. The amount of the government's liability to shippers for loss or damage is limited by law, and action must be brought therefor within a specified time. The commission is not allowed to give undue or unreasonable preferences, or subject anyone to undue or unreasonable disadvantages; it must afford reasonable, proper, and equal facilities for interchange of traffic between lines, and must post rates at stations. The law, in relation to accidents, is similar to that of England.

The commission reports to Parliament annually its proceedings, and all matters of interest relative to the construction, operation and equipment of the roads.

___

THE STATUS OF RAILWAYS IN GERMANY.

Railways began to be constructed in Germany in 1835. Ninety per cent. of the mileage is now owned by the government. Under the law, the government is required to manage the railways "in the interest of general traffic as a single system."* It may cause the construction of new roads, which must be equipped according to standard specifications; it has power to enforce uniform traffic and police regulations; it must keep the roads in good condition and equip them according to the requirements of traffic; it must provide necessary cars for through traffic and making connection with other roads, on payment of proper compensation; it has control of tariffs; the government determines the standard of construction and equipment.

The railways are controlled by a board of five members known as the "imperial railway board," and the few private railways are controlled by State boards. Private roads have their maximum rates fixed by their charters. The government operates

___

* Article 42, Constitution of German Empire.

all the railways owned by the State. Rates must be published; pools are recognized; undue or unreasonable preference is forbidden in regard to rates. In regard to the basis of rates, a writer * says : " In Germany, where the railways are almost exclusively owned by the State governments, and interior competition thus minimized, there is no hard and fast rule. The short-haul principle is accepted as a general rule in Prussia, but exceptions may be admitted by the minister of public works. The Bundesrath of the empire also enunciated the same principle, but expressly inserted the proviso that particular circumstances might justify an infraction of the rule. These exceptions are of frequent occurrence. The short-haul principle does not apply to through transit rates, to import or export tariffs, or to any competitive centers where the competition is caused by water-ways or foreign railways. After the purchase of the Prussian railways by the State, a few years ago, the attempt was made to enforce the short-haul rule strictly, but it failed. A large number of special rates permit charges in derogation of the short-haul principle. Even the earnest defenders of State railways confess that numerous exceptions are indispensable."

In 1886, the government issued a code of regulations applicable to the whole railway system of Germany. It deals with the condition of the permanent way; provisions requisite for bridges, crossings, signals, etc.; the construction of locomotives;

* Professor Seligman, *Political Science Quarterly*, 1887, page 261.

the testing of locomotives and tenders; the construction of rolling stock, with specific regulations regarding wheels, tires, axles, etc.; the periodical examination of locomotives, carriages, and wagons; the weight and working of trains; the rate of speed for different kinds of traffic; the movement of trains; the conditions of working fast and slow traffic; the transportation of passengers on freight trains, and vice versa; communication between passengers and conductors; the character of electric communication, signals, and regulations affecting the public.*

THE STATUS OF RAILWAYS IN FRANCE.

The history of the French railway system is varied and complicated. The laws and regulations affecting it are voluminous. The State has always actively interfered. There have been, at different periods in French history, lines constructed by contributions made in part by the general government, in part by local districts, and in part by private companies; by the government alone; by private

---

* The government officials of Germany show great expertness. But they have not been able to make the railways conform to the comfort and varying practical needs of the public. Their theories are admirable, but their practices are not satisfactory. They are not different in this respect from government servants the world over. They have no commercial instincts, and when called upon to act in cases requiring such intuition, respond with general rules and regulations that would be appropriate enough, perhaps, to army or navy life, but are utterly inadequate to the needs of trade. They meet the needs of commerce just as they drill soldiers or provide pigeon-holes for letters.

companies unaided, and by the general government and private owners conjointly. There have been leases of State roads to private companies; surrenders of State lines to private companies; competition between State and private roads; schemes of nationalization, and provision made for governmental purchase.

The French railway system dates from 1842. In that year an act was passed for the "Establishment of grand lines of railroad." The lines were to diverge from the capital, Paris, and this conception still governs. The cost of construction was to be borne in part by the general government, in part by the local districts through which the roads passed, and in part by the companies operating them. The latter contributed about one-half of the cost. At the expiration of a given period, about thirty-six years, the roads were to become the absolute property of the State. This latter part of the plan did not, however, come into effect because of the financial crisis in 1847, and the political revolutions intervening, which stopped railway construction. It then became necessary to make new arrangements, and under a law passed in 1859, the State assumed supervision over all railway construction; it also took cognizance of rates. This act forbade discrimination, and under it the French railway system became of a dual character—owned partly by the State and partly by private companies. Under this law, it was provided that all railways should become government property in about 1950. The plan of mixed ownership was not found to work satisfac-

torily. Under it the government suffered much by
the competition of the private roads, and was ultimately forced, by reason of such competition, to
lease to its rivals such parts of the lines as were
valuable to them.

After the Franco-Prussian war, the government
contemplated nationalizing the whole railway system, but insurmountable financial obstacles prevented, and in 1883 the situation was such that the
government was compelled practically to surrender
the right it possessed of purchasing private roads,
except upon prohibitory terms. Moreover, at this
period, also, the government was compelled by financial considerations to cease the construction of more
lines ; to cede to the private companies such roads
as it had recently constructed, and to authorize the
latter to construct additional lines.

With regard to railway construction after that
date, the arrangement is as follows : " The companies undertake to contribute a specified amount
per mile towards construction, and to furnish the
rolling stock, and the furniture and fixtures of the
stations. The remaining expenses of construction and
equipment are to be ultimately borne by the State ;
but in the first instance the companies advanced the
money for the State, and an annual payment is made
by the State to the companies, to meet interest on
the amount of advances, and to create a sinking
fund, which will extinguish the principal by the
time when the concessions of the companies terminate and the properties vest in the State. The
amounts of annual payments by the State to the

companies on account of moneys advanced for new construction are, under certain circumstances, liable to be diminished by the payments made by the State, under its guaranty of interest and sinking fund, on the bonds issued by the companies for the extension of original lines."*

At the present date, by far the larger portion of the French railway system is owned and operated by private companies, each company serving a definite territory, and being comparatively free from competitive lines.

French railway legislation has provided for the publication of tariffs and traffic regulations; the railways make their own rates, but a government bureau reviews them; reductions can only go into effect after three months' notice, and increases after a year's notice, except in the case of certain international traffic, the rates on which can be changed on twenty-four hours' notice, or under certain circumstances, without any notice.

Freight and passenger traffic are divided into classes as follows:

Freight—Fast freight (grande vitesse); slow freight (pepite vitesse).

Passenger—First, second, and third class.

The classification of freight is generally based on value, but is subject to government control. Special rates are allowed, subject to the sanction of the government.

---

* "Fourth Annual Report, Interstate Commerce Commission," page 340.

THE STATUS OF RAILWAYS IN AUSTRIA-HUNGARY.

In Austria, more than a third of the railways are owned by the government. The residue is owned by private companies. Concessions, or charters for the construction of railways, expire at a stipulated period not exceeding ninety years. Upon their expiration the lines, lands, and buildings revert to the State, but the equipment remains the property of the company. Before a railway is opened it must be approved by the minister of commerce. The tariffs of State roads are fixed by the government; those of private companies are subject to revision by the government every three years, and the government has power to reduce rates, if the net earnings exceed fifteen per cent. In most cases, the maximum rates of private roads are fixed in their charters, and where this is not the case, the government fixes the maximum. Unjust discrimination is prohibited and publication of rates is required. Special rates are allowed, subject to the approval of the government. The police regulations made by the government for the roads are binding upon private companies. The government is empowered to exact any information it requires from private roads, and each road must keep a "book of complaint" at each station, in which patrons may enter their grievances. Private companies must furnish the government with a list of all officers and employes, and must keep their accounts under the general supervision of the government.

The Hungarian railways are owned entirely by the State.

Any reference to the railways of Austria-Hungary would be incomplete without referring to the zone system of passenger fares, recently adopted. This is a departure from all previous methods of fixing passenger fares. Its application is not identical in Austria and Hungary, for the reason that the railways of Hungary are owned entirely by the State, and have been constructed so as to make them all tributary to its capital, Buda-Pesth, while in Austria only a portion of the railways is owned by the State, and some of its most important lines have no direct connection with the capital, Vienna. A supposed object of the introduction of the zone system of passenger fares, was to encourage long-distance travel between the capital and the provinces; to modify, as far as possible, the element of distance in favor of the traveling public; to unify the interests of all sections, and promote the welfare of the capital cities.*

---

*The zone tariff is a mechanical device. Government officials who meddle in commercial affairs always affect devices of this kind, because they have neither the experience nor skill to conform to the actual needs of trade. Government officials the world over confine themselves to a few general patterns, which everybody is expected to use. Thus, if a man happens to have a little bigger head than his neighbor, he must go without a hat, or perch it on the top of his head; if his head is a little smaller than his neighbor's, his hat will drop over his eyes. If his feet are long, his toes will stick out from his shoes; if short, his shoes will curl up. The efforts of government officials are constantly directed towards the reduction of mankind into a few general classes, instead of considering their individual needs. And herein is the difference between commercial enterprises carried on by owners and those carried on by the government. The former listen and conform to the needs of each particular patron. On the other hand, the government official is constitutionally incapacitated

The Hungarian zone system is described as follows: "Each railway is divided into sections, called zones; and, all the railways having a common center at Buda-Pesth, the zones are established to and from that center. The first zone is shortest, extending a distance of twenty-five kilometers from the starting-point; the second, and each succeeding zone, up to the twelfth, is fifteen kilometers longer than the zone immediately preceding it; the twelfth and thirteenth zones are each twenty-five kilometers longer than its immediately preceding zone, and all distances exceeding 225 kilometers from the starting-point are included in a single zone, the fourteenth. Passenger rates are fixed, not per mile or kilometer, but at so much per zone, the charge for every fraction of a zone being the same as for a full zone. The effect of the system is a constantly diminishing rate per mile, or per kilometer, in proportion to distance traveled. On certain classes of trains, special local rates are made to the first and second stations from the starting-point, regardless of the zone system; also, after the twelfth zone is passed, the rate per zone, or part of zone, is slightly increased." *

---

from studying the individual needs of men, and in those cases where he is not, the rules and regulations that surround him, prevent him making any exceptions. It is because of this disposition and environment that he is disposed to look upon the efforts of common carriers to satisfy the individual needs of patrons as unjust discrimination. Unhappy the country whose commerce is hampered by the meddling of government servants! With the best intentions in the world, coupled with executive talents of the highest order, they utterly lack the adaptable qualities that those who have to do with trade must possess.

* "Fourth Annual Report, Interstate Commerce Commission," page 245.

The Austrian zone tariff (which differs from the Hungarian for the reasons given), is not limited to lines radiating from the capital, and the rates are measured by kilometers as before, though this measurement is modified by the principle of zones. It may be described as follows: "The first five zones from the starting-point are each ten kilometers in length; the next two are fifteen kilometers each; the eighth is twenty kilometers; the following four are twenty-five kilometers each, and all zones above the twelfth are fifty kilometers in length. From the starting-point to a point within any one of the zones, the charge is at a fixed rate per kilometer to the farthest limit of that zone. . . . . A third-class ticket to any point within the first zone of ten kilometers' length is ten kreutzers.* . . . The average rate to any point in the second zone is one and one-third kreutzers per kilometer, while the rate to the farthest point of the zone is one kreutzer per kilometer. The average rate to any point in the third zone is one and one-fifth kreutzers per kilometer; in the fourth zone, one and one-seventh kreutzers per kilometer; in the fourteenth zone, one and one-eleventh kreutzers per kilometer. The charge to the farthest limit of any zone is always at the rate of one kreutzer per kilometer."†

---

*A kilometer is 3,280 feet; a kreutzer is about four-tenths of a cent.

†"Fourth Annual Report, Interstate Commerce Commission," page 348.

THE STATUS OF RAILWAYS IN BELGIUM.

With minor and unimportant exceptions, Belgian railways are owned and operated by the State. The roads not now owned by the government will, under the terms of their charters, ultimately revert to it. Railway affairs are administered by a government department of "railways, post offices, and telegraphs," under the laws of the kingdom. The laws regulate tariffs. Railways are exempted from taxation.

THE STATUS OF RAILWAYS IN SPAIN AND PORTUGAL.

The railways in these countries are owned and operated by private companies. Most of them, however, have been aided by the government by subsidies or guarantees. Where such aid has been granted, it has always been conditional upon the roads reverting to the government in ninety-nine years.

THE STATUS OF RAILWAYS IN ITALY.

The railway problem in Italy has been a vexed one. Speaking of Italy's experience, Professor Hadley says:* "Italy has tried both State railroads and private railroads; has tried almost every possible relation between the State and the railroads. Each of three or four main systems received its original charter from a different govern-

---

* "Railroad Transportation," page 220.

.

ment. One derived its being from the Emperor of Austria; another from the Pope. Each charter has been amended over and over again. There has been State assistance of every kind—guarantees of interest, advances of capital, subsidies for building, subsidies for running. The State has built some of the roads; others it has bought and paid for. It has tried various forms of management—direct State action, lease, and participation in profits."

In 1878 a commission investigated the whole subject in a comprehensive and thorough manner. Its inquiries were not simply local, or confined to Italy alone, but extended over all Europe; it spared neither time nor expense in obtaining information; its labors were painstaking and complete, and after working assiduously for nearly three years, the result of its labors was embodied in a lengthy report which forms, it is probable, the most complete work of its kind. The outcome of such investigation was decidedly adverse to State management, as pointed out elsewhere in this volume. The result was a reorganization of the whole railway system, and the establishment of the present status.

Prior to 1859, Italy was divided into small States, each one of which had its own system of lines, if it had any railways at all; they were local, independent, and isolated in their nature; these systems were not adapted to through traffic, because they ran crosswise through the country, while the direction of through traffic was lengthwise. In course of time, political events brought about consolidation into a few systems, known as the "Alta Italia"

(Upper Italian) and "Romane" (Roman), which were
directly worked by the State; the "Calabro-Sicule"
(Calabria and Sicily) worked at the State's expense
and on its account by a private company, which
also worked on its own account another system,
called the "Meridionale," of which it was grantee.

In July, 1885, these four systems were, by a law
of that year, combined into three systems, divided
according to their longitudinal sections, in order to
accommodate through traffic; they are known as
the "Mediterranean," the "Adriatic," and the
"Sicilian" systems. In order to bring this about,
it was necessary to make the "Meridionale" company (a private one) renounce its right to work its
lines. This was done by an arrangement with that
company, by which it received certain subventions
from the State, and was given the management of one
of the three new systems—the "Adriatic." These
three systems were, on 1st July, 1885, taken over by
private companies under contract with the government. The contracts run for sixty years, with an
option for either the government or the companies
to terminate them at the end of twenty or forty
years, upon a two years' notice. The companies
purchased the rolling stock and equipment from
the State; this they keep in repair at their own cost,
as an operating expense, but they receive from the
State annual subventions, equal to about five per
cent. on the investment they have made in such
rolling stock and equipment. The provisions made
for the maintenance of the roads and for extraordinary expenditures are complicated. A number of

reserve funds are provided. A certain amount per mile of track, on account of certain contingencies, such as "extraordinary repairs," "renewal of rails," "renewal of rolling stock," is deducted periodically from the gross receipts and applied to reserve funds to provide for these expenditures. Increase of accommodations or supplies is provided for by yet another fund. The revenues are apportioned in stipulated percentages. Part goes to the companies for operating expenses and profits, part to the State as the owner of the lines, part to the reserve funds mentioned, and another part goes to reimburse the government for its annual subventions. If a company should earn sufficient to pay more than seven and a half per cent. profits, one-half of the excess goes to the government.

Under this arrangement, tariffs are made generally uniform, with decreasing rates by zones of fifty and a hundred kilometers, as the distance run increases. Special tariffs, however, are allowed under certain circumstances. To increase tariffs, a new law is required to be passed for that purpose, but reductions may be made by agreement between the companies and the State, or by the State alone. A body known as "Council of the Tariffs," has jurisdiction over rates; it is composed of delegates representing the State, agriculture, commerce and industry, and . the railways.

The accounts of the railways are under the supervision of a government inspector. The companies managing the railways can not transfer the management of their properties, unless authorized by law.

The government may contract with the companies to build new lines upon certain terms. Controversies between the companies and the State are settled by arbitration.

THE STATUS OF RAILWAYS IN RUSSIA.

In Russia the government owns and operates about one-third of the railways of the country; the remainder are owned and operated by private companies. In many cases, however, the latter have received aid from the government by subsidies or guarantees.

The State railways are managed by a board, the members of which are appointed by the government. This board supervises their financial affairs, makes rates, etc., and in its general powers resembles the directory of a private corporation. Each State line has, also, its general manager or executive officer, and is administered generally on the same plan as a private railway; should the expenses of working exceed the earnings, the government makes appropriations to cover the deficit.

Private railroads are built under charters granted by the government. Before granting these, it requires to be convinced that the road is in the public interest; promoters must also satisfy the government that they are able to carry out the construction of the road, and when once a charter is granted, the road must be constructed within the time specified therein; it must be built according to plans and specifications approved by the government, and when finished, can not be opened until the work has been approved, and permission granted by the government. Private companies can not transfer their privileges without the State's consent. Charters generally specify maximum rates. Rates can not, however, be changed except with the consent of the government. A "tariff council" exists to administer the law regarding rates. The government takes cognizance of the operations of all railroads, and prescribes rules relating to construction and maintenance, both of permanent way and equipment, signals, speed of trains, etc. It appoints an inspector for each private railway, whose duty it is to see that the State regulations are observed. When a private road receives governmental aid, the State is represented on its directorate by two or more members, whose recommendation is required for all expenditures, declarations of dividends, etc., which must also be approved by the government.

THE STATUS OF RAILWAYS IN JAPAN.

In Japan there appears to have been, up to 1875, three classes of railways, namely, "State," "Prefecture," and "Village" roads. State roads are maintained at national expense, but their regulation and repair is in the hands of the prefectures through which they pass. Prefecture roads are maintained by equal contributions from the general government and particular districts or prefectures. Village roads serve petty local districts, and are maintained at their expense.

In 1885 comparatively extended railway construction commenced by private corporations, and in 1887 the government promulgated an ordinance entitled, "Private railway regulations," which provides that in the construction of railways leave must first be obtained of the government before they are built. The government will not grant this permission if the new enterprise will interfere with any existing railway, or there is no local necessity for it. If satisfied on these points, it grants a charter, under which the construction of the railway must be commenced within three months and the work completed within a specified time. The ordinance relating to railway regulation fixes the gauge of all railways at three feet six inches, and no company may change its methods of working without permission. Rates are fixed subject to the approval of the government, and all changes of time for trains, their number, etc., must also be approved by it. When a charter is granted for a limited period, the government has the right, at its expiration, to purchase the property at a price calculated from the average price of the shares during five years previous to the date of purchase.

INDEX TO AUTHORITIES QUOTED.

22   (337)

In addition to the foregoing, the writer is indebted to the following gentlemen, whose views on questions discussed in this book have been profitable to him in elucidating the subject :

> HON. WILLIAM R. MORRISON,
> MR. T. B. BLACKSTONE,
> MR. CORNELIUS VANDERBILT,
> SENATOR JOHN SHERMAN,
> MR. MARVIN HUGHITT,
> PRESIDENT HARRISON,
> MR. JOHN NEWELL,
> SENATOR JOHN H. REAGAN,
> MR. J. W. MIDGELY.

GENERAL INDEX.

352 *GENERAL INDEX.*

23